Similarity Search
The Metric Space Approach

ADVANCES IN DATABASE SYSTEMS

Series Editor

Ahmed K. Elmagarmid

Purdue University
West Lafayette, IN 47907

Other books in the Series:

STREAM DATA MANAGEMENT, *Nauman Chaudhry, Kevin Shaw, Mahdi Abdelguerfi,* ISBN: 0-387-24393-3

FUZZY DATABASE MODELING WITH XML, *Zongmin Ma,* ISBN: 0-387-24248-1

MINING SEQUENTIAL PATTERNS FROM LARGE DATA SETS, *Wei Wang and Jiong Yang;* ISBN: 0-387-24246-5

ADVANCED SIGNATURE INDEXING FOR MULTIMEDIA AND WEB APPLICATIONS, *Yannis Manolopoulos, Alexandros Nanopoulos, Eleni Tousidou;* ISBN: 1-4020-7425-5

ADVANCES IN DIGITAL GOVERNMENT, *Technology, Human Factors, and Policy, edited by William J. McIver, Jr. and Ahmed K. Elmagarmid;* ISBN: 1-4020-7067-5

INFORMATION AND DATABASE QUALITY, *Mario Piattini, Coral Calero and Marcela Genero;* ISBN: 0-7923- 7599-8

DATA QUALITY, *Richard Y. Wang, Mostapha Ziad, Yang W. Lee:* ISBN: 0-7923-7215-8

THE FRACTAL STRUCTURE OF DATA REFERENCE: *Applications to the Memory Hierarchy, Bruce McNutt;* ISBN: 0-7923-7945-4

SEMANTIC MODELS FOR MULTIMEDIA DATABASE SEARCHING AND BROWSING, *Shu-Ching Chen, R.L. Kashyap, and Arif Ghafoor;* ISBN: 0-7923-7888-1

INFORMATION BROKERING ACROSS HETEROGENEOUS DIGITAL DATA: **A Metadata-based Approach,** *Vipul Kashyap, Amit Sheth;* ISBN: 0-7923-7883-0

DATA DISSEMINATION IN WIRELESS COMPUTING ENVIRONMENTS, *Kian-Lee Tan and Beng Chin Ooi;* ISBN: 0-7923-7866-0

MIDDLEWARE NETWORKS: Concept, Design and Deployment of Internet Infrastructure, *Michah Lerner, George Vanecek, Nino Vidovic, Dad Vrsalovic;* ISBN: 0-7923-7840-7

ADVANCED DATABASE INDEXING, *Yannis Manolopoulos, Yannis Theodoridis, Vassilis J. Tsotras;* ISBN: 0-7923-7716-8

MULTILEVEL SECURE TRANSACTION PROCESSING, *Vijay Atluri, Sushil Jajodia, Binto George* ISBN: 0-7923-7702-8

FUZZY LOGIC IN DATA MODELING, *Guoqing Chen* ISBN: 0-7923-8253-6

INTERCONNECTING HETEROGENEOUS INFORMATION SYSTEMS, *Athman Bouguettaya, Boualem Benatallah, Ahmed Elmagarmid* ISBN: 0-7923-8216-1

For a complete listing of books in this series, go to http://www.springeronline.com

Similarity Search
The Metric Space Approach

Pavel Zezula
Masaryk University, Czech Republic

Giuseppe Amato
ISTI-CNR, Italy

Vlastislav Dohnal
Masaryk University, Czech Republic

Michal Batko
Masaryk University, Czech Republic

Pavel Zezula
Masaryk University, Czech Republic

Giuseppe Amato
ISTI-CNR, Italy

Vlastislav Dohnal
Masaryk University, Czech Republic

Michal Batko
Masaryk University, Czech Republic

ISBN-13: 978-1-4419-3972-2

e-ISBN-10: 0-387-29151-2
e-ISBN-13: 978-0387-29151-2

springeronline.com

*This book is dedicated to the
10th anniversary of the
Faculty of Informatics,
Masaryk University in Brno*

Contents

Dedication   v
Foreword   xiii
Preface   xv
Acknowledgments   xvii

Part I Metric Searching in a Nutshell

Overview   3

1. FOUNDATIONS OF METRIC SPACE SEARCHING   5
   1   The Distance Searching Problem   6
   2   The Metric Space   8
   3   Distance Measures   9
       3.1   Minkowski Distances   10
       3.2   Quadratic Form Distance   11
       3.3   Edit Distance   12
       3.4   Tree Edit Distance   13
       3.5   Jaccard's Coefficient   13
       3.6   Hausdorff Distance   14
       3.7   Time Complexity   14
   4   Similarity Queries   15
       4.1   Range Query   15
       4.2   Nearest Neighbor Query   16
       4.3   Reverse Nearest Neighbor Query   17
       4.4   Similarity Join   17
       4.5   Combinations of Queries   18
       4.6   Complex Similarity Queries   18

5   Basic Partitioning Principles   20
    5.1   Ball Partitioning   20
    5.2   Generalized Hyperplane Partitioning   21
    5.3   Excluded Middle Partitioning   21
    5.4   Extensions   21
6   Principles of Similarity Query Execution   22
    6.1   Basic Strategies   22
    6.2   Incremental Similarity Search   25
7   Policies for Avoiding Distance Computations   26
    7.1   Explanatory Example   27
    7.2   Object-Pivot Distance Constraint   28
    7.3   Range-Pivot Distance Constraint   30
    7.4   Pivot-Pivot Distance Constraint   31
    7.5   Double-Pivot Distance Constraint   33
    7.6   Pivot Filtering   34
8   Metric Space Transformations   35
    8.1   Metric Hierarchies   36
    8.1.1 Lower-Bounding Functions   36
    8.2   User-Defined Metric Functions   38
    8.2.1 Searching Using Lower-Bounding Functions   38
    8.3   Embedding Metric Space   39
    8.3.1 Embedding Examples   39
    8.3.2 Reducing Dimensionality   40
9   Approximate Similarity Search   41
    9.1   Principles   41
    9.2   Generic Algorithms   44
    9.3   Measures of Performance   46
    9.3.1 Improvement in Efficiency   46
    9.3.2 Precision and Recall   46
    9.3.3 Relative Error on Distances   48
    9.3.4 Position Error   49
10 Advanced Issues   50
    10.1   Statistics on Metric Datasets   51
    10.1.1 Distribution and Density Functions   51
    10.1.2 Distance Distribution and Density   52
    10.1.3 Homogeneity of Viewpoints   54
    10.2   Proximity of Ball Regions   55
    10.3   Performance Prediction   58

	10.4	Tree Quality Measures	60
	10.5	Choosing Reference Points	63
2.	SURVEY OF EXISTING APPROACHES		67
1	Ball Partitioning Methods		67
	1.1	Burkhard-Keller Tree	68
	1.2	Fixed Queries Tree	69
	1.3	Fixed Queries Array	70
	1.4	Vantage Point Tree	72
	1.4.1	Multi-Way Vantage Point Tree	74
	1.5	Excluded Middle Vantage Point Forest	75
2	Generalized Hyperplane Partitioning Approaches		76
	2.1	Bisector Tree	76
	2.2	Generalized Hyperplane Tree	77
3	Exploiting Pre-Computed Distances		78
	3.1	AESA	78
	3.2	Linear AESA	79
	3.3	Other Methods	80
4	Hybrid Indexing Approaches		81
	4.1	Multi Vantage Point Tree	81
	4.2	Geometric Near-neighbor Access Tree	82
	4.3	Spatial Approximation Tree	85
	4.4	M-tree	87
	4.5	Similarity Hashing	88
5	Approximate Similarity Search		89
	5.1	Exploiting Space Transformations	89
	5.2	Approximate Nearest Neighbors with BBD Trees	90
	5.3	Angle Property Technique	92
	5.4	Clustering for Indexing	94
	5.5	Vector Quantization Index	95
	5.6	Buoy Indexing	97
	5.7	Hierarchical Decomposition of Metric Spaces	97
	5.7.1	Relative Error Approximation	98
	5.7.2	Good Fraction Approximation	98
	5.7.3	Small Chance Improvement Approximation	98
	5.7.4	Proximity-Based Approximation	99
	5.7.5	PAC Nearest Neighbor Search	99

Part II   Metric Searching in Large Collections of Data

Overview   103

3. CENTRALIZED INDEX STRUCTURES   105
    1   M-tree Family   105
        1.1   The M-tree   105
        1.2   Bulk-Loading Algorithm of M-tree   109
        1.3   Multi-Way Insertion Algorithm   112
        1.4   The Slim Tree   113
        1.4.1   Slim-Down Algorithm   114
        1.4.2   Generalized Slim-Down Algorithm   116
        1.5   Pivoting M-tree   118
        1.6   The M^+-tree   121
        1.7   The M^2-tree   124
    2   Hash-based metric indexing   125
        2.1   The D-index   126
        2.1.1   Insertion and Search Strategies   129
        2.2   The eD-index   131
        2.2.1   Similarity Self-Join Algorithm with eD-index   133
    3   Performance Trials   136
        3.1   Datasets and Distance Measures   137
        3.2   Performance Comparison   138
        3.3   Different Query Types   140
        3.4   Scalability   141

4. APPROXIMATE SIMILARITY SEARCH   145
    1   Relative Error Approximation   145
    2   Good Fraction Approximation   148
    3   Small Chance Improvement Approximation   150
    4   Proximity-Based Approximation   152
    5   PAC Nearest Neighbor Searching   153
    6   Performance Trials   154
        6.1   Range Queries   155
        6.2   Nearest Neighbors Queries   156
        6.3   Global Considerations   159

5.	PARALLEL AND DISTRIBUTED INDEXES		161
	1	Preliminaries	161
		1.1 Parallel Computing	162
		1.2 Distributed Computing	163
		1.2.1 Scalable and Distributed Data Structures	163
		1.2.2 Peer-to-Peer Data Networks	164
	2	Processing M-trees with Parallel Resources	164
		2.1 CPU Parallelism	165
		2.2 I/O Parallelism	165
		2.3 Object Declustering in M-trees	167
	3	Scalable Distributed Similarity Search Structure	167
		3.1 Architecture	168
		3.2 Address Search Tree	169
		3.3 Storage Management	169
		3.3.1 Bucket Splitting	170
		3.3.2 Choosing Pivots	171
		3.4 Insertion of Objects	171
		3.5 Range Search	172
		3.6 Nearest Neighbor Search	173
		3.7 Deletions and Updates of Objects	174
		3.8 Image Adjustment	175
		3.9 Logarithmic Replication Strategy	177
		3.10 Joining the Peer-to-Peer Network	178
		3.11 Leaving the Peer-to-Peer Network	178
	4	Performance Trials	179
		4.1 Datasets and Computing Infrastructure	180
		4.2 Performance of Similarity Queries	180
		4.2.1 Global Costs	181
		4.2.2 Parallel Costs	183
		4.2.3 Comparison of Search Algorithms	188
		4.3 Data Volume Scalability	189
Concluding Summary			193
References			197
Author Index			211
Index			215
Abbreviations			219

Foreword

The area of similarity searching is a very hot topic for both research and commercial applications. Current data processing applications use data with considerably less structure and much less precise queries than traditional database systems. Examples are multimedia data like images or videos that offer query-by-example search, product catalogs that provide users with preference-based search, scientific data records from observations or experimental analyses such as biochemical and medical data, or XML documents that come from heterogeneous data sources on the Web or in intranets and thus does not exhibit a global schema. Such data can neither be ordered in a canonical manner nor meaningfully searched by precise database queries that would return exact matches.

This novel situation is what has given rise to similarity searching, also referred to as content-based or similarity retrieval. The most general approach to similarity search, still allowing construction of index structures, is modeled in metric space. In this book, Prof. Zezula and his co-authors provide the first monograph on this topic, describing its theoretical background as well as the practical search tools of this innovative technology.

In Part I, the authors describe ideas and principles, as well as generic partitioning, search and transformation strategies which have been developed for similarity search in metric spaces. Their use is illustrated in an extensive survey of available indexes. Part II concentrates on similarity search techniques for large collections of data. In particular, it starts with the pioneering work on the M-tree, developed by Prof. Zezula as one of the authors, and continues with the description of hash-based techniques for similarity searching, which formed the main topic of Dr. Dohnal's PhD dissertation. The approximate similarity search, representing another important chapter of this book, was mainly developed in the PhD dissertation of Dr. Amato. The final chapter on scalable and distributed index structures for similarity searching reports the latest efforts of the PhD candidate Dr. Batko. All these PhD dissertations have been supervised by Prof. Zezula.

This monograph is a very valuable resource for scientists who are working or want to work on the many aspects of similarity search. The authors are not only leading experts in this field, but also pedagogically first-rate scholars. Their explanations nicely combine mathematical rigor with intuitive examples and illustration. I believe this book will be a great asset for students and researchers alike.

Prof. Gerhard Weikum
Max-Planck Institute of Computer Science
Saarbruecken, Germany

Preface

In the Information Society, information holds the master key to economic influence and success. But the usefulness of information depends critically upon its quality and the speed at which it can be transferred. In domains as diverse as multimedia, molecular biology, computer-aided design and marketing and purchasing assistance, the number of data resources is growing rapidly, both with regard to database size and the variety of forms in which data comes packaged. To cope with the resulting information overkill, it is vital to find tools to search these resources efficiently and effectively. Hence the intense interest in Computer Science in searching digital data repositories.

But traditional retrieval techniques, typically based upon sorting routines and hash tables, are not appropriate for a growing number of newly-emerging data domains. More flexible methods must be found instead which take into account the needs of particular users and particular application domains.

This book is about finding efficient ways to locate user-relevant information in collections of objects which have been quantified using a pairwise distance measure between object instances. It is written in direct response to recent advances in computing, communication and storage which have led to the current flood of digital libraries, data warehouses and the limitless heterogeneity of Internet resources. The scale of the problem can be gauged by noting that almost everything we see, hear, read, write or measure will soon be available to computerized information systems. In such an environment, varied data modalities such as multimedia objects, scientific observations and measurements, statistical analyses and many others, are massively extending more traditional attribute-like data types.

Ordinary retrieval techniques are inadequate in many of these newer data domains because sorting is simply impossible. To illustrate, consider a collection of bit patterns compared using the Hamming distance, i.e., the number of bits by which a given pair of patterns differs. There is no way to sort the patterns linearly so that, selecting any arbitrary member, the other objects can be ordered in terms of steadily increasing Hamming distance. The same applies to the spectrum of colors. Obviously, we can sort colors according to their similarity with respect to a specific hue, for example pink. But we can't sort the set of all colors in such a way that, for each hue, its immediate neighbor is the hue most similar to it.

This is what has given rise to a novel indexing paradigm based upon distance. From a formal standpoint, the search problem is modelled in metric space. The collection of objects to be searched forms a subset of the metric space domain, and the distance measure applied to pairs of objects is a metric distance function. This approach significantly extends the scope of traditional search approaches and supports execution of similarity queries. By considering exact, partial, and range queries as special cases, the distance search approach is highly extensible. In the last ten years, its attractiveness has prompted major research efforts, resulting in a number of specific theories, techniques, implementation paradigms and analytic tools aimed at making the distance-based approach viable.

This book focuses on the state of the art in developing index structures for searching metric space. It consists of two parts. Part I presents the metric search approach in a nutshell. It defines the problem, describes major theoretical principles, and provides an extensive survey of specific techniques for a large range of applications. This part is self-contained and does not require any specific prerequisites. Part II concentrates on approaches particularly designed for searching in large collections of data. After describing the most popular centralized disk-based metric indexes, approximation techniques are presented as a way to significantly speed up search time at the expense of some imprecision in query results. The final chapter of the book concentrates on scalable and distributed metric structures, which can deal with data collections that for practical purposes are arbitrarily large, provided sufficient computational power is available in the computer network. In order to properly understand Part II, we recommend at a minimum reading Chapter 1 of Part I.

PAVEL ZEZULA, GIUSEPPE AMATO,

VLASTISLAV DOHNAL, AND MICHAL BATKO

Acknowledgments

We wish to acknowledge all the people who have helped us directly or indirectly in completing this book. First of all, we would like to thank Paolo Ciaccia and Marco Patella for their enthusiastic cooperation and important contribution to the development of metric search techniques. We would also like to mention our other collaborators, mainly Fausto Rabitti, Paolo Tiberio, Claudio Gennaro, and Pasquale Savino, who encouraged us to finish the preparation of this book. We are grateful to Melissa Fearon and Valerie Schofield from Springer for their technical support during the preparation phase. And we are indebted to Mark Alexander for his comments, suggestions, and modifications concerning language and style. Many technical details have been corrected due to observations by Matej Lexa, David Novák, Petr Liška and Fabrizio Falchi who have read a preliminary version of the book. We would also like to acknowledge the support of the EU Network of Excellence DELOS - No. 507618, which made this international publication possible by underwriting travel expenses, and which has served as an excellent forum for discussing the book's subject matter. The work was also partially supported by the National Research Program of the Czech Republic Project number 1ET100300419.

Acknowledgment

PART I

METRIC SEARCHING IN A NUTSHELL

Overview

As the growth of digital data accelerates in variety and extent, huge data repositories are becoming available on computer networks. For users to be able to access selected data objects, the objects need to be structured and manipulated efficiently but also effectively.

In contrast to traditional databases made up of simple attribute data, contemporary data is bulkier and more complex in nature. To deal with the increased bulk, data reduction techniques are employed as in [Barbará et al., 1997]. These approaches typically result in high-dimensional vectors or other objects for which nothing beyond pairwise distances can be measured. Such data are sometimes designated *distance-only* data. A similar situation can occur with multimedia data. Here, the standard approach is to search not at the level of the actual multimedia objects, but rather using characteristic features extracted from these objects. In such environments, an *exact match* has little meaning, and *proximity* concepts (*similarity*, *dissimilarity*) are typically much more fruitful for searching.

Proximity searching has become a fundamental computational task in a variety of application areas, including multimedia information retrieval, data mining, pattern recognition, machine learning, computer vision, biomedical databases, data compression and statistical data analysis. It was originally studied mostly within computational geometry, but has recently attracted increasing attention in the database community, because of the growing need for dealing with a large, often distributed, volume of data. As a consequence, performance has become an important criterion for a successful design. It is well-known that performance is a noteworthy constraint on software systems, and a lack of it is the leading cause for failure. In applications such as data warehousing, with huge repositories of heterogeneous data, it's easy to see how important search speed is and how difficult it can be to achieve the necessary response time. Other good examples of data intensive applications are data mining and multimedia content-based retrieval, where the amount of data processed is usually counted in terabytes or more.

The primary objective of doing a similarity search in metric space is not terribly different from that in other kinds of searching. In each case the task is to retrieve subsets from available data collections. But there are many aspects of similarity searching in metric spaces which make it distinct. In order to systematically explain the principles which have led to the development of numerous specific proposals, we first explain in Chapter 1 how distances can be used to formalize the problem of proximity and how metric space postulates can be applied to data partitioning and pruning for different search methods. Chapter 2 is devoted to a structured survey of existing indexing techniques designed especially for metric data storage and retrieval.

Chapter 1

FOUNDATIONS OF METRIC SPACE SEARCHING

The search problem is constrained in general by the type of data stored in the underlying database, the method of comparing individual data instances, and the specification of the query by which users express their information needs. Treating data collections as metric objects brings a great advantage in generality, because many data classes and information-seeking strategies conform to the metric view. Accordingly, a single metric indexing technique can be applied to many specific search problems quite different in nature. In this way, the important *extensibility* property of indexing structures is automatically satisfied. An indexing scheme that allows various forms of queries, or which can be modified to provide additional functionality, is of more value than an indexing scheme otherwise equivalent in power or even better in certain respects, but which cannot be extended.

Because of the solid mathematical foundations underlying the notion of *metric space*, straightforward but precise partitioning and pruning rules can be constructed. This is very important for developing index structures, especially in cases where query execution costs are not only I/O-bound but also CPU-bound. In this chapter, we put clear constraints on the scope and capability of metric searching and define principles which are used to construct corresponding search indexes.

In Section 1, we introduce the problem of metric searching and justify its importance with respect to other approaches. After defining a metric space in Section 2, we show examples of several distance measures which are used for searching in diverse data collections in Section 3. Another issue closely related to distance measures is the problem of posing queries presented in Section 4. A specification of basic partitioning principles in Section 5 helps to understand principles of query execution in Section 6. The remaining sections in Chapter 1 are devoted to performance related issues. Specifically, techniques aimed at reducing the number of distance computations are discussed in Section 7, useful metric space transformations are presented in Section 8, and concepts of approximate similarity search are explained in Section 9. Finally, Section 10 provides a collection of analytic tools and approaches especially developed for metric index structures.

1. The Distance Searching Problem

Searching has always been one of the most prominent data processing operations. However, exact-match retrieval, typical for traditional databases, is neither feasible nor meaningful for data types in the present digital age. The reason is that the constantly expanding data of modern digital collections lacks structure and precision. Because of this, what constitutes a match to a request is often different from that implied in more traditional, well-established areas.

A very useful, if not necessary, search paradigm is to quantify the *proximity*, *similarity*, or *dissimilarity* of a query object versus the objects stored in a database to be searched. Roughly speaking, objects that are *near* a given query object form the query response set. A useful abstraction for nearness is provided by the mathematical notion of *metric space* [Kelly, 1955]. We consider the problem of organizing and searching large datasets from the perspective of *generic* or *arbitrary* metric spaces, sometimes conveniently labelled *distance spaces*. In general, the search problem can be described as follows:

PROBLEM 1.1 *Let $\mathcal{D}$ be a domain, d a distance measure on $\mathcal{D}$, and $(\mathcal{D}, d)$ a metric space. Given a set $X \subseteq \mathcal{D}$ of n elements, preprocess or structure the data so that proximity queries are answered efficiently.*

From a practical point of view, X can be seen as a file (a dataset or a collection) of objects that takes values from the domain $\mathcal{D}$, with d as the proximity measure, i.e., the distance function defined for an arbitrary pair of objects from $\mathcal{D}$. Though several types of similarity queries exist and others are expected to appear in the future, the basic types are known as the *similarity range* and the *nearest neighbor(s)* queries.

In a distance space, the only possible operation on data objects is the computation of a distance function on pairs of objects which satisfies the *triangle inequality*. In contrast, objects in a *coordinate space* – coordinate space being a special case of metric space – can be seen as vectors. Such spaces satisfy some additional properties that can be exploited in storage (index) structure designs. Naturally, the distance between vectors can be computed, but each vector can also be uniquely located in coordinate space. Further, vector representation allows us to perform operations like vector addition and subtraction. Thus, new vectors can be constructed from prior vectors. For more information, see e.g., [Gaede and Günther, 1998, Böhm et al., 2001] for surveys of techniques that exploit the properties of coordinate space.

Since many data domains in use are represented by vectors, there might seem to be little point in hunting efficient index structures in pure metric spaces, where the number of possible geometric properties would seem limited. The following discussion should clarify the issue and provide sufficient evidence of the importance of the distance searching problem.

Applications managing non-vector data like character strings (natural language words, DNA sequences, etc.) do exist, and their number is growing. But even when the objects processed are vectors, the properties of the underlying coordinate space cannot always be easily exploited. If the individual vectors are correlated, i.e., there is *cross-talk* between them, the neighborhood of the vectors seen through the lens of the distance measure between them will not map directly to their coordinate space, and vice versa. Distance functions which allow user-defined weights to be specified better reflect the user's perception of the problem and are therefore preferable. This occurs, for instance, when searching images using color similarity, where cross-talk between color components is a factor that must be taken into account.

Existing solutions for searching in coordinate space suffer from the so-called *dimensionality curse* – such structures either become slower than naive algorithms with linear search times or they use too much space. Though the structure of indexed data may be intrinsically much simpler (the data may, e.g., lie in a lower-dimensional hyperplane), this is typically difficult to ascertain. Moreover, some spaces have coordinates restricted to small sets of possible values (perhaps even binary), so that the use of such coordinates is not necessarily helpful.

Depending on the data objects, the distance measure and the dimensionality of a given space, we agree that the use of coordinates can be advantageous in special cases, resulting in non-extensible solutions. But we also agree with [Clarkson, 1997], that

> *to strip the problem down to its essentials by only considering distances,*
> *it is reasonable to find the minimal properties needed for fast algorithms.*

In summary, the primary reasons for looking at the distance data search problem seriously are the following:

1 There are numerous applications where the proximity criteria offer no special properties but distance, so a metric search becomes the sole option.

2 Many specialized solutions for proximity search perform no better than indexing techniques based on distances. Metric search thus forms a viable alternative.

3 If a good solution utilizing generic metric space can be found, it will provide high extensibility. It has the potential to work for a large number of existing proximity measures, as well as many others to be defined in the future.

2.   The Metric Space

A similarity search can be seen as a process of obtaining data objects in order of their distance or dissimilarity from a given query object. It is a kind of *sorting, ordering,* or *ranking* of objects with respect to the query object, where the ranking criterion is the distance measure. Though this principle works for any distance measure, we restrict the possible set of measures by the *metric postulates.*

Suppose a metric space $\mathcal{M} = (\mathcal{D}, d)$ defined for a domain of objects (or the objects' *keys* or *indexed features*) $\mathcal{D}$ and a total (distance) function d. In this metric space, the properties of the function $d : \mathcal{D} \times \mathcal{D} \mapsto \mathbb{R}$, sometimes called the metric space postulates, are typically characterized as:

$$\forall x, y \in \mathcal{D}, d(x, y) \geq 0 \qquad\qquad \text{non-negativity,}$$

$$\forall x, y \in \mathcal{D}, d(x, y) = d(y, x) \qquad\qquad \text{symmetry,}$$

$$\forall x, y \in \mathcal{D}, x = y \Leftrightarrow d(x, y) = 0 \qquad\qquad \text{identity,}$$

$$\forall x, y, z \in \mathcal{D}, d(x, z) \leq d(x, y) + d(y, z) \qquad\qquad \text{triangle inequality.}$$

For brevity, some authors call the *metric function* simply the *metric*. There are also several variations of metric spaces. In order to specify them more easily, we first transform the metric space postulates above into an equivalent form in which the identity postulate is decomposed into (p3) and (p4):

(p1) $\forall x, y \in \mathcal{D}, d(x, y) \geq 0$ non-negativity,

(p2) $\forall x, y \in \mathcal{D}, d(x, y) = d(y, x)$ symmetry,

(p3) $\forall x \in \mathcal{D}, d(x, x) = 0$ reflexivity,

(p4) $\forall x, y \in \mathcal{D}, x \neq y \Rightarrow d(x, y) > 0$ positiveness,

(p5) $\forall x, y, z \in \mathcal{D}, d(x, z) \leq d(x, y) + d(y, z)$ triangle inequality.

If the distance function does not satisfy the positiveness property (p4), it is called a *pseudo-metric*. In this book, we do not consider pseudo-metric functions separately, because such functions can be transformed to the standard metric by regarding any pair of objects with zero distance as a single object. Such a transformation is correct: if the triangle inequality (p5) holds, we can prove that $d(x, y) = 0 \Rightarrow \forall z \in \mathcal{D}, d(x, z) = d(y, z)$. Specifically, by combining the triangle inequalities

$$d(x, z) \leq d(x, y) + d(y, z)$$

and

$$d(y, z) \leq d(x, y) + d(x, z),$$

we get $d(x, z) = d(y, z)$, if $d(x, y) = 0$.

If, on the other hand, the symmetry property (p2) does not hold, we talk about a *quasi-metric*. For example, let the objects be different locations within a city, and the distance function the physical distance a car must travel between them. The existence of one-way streets implies the function must be asymmetrical. There are techniques to transform asymmetric distances into symmetric form, for example:

$$d_{sym}(x, y) = d_{asym}(x, y) + d_{asym}(y, x).$$

To round out our list of possible metric distance function variants, we conclude this section with a version which satisfies a stronger constraint on the triangle inequality. It is called the *super-metric* or the *ultra-metric*. Such a function satisfies the following tightened triangle inequality:

$$\forall x, y, z \in \mathcal{D}, d(x, z) \leq \max\{d(x, y), d(y, z)\}.$$

The geometric characterization of the super-metric requires every triangle to have at least two sides of equal length, i.e., to be *isosceles*, which implies that the third side must be shorter than the others. Ultra-metrics are widely used in the field of biology, particularly in evolutionary biology. By comparing the DNA sequences of pairs of species, evolutionary biologists obtain an estimate of the time which has elapsed since the species separated. From these distances, an evolutionary tree (sometimes called phylogenetic tree) can be reconstructed, where the weights of the tree edges are determined by the time elapsed between two speciation events [Parnas and Ron, 2001, Rammal et al., 1986]. Having a set of extant species, the evolutionary tree forms an ultra-metric tree with all the species stored in leaves and an identical distance from root to leaves. The ultra-metric tree is a model of the underlying ultra-metric distance function.

3. Distance Measures

The distance functions of metric spaces represent a way of quantifying the closeness of objects in a given domain. In the following, we present examples of distance functions used in practice on various types of data. Distance functions are often tailored to specific applications or a class of possible applications. In practice, distance functions are specified by domain experts, however, no distance function restricts the range of queries that can be asked with this metric.

Depending on the character of values returned, distance measures can be divided into two groups:

- **discrete** – distance functions which return only a small (predefined) set of values, and

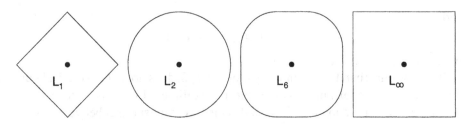

Figure 1.1. The sets of points at a constant distance from the central point for different L_p distance functions.

- **continuous** – distance functions in which the cardinality of the set of values returned is very large or infinite.

An example of a continuous function is the *Euclidean distance* between vectors, while the *edit distance* on strings represents a discrete function. As we will see in Chapter 2, some metric structures are applicable only in the area of discrete metric functions. In the following, we mainly survey metric functions used for complex data types like multidimensional vectors, strings or sets. However, even domains as simple as the real numbers ($\mathcal{D} = \mathbb{R}$) can be seen in terms of metric data, by defining the distance function as $d = |o_i - o_j|$, that is, as the absolute value of the difference of any pair of numbers (o_i, o_j) from $\mathcal{D}$.

3.1 Minkowski Distances

The *Minkowski distance* functions form a whole family of metric functions, designated as the L_p metrics, because the individual cases depend on the numeric parameter p. These functions are defined on n-dimensional vectors of real numbers as:

$$L_p[(x_1, \ldots, x_n), (y_1, \ldots, y_n)] = \sqrt[p]{\sum_{i=1}^{n} |x_i - y_i|^p} \,,$$

where the L_1 metric is known as the *Manhattan distance* (also the *City-Block distance*), the L_2 distance denotes the well-known Euclidean distance, and the $L_\infty = \max_{i=1}^{n} |x_i - y_i|$ is called the *maximum distance*, the *infinite distance* or the *chessboard distance*. Figure 1.1 illustrates some members of the L_p family, where the shapes denote points of a 2-dimensional vector space that are at the same distance from the central point. The L_p metrics find use in a number of cases where numerical vectors have independent coordinates, e.g., in measurements of scientific experiments, environmental observations, or the study of different aspects of the business process.

3.2   Quadratic Form Distance

Several applications using vector data have individual components, i.e., feature dimensions, correlated, so a kind of cross-talk exists between individual dimensions. Consider, for example, color histograms of images, where each dimension represents a specific color. To compute a distance, the red component, for example, must be compared not only with the dimension representing the red color, but also with the pink and orange, because these colors are similar. The Euclidean distance L_2 does not reflect any correlation of features of color histograms. A distance model that has been successfully applied to image databases in [Faloutsos et al., 1994], and that has the power to model dependencies between different components of features, is provided by the *quadratic form distance* functions in [Hafner et al., 1995, Seidl and Kriegel, 1997]. In this approach, the distance measure of two n-dimensional vectors is based on an $n \times n$ positive semi-definite matrix $M = [m_{i,j}]$, where the *weights* $m_{i,j}$ denote how strong the connection between two components i and j of vectors $\vec{x}$ and $\vec{y}$ is, respectively. These weights are usually normalized so that $0 \le m_{i,j} \le 1$ with the diagonal elements $m_{i,i} = 1$. The following expression represents a generalized quadratic distance measure d_M, where the superscript T denotes vector transposition:

$$d_M(\vec{x}, \vec{y}) = \sqrt{(\vec{x} - \vec{y})^T \cdot M \cdot (\vec{x} - \vec{y})} \; .$$

Observe that this definition of distance also subsumes the Euclidean distance when the matrix M is equal to the identity matrix. Also the weighted Euclidean distance measure can be expressed using the matrix with non-zero elements on the diagonal representing weights of the individual dimensions, i.e., $M = diag(w_1, \ldots, w_n)$. Applying such a matrix, the quadratic form distance formula turns out to be as follows, yielding the general formula for the weighted Euclidean distance:

$$d_M(\vec{x}, \vec{y}) = \sqrt{\sum_{i=1}^{n} w_i (x_i - y_i)^2} \; .$$

As an example, consider simplified color histograms with three different colors (blue, red, orange) represented as 3-D vectors. Assuming three normalized histograms of a pure red image $\vec{x} = (0, 1, 0)$, a pure orange image $\vec{y} = (0, 0, 1)$ and a pure blue image $\vec{z} = (1, 0, 0)$, the Euclidean distance evaluates to the following distances: $L_2(\vec{x}, \vec{y}) = \sqrt{2}$ and $L_2(\vec{x}, \vec{z}) = \sqrt{2}$. This implies that the orange and the blue images are equidistant from the red. However, human color perception is quite different and perceives red and orange to be more alike than red and blue. This can be modeled with the matrix M shown below, yielding a

$\vec{x}, \vec{y}$ distance equal to $\sqrt{0.2}$, while the distance $\vec{x}, \vec{z}$ evaluates to $\sqrt{2}$.

$$M = \begin{bmatrix} 1.0 & 0.0 & 0.0 \\ 0.0 & 1.0 & 0.9 \\ 0.0 & 0.9 & 1.0 \end{bmatrix}$$

The quadratic form distance measure may be computationally expensive, depending upon the dimensionality of the vectors. Color image histograms are typically high-dimensional vectors consisting of 64 or 256 distinct colors (vector dimensions).

3.3 Edit Distance

The closeness of sequences of symbols (strings) can be effectively measured by the *edit distance*, also called the *Levenshtein distance*, presented in [Levenshtein, 1965]. The distance between two strings $x = x_1 \cdots x_n$ and $y = y_1 \cdots y_m$ is defined as the minimum number of atomic edit operations (insert, delete, and replace) needed to transform string x into string y. The atomic operations are defined formally as follows:

- **insert** the character c into the string x at the position i:
  $ins(x, i, c) = x_1 x_2 \cdots x_i c x_{i+1} \cdots x_n$;

- **delete** the character at the position i from the string x:
  $del(x, i) = x_1 x_2 \cdots x_{i-1} x_{i+1} \cdots x_n$;

- **replace** the character at the position i in x with the new character c:
  $replace(x, i, c) = x_1 x_2 \cdots x_{i-1} c x_{i+1} \cdots x_n$.

The generalized edit distance function assigns weights (positive real numbers) to individual atomic operations. Hence, the distance between strings x and y is the minimum value of the sum of weighted atomic operations needed to transform x into y. If the weights of insert and delete operations differ, the edit distance is not symmetric (violating property (p2) defined in Section 2) and therefore not a metric function. To see why, consider the following example, where the weights of atomic operations are set as $w_{ins} = 2$, $w_{del} = 1$, $w_{replace} = 1$:

$$d_{edit}(\text{``combine''}, \text{``combination''}) = 9$$
$$- \text{ replacement } e \rightarrow a, \text{ insertion of } t, i, o, n$$
$$d_{edit}(\text{``combination''}, \text{``combine''}) = 5$$
$$- \text{ replacement } a \rightarrow e, \text{ deletion of } t, i, o, n$$

Within this book, we only assume metric functions, thus the weights of insert and delete operations must be the same. However, the weight of the replace operation can differ. Usually, the edit distance is defined with all weights equal to one. An excellent survey on string matching can be found in [Navarro, 2001].

Using weighting functions, we can define a most generic edit distance which assigns different costs even to operations on individual characters. For example, the replacement $a \rightarrow b$ can be assigned a different weight than $a \rightarrow c$. To retain the metric postulates, some additional limits must be placed on weight functions, e.g. symmetry of substitutions – the cost of $a \rightarrow b$ must be the same as the cost of $b \rightarrow a$.

3.4 Tree Edit Distance

The *tree edit distance* is a well-known proximity measure for trees, extensively studied in [Sankoff and Kruskal, 1983, Apostolico and Galil, 1997]. The tree edit distance function defines a distance between two tree structures as the minimum cost needed to convert the source tree to the target tree using a predefined set of tree edit operations, such as the insertion or deletion of a node. In fact, the problem of computing the distance between two trees is a generalization of the edit distance to labeled trees. The individual cost of edit operations (atomic operations) may be constant for the whole tree, or may vary with the level in the tree at which the operation is carried out. The reason for having different weights for tree levels is that the insertion of a single node near the root may be more significant than adding a new leaf node. This will, of course, depend on the application domain. Several strategies for setting costs and computing the tree edit distance are described in the doctoral thesis by Lee [Lee, 2002]. Since XML documents are typically modeled as rooted labeled trees, the tree edit distance can also be used to measure the structural dissimilarity of XML documents [Guha et al., 2002, Cobena et al., 2002].

3.5 Jaccard's Coefficient

Let us now focus on a different type of data and present a similarity measure that is applicable to sets. Assuming two sets A and B, *Jaccard's coefficient* is defined as

$$d(A, B) = 1 - \frac{|A \cap B|}{|A \cup B|} .$$

This distance function is simply based on the ratio between the cardinalities of intersection and union of the compared sets. As an example of an application that deals with sets, suppose we have access to a log file of web addresses (URLs) accessed by visitors to an Internet Café. Along with the addresses, visitor identifications are also stored in the log. The behavior of a user browsing the Internet can be expressed as the set of visited network sites and Jaccard's coefficient can be applied to assess the similarity (or dissimilarity) of individual users' search interests.

An application of this metric to vector data is called the *Tanimoto similarity* measure (see for example [Kohonen, 1984]), the distance version of which can be defined as:

$$d_{TS}(\vec{x}, \vec{y}) = 1 - \frac{\vec{x} \cdot \vec{y}}{\|\vec{x}\|^2 + \|\vec{y}\|^2 - \vec{x} \cdot \vec{y}},$$

where $\vec{x} \cdot \vec{y}$ is the scalar product of $\vec{x}$ and $\vec{y}$, and $\|\vec{x}\|$ is the Euclidean norm of $\vec{x}$.

3.6 Hausdorff Distance

An even more complicated distance measure defined on sets is the *Hausdorff distance* [Huttenlocher et al., 1993]. In contrast to Jaccard's coefficient, where any two elements of sets must be either equal or completely distinct, the Hausdorff distance matches elements based upon a distance function d_e. Specifically, the Hausdorff distance is defined as follows. Assume:

$$
\begin{aligned}
d_p(x, B) &= \inf_{y \in B} d_e(x, y), \\
d_p(A, y) &= \inf_{x \in A} d_e(x, y), \\
d_s(A, B) &= \sup_{x \in A} d_p(x, B), \\
d_s(B, A) &= \sup_{y \in B} d_p(A, y).
\end{aligned}
$$

Then the Hausdorff distance over sets A, B is:

$$d(A, B) = \max\{d_s(A, B), d_s(B, A)\}.$$

The distance $d_e(x, y)$ between two elements of sets A and B can be an arbitrary metric, e.g. the Euclidean distance, and is application-specific. Succinctly put, the Hausdorff distance measures the extent to which each point of the "model" set A lies near some point of the "image" set B and vice versa. In other words, two sets are within the Hausdorff distance r from each other if and only if any point of one set is within the distance r from some point of the other set. A typical application is the comparison of shapes in image processing, where each shape is defined by a set of points in a 2-dimensional space.

3.7 Time Complexity

In general, computing a distance is a nontrivial process which will certainly be much more computationally intensive than a keyword comparison as used in traditional search structures. For example, the L_p norms (metrics) are computed in linear time dependent on the dimensionality n of the space. However, the quadratic form distance is much more expensive because it involves multiplications by a matrix M. Thus, the time complexity in principle is $\mathcal{O}(n^2 + n)$. Existing dynamic programming algorithms which evaluate the edit distance on two strings of length n and m have time complexity $\mathcal{O}(nm)$. Tree edit distance is even more demanding and has a worst-case time complexity of $\mathcal{O}(n^4)$, where n refers to the number of tree nodes. For more details see for example [Lee, 2002]. Similarity metrics between sets are also very time-intensive to evaluate. The Hausdorff distance has a time complexity of $\mathcal{O}(nm)$ for sets of size n and m. A more sophisticated algorithm by [Alt et al., 1991] can reduce its complexity to $\mathcal{O}((n + m)log(n + m))$.

In summary, the high computational complexity of metric distance functions gives rise to an important objective for metric index structures, namely minimizing the number of distance evaluations. Practical uses for the theoretical underpinnings discussed in Section 7 are demonstrated in the survey in Chapter 2.

4.   Similarity Queries

A similarity query is defined explicitly or implicitly by a query object q and a constraint on the form and extent of proximity required, typically expressed as a distance. The response to a query returns all objects which satisfy the selection conditions, presumed to be those objects close to the given query object. In the following, we first define elementary types of similarity queries, and then discuss possibilities for combining them.

4.1   Range Query

Probably the most common type of similarity query is the *similarity range query* $R(q, r)$. The query is specified by a query object $q \in \mathcal{D}$, with some query radius r as the distance constraint. The query retrieves all objects found within distance r of q, formally:

$$R(q, r) = \{o \in X, d(o, q) \leq r\}.$$

If needed, individual objects in the response set can be ranked according to their distance with respect to q. Observe that the query object q need not exist in the collection $X \subseteq \mathcal{D}$ to be searched, and the only restriction on q is that it belongs to the metric domain $\mathcal{D}$. For convenience, Figure 1.2a shows an example of a range query. In a geographic application, a range query can formulate the requirement: *Give me all museums within a distance of two kilometers from my hotel.*

When the search radius is zero, the range query $R(q, 0)$ is called a *point query* or *exact match*. In this case, we are looking for an identical copy (or copies) of the query object q. The most usual use of this type of query is in delete algorithms, when we want to locate an object to remove from the database.

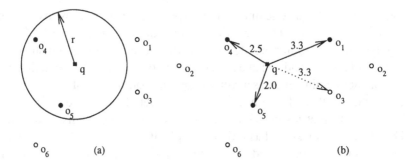

Figure 1.2. (a) Range query $R(q, r)$ and (b) nearest neighbor query $3NN(q)$.

4.2   Nearest Neighbor Query

Whenever we want to search for similar objects using a range search, we must specify a maximal distance for objects to qualify. But it can be difficult to specify the radius without some knowledge of the data and the distance function. For example, the range $r = 3$ of the edit distance metric represents less than four edit operations between compared strings. This has a clear semantic meaning. However, a distance of two color-histogram vectors of images is a real number whose quantification cannot be so easily interpreted. If too small a query radius is specified, the empty set may be returned and a new search with a larger radius will be needed to get any result. On the other hand, if query radii are too large, the query may be computationally expensive and the response sets contain many nonsignificant objects.

An alternative way to search for similar objects is to use *nearest neighbor queries*. The elementary version of this query finds the closest object to the given query object, that is the nearest neighbor of q. The concept can be generalized to the case where we look for the k nearest neighbors. Specifically, $kNN(q)$ query retrieves the k nearest neighbors of the object q. If the collection to be searched consists of fewer than k objects, the query returns the whole database. Formally, the response set can be defined as follows:

$$kNN(q) = \{R \subseteq X, |R| = k \wedge \forall x \in R, y \in X - R : d(q, x) \leq d(q, y)\}.$$

When several objects lie at the same distance from the k-th nearest neighbor, the ties are solved arbitrarily. Figure 1.2b illustrates the situation for a $3NN(q)$ query. Here the objects o_1, o_3 are both at distance 3.3 and the object o_1 is chosen as the third nearest neighbor (at random), instead of o_3. If we continue with our geographic application, we can pose a query: *Tell me which three museums are the closest to my hotel.*

4.3 Reverse Nearest Neighbor Query

In many situations, it is interesting to know how a specific object is perceived or ranked in terms of distance by other objects in the dataset, i.e., which objects view the query object q as their nearest neighbor. This is known as a *reverse nearest neighbor* search. The generic version, conveniently designated $kRNN(q)$, returns all objects with q among their k nearest neighbors. An example is illustrated in Figure 1.3a, where the dotted circles denote the distance to the second nearest neighbor of objects o_i. The objects o_4, o_5, o_6 satisfying the $2RNN(q)$ query, that is those objects with q among their two nearest neighbors, are represented by black points.

Recent work, such as [Korn and Muthukrishnan, 2000, Stanoi et al., 2001, Yang and Lin, 2001, Stanoi et al., 2000, Kollios et al., 1999], has highlighted the importance of reverse nearest neighbor queries in decision support systems, profile-based marketing, document repositories, and management of mobile devices. The response set of the general $kRNN(q)$ query may be defined as follows:

$$kRNN(q) \quad = \quad \{R \subseteq X, \forall x \in R : q \in kNN(x) \wedge$$
$$\forall x \in X - R : q \notin kNN(x)\}.$$

Observe that even an object located far from the query object q can belong to the $kRNN(q)$ response set. At the same time, an object near q need not necessarily be a member of the $kRNN(q)$ result. This characteristic of the reverse nearest neighbor search is called the *non-locality property*. A specific query can ask for: *all hotels with a specific museum as the nearest cultural heritage site.*

4.4 Similarity Join

The development of Internet services often requires the integration of heterogeneous sources of data. Such sources are typically unstructured whereas the intended services often require structured data. An important challenge here is to provide consistent and error-free data, which entails some kind of *data cleaning* or *integration* typically implemented by a process called a *similarity join*. The similarity join between two datasets $X \subseteq \mathcal{D}$ and $Y \subseteq \mathcal{D}$ retrieves all pairs of objects $(x \in X, y \in Y)$ whose distance does not exceed a given threshold $\mu \geq 0$. Specifically, the result of the similarity join $J(X, Y, \mu)$ is defined as:

$$J(X, Y, \mu) = \{(x, y) \in X \times Y : d(x, y) \leq \mu\}.$$

If $\mu = 0$, we get the traditional *natural join*. If the datasets X and Y coincide, i.e., $X = Y$, we talk about the *similarity self join* and denote it as $SJ(\mu) = J(X, X, \mu)$, where X is the searched dataset. Figure 1.3b presents an example of a similarity self join $SJ(2.5)$. For illustration, consider a bibliographic database obtained from diverse resources. In order to clean the data, a similarity

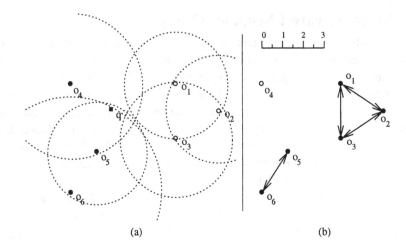

Figure 1.3. (a) A reverse nearest neighbor query $2RNN(q)$ and (b) a similarity self join query $SJ(2.5)$. Qualifying objects are filled.

join request might identify all document titles with an edit distance smaller than two. Another application might maintain a collection of hotels and a collection of museums. The user might wish to find *all pairs of hotels and museums which are a five minute walk apart.*

4.5   Combinations of Queries

As an extension of the query types defined above, we can define additional types of queries as combinations of the previous ones. For example, we might combine a range query with a nearest neighbor query to get $kNN(q, r)$ with the response set:

$$kNN(q,r) = \{R \subseteq X, |R| \leq k \wedge \forall x \in R, y \in X - R :$$
$$d(q,x) \leq d(q,y) \wedge d(q,x) \leq r\}.$$

In fact, we have constrained the result from two sides. First, all objects in the result-set should lie at a distance not greater than r, and if there are more than k of them, just the first (i.e., the nearest) k are returned. By analogy, we can combine a similarity self join and a nearest neighbor search. In such queries, we limit the number of pairs returned for a specific object to the value k.

4.6   Complex Similarity Queries

Efficient processing of queries consisting of more than one similarity predicate, i.e., *complex similarity queries*, differs substantially from traditional (Boolean) query processing. The problem was studied first by [Fagin, 1996, Fagin, 1998]. The basic lesson learned is that the similarity score (or grade) a retrieved object receives as a whole depends not only on the scores it gets for individual predicates, but also on how such scores are combined. In order to understand the problem, consider a query for circular shapes of red color. In order to find the best match, it is not enough to retrieve the best matches for the color features and the shapes. Naturally, the best match for the whole query need not be the best match for a single (color or shape) predicate.

To this aim, [Fagin, 1996] has proposed the so-called $\mathcal{A}_0$ algorithm which solves the problem. This algorithm assumes that for each query predicate we have an index structure able to return objects of decreasing similarity. For every predicate i, the algorithm successively creates a set X_i containing objects which best match the query predicate. This building phase continues until all sets X_i contain at least k common objects, i.e., $|\bigcap_i X_i| = k$. This implies that the cardinalities of sets X_i are not known in advance, so a rather complicated incremental similarity search is needed (please refer to Section 6.2 for details). For all objects $o \in \bigcup_i X_i$, the algorithm evaluates all query predicates and establishes their final ranks. Then the first k objects are returned as a result. This algorithm is correct, but its performance is not very optimal and the expected query execution costs can be quite high.

[Ciaccia et al., 1998b] have concentrated on complex similarity queries expressed through a generic language. On the other hand, they assume that query predicates are from a single feature domain, i.e., from the same metric space. Contrary to the language level that deals with similarity scores, the proposed evaluation process is based on distances between feature values, because metric indexes can use just distances to evaluate predicates. The proposed solution suggests that the index should process complex queries as a whole, evaluating multiple similarity predicates at a time. The flexibility of this approach is demonstrated by considering three different similarity languages: fuzzy standard, fuzzy algebraic and weighted sum. The possibility to implement such an approach is demonstrated through an extension of the M-tree [Ciaccia et al., 1997b]. Experimental results show that performance of the extended M-tree is consistently better than the $\mathcal{A}_0$ algorithm. The main drawback of this approach is that even though it is able to employ more features during the search, these features are compared using a single distance function. An extension of the M-tree [Ciaccia and Patella, 2000a] which goes further is able to compare different features with arbitrary distance functions. This index structure outperforms the $\mathcal{A}_0$ algorithm as well. Details of this structure are given in Chapter 3.

A *similarity algebra with weights* has been introduced in [Ciaccia et al., 2000]. This is a generalization of relational algebra to allow the formulation of complex similarity queries over multimedia databases. The main contribution of this work is that it combines within a single framework several relevant

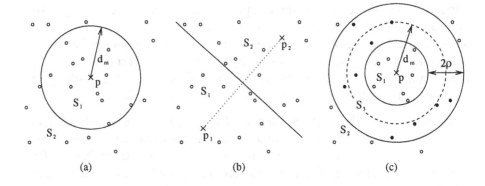

Figure 1.4. Examples of partitioning: (a) the ball partitioning, (b) the generalized hyperplane partitioning, and (c) the excluded middle partitioning.

aspects of the similarity search, such as new operators (Top and Cut), weights to express user preferences, and scores to rank search results.

5. Basic Partitioning Principles

Partitioning, in general, is one of the most fundamental principles of any storage structure, aiming at dividing the search space into sub-groups, so that once a query is given, only some of these groups are searched. Given a set $S \subseteq \mathcal{D}$ of objects in metric space $\mathcal{M} = (\mathcal{D}, d)$, [Uhlmann, 1991] defines *ball partitioning* and *generalized hyperplane partitioning*, while [Yianilos, 1999] suggests *excluded middle partitioning*. In the following, we briefly characterize these techniques.

5.1 Ball Partitioning

Ball partitioning breaks the set S into subsets S_1 and S_2 using a spherical cut with respect to $p \in \mathcal{D}$, where p is the *pivot*, chosen arbitrarily. Let d_m be the median of $\{d(o_i, p), \forall o_i \in S\}$. Then all $o_j \in S$ are distributed to S_1 or S_2 according to the following rules:

- $S_1 \leftarrow \{o_j \mid d(o_j, p) \leq d_m\}$,

- $S_2 \leftarrow \{o_j \mid d(o_j, p) \geq d_m\}$.

The redundant conditions $\leq$ and $\geq$ assure balance when the median value is not unique. This is accomplished by assigning each element at the median distance to one of the subsets in an arbitrary, but balanced, fashion. An example of a data space containing twenty-three objects is depicted in Figure 1.4a. The selected pivot p and the median distance d_m establish the ball partitioning.

5.2   Generalized Hyperplane Partitioning

Generalized hyperplane partitioning can be considered as an orthogonal principle to ball partitioning. This partitioning also breaks the set S into subsets S_1 and S_2. This time, though, two reference objects (pivots) $p_1, p_2 \in \mathcal{D}$ are arbitrarily chosen. All other objects $o_j \in S$ are assigned to S_1 or S_2 depending upon their distances from the selected pivots as follows:

- $S_1 \leftarrow \{o_j \mid d(p_1, o_j) \leq d(p_2, o_j)\}$,

- $S_2 \leftarrow \{o_j \mid d(p_1, o_j) \geq d(p_2, o_j)\}$.

In contrast to ball partitioning, the generalized hyperplane does not guarantee a balanced split, and a suitable choice of reference points to achieve this objective is an interesting challenge. An example of a balanced split of a hypothetical dataset is given in Figure 1.4b.

5.3   Excluded Middle Partitioning

Excluded middle partitioning [Yianilos, 1999] divides S into three subsets S_1, S_2 and S_3. In principle, it is an extension of ball partitioning which has been motivated by the following fact: Though similarity queries search for objects lying within a small vicinity of the query object, whenever a query object appears near the partitioning threshold, the search process typically requires accessing both of the ball-partitioned subsets. The central idea of excluded middle partitioning is therefore to leave out points near the threshold d_m in defining the two subsets S_1 and S_2. The excluded points form the third subset S_3. An illustration of excluded middle partitioning can be seen in Figure 1.4c, where the dark objects fall into the exclusion zone. With such an arrangement, the search for similar objects always ignores at least one of the subsets S_1 or S_2, provided that the search selectivity is smaller than the *thickness* of the exclusion zone. Naturally, the excluded points cannot be lost, so they can either be considered to form a third subset or, if the set is large, the basis of a new partitioning process. Given the thickness of the exclusion zone 2ρ, the partitioning can be defined as follows:

- $S_1 \leftarrow \{o_j \mid d(o_j, p) \leq d_m - \rho\}$,

- $S_2 \leftarrow \{o_j \mid d(o_j, p) > d_m + \rho\}$,

- $S_3 \leftarrow$ otherwise.

Figure 1.4c also depicts a situation where the split is balanced, i.e., the cardinalities of S_1 and S_2 are the same. However, this is not always guaranteed.

5.4   Extensions

Naturally, the basic partitioning principles can be generalized and extended in several ways. In principle,

- The binary partitioning can be extended into multiple partitioning by considering several thresholds, i.e., the set S can be divided into $k > 2$ groups.

- The partitioning process can continue recursively so that a tree organization can be built in a top-down way.

Specific combinations of these strategies have resulted in numerous practical storage structure designs, a survey of which is the subject of Chapter 2.

6. Principles of Similarity Query Execution

In the following, we discuss some general, rather abstract, principles of similarity query execution. In addition to partitioning principles, strategies for query execution form another important part of any search structure because they can significantly influence the efficiency of answering queries. In Section 6.1 we first concentrate on similarity range and nearest neighbor queries using two model structures: the sequential scan and a class of hierarchically partitioned structure. Section 6.2 is devoted to the more generic case of the so-called incremental similarity search.

6.1 Basic Strategies

The simplest, not always inefficient, strategy for executing similarity queries can be defined on a *sequential* organization of objects. Since the query object q is a search parameter which varies from search to search, the ordering of data objects with respect to q cannot be guaranteed, and all objects of a given file must therefore be processed. For a similarity range query, the response set is obtained by consecutively computing distances of data objects to q, and objects inside of the threshold r incrementally form the response set. The construction of the set of nearest neighbors is also an incremental process. Assuming $k \leq n$, the initial version of such a set is formed by the first k objects ordered with respect to their distance from q. For all the others, an object o_i is inserted in the response set if and only if $d(q, o_i) < d(q, o_k)$, where o_k is the k-th nearest neighbor of q at a given stage of query execution. Whenever a new object is inserted in the response set, the previous k-th nearest neighbor is eliminated.

To achieve sub-linear search complexity, numerous similarity search structures have been proposed (see Chapter 2 for a survey of the most important). These separate data objects into subsets in such a way that only some of the subsets need to be accessed to solve a given query. As we will see later, organizational strategies differ wildly, depending upon their underlying partitioning principles (see Section 5) and connecting structures.

In order to demonstrate the generic principles of search strategies used in index structures, we assume a kind of hypothetical organization of metric data. Specifically, an entry $N = (G, \mathcal{R}(G))$ of the structure consists of a set G of metric objects or other entries, and a specification of the *bounding region*

Range Search Algorithm
Input: query region $\mathcal{R}(Q)$.
Output: response set `response`.

Enter information about an available entry into PR.
`response` $\leftarrow \emptyset$
while PR $\neq \emptyset$ **do**
   Extract entry $N = (G, \mathcal{R}(G))$ from PR.
   foreach object entry $o_j \in G$ **do**
      if $d(q, o_j) \leq r$ **then**
         $o_j \rightarrow$ `response`
   enddo
   foreach non-object entry $N' = (G', \mathcal{R}(G')) \in G$ **do**
      if $\mathcal{R}(G')$ and $\mathcal{R}(Q)$ intersect **then**
         Insert the entry N' into PR.
   enddo
enddo

Figure 1.5. Search algorithm for range queries $Q = R(q, r)$.

$\mathcal{R}(G)$. A bounding region of G represents a constraint on the metric that must be satisfied by all elements $e \in G$. For example, a bounding region of a set G of objects specified by a preselected object p and a radius r implies that $\forall o \in G, d(o, p) \leq r$. For convenience, such bounding regions are often called *ball regions*. In practice, bounding regions can be formed by more complex conditions. As a rule, each element belongs to exactly one group (one set G) while the individual bounding regions may overlap. For simplicity, we assume that entries form a hierarchy and that the search always starts at the root entry. Since any similarity query Q returns a set of objects, we can always define a bounding region around the objects by analogy. We designate such region by $\mathcal{R}(Q)$.

To outline the principles of search algorithms, we assume the properties (bounding constraints) of data regions are known, including pointers to their instance sets. Since an entry can contain other entries, search algorithms are recursive and an implementation without recursion requires a queue of *Pending Requests*, PR, as an auxiliary data structure. The similarity range query $Q = R(q, r)$ can be solved using the algorithm presented in Figure 1.5. We also present the algorithm for executing the nearest neighbor query $Q = kNN(q)$, see Figure 1.6.

Nearest Neighbor Search Algorithm
Input: query object q, number of neighbors k.
Output: response set response of cardinality k.

Enter information about an available entry into PR.
Fill response with k (random) objects from X.
Adjust $\mathcal{R}(Q)$ according to the maximum distance from q
    in the response designated as r.
Sort entries in PR with decreasing region proximity to $\mathcal{R}(Q)$.
while PR $\neq \emptyset$ **do**
    Extract the first entry $N = (G, \mathcal{R}(G))$ from PR.
    foreach object entry $o_j \in G$ **do**
        if $d(q, o_j) \leq r$ **then**
            Update the response, r, and $\mathcal{R}(Q)$ by inserting o_j and
             removing the most distant object from q.
            Remove all entries $N' = (G', \mathcal{R}(G'))$ from PR
             which no longer intersects $\mathcal{R}(Q)$.
        endif
    enddo
    foreach non-object entry $N' = (G', \mathcal{R}(G')) \in G$ **do**
        if $\mathcal{R}(G')$ and $\mathcal{R}(Q)$ intersect **then**
            Insert the entry N' into PR.
        endif
    enddo
    Sort entries in PR with decreasing region proximity to $\mathcal{R}(Q)$.
enddo

Figure 1.6.   Search algorithm for nearest neighbor queries.

Partitioned organizations for similarity queries typically consist of many subsets, usually characterized by bounding spheres, i.e., ball regions. Aggregate information of this type is used for querying, specifically for pruning subsets that cannot contain qualifying objects. When a range query is considered, it is easy to see that ball regions having zero overlap with the query region can safely be ignored. On the other hand, all regions overlapping the query region should be accessed and the queue PR is used to keep track of such regions encountered during query execution.

Even with nearest neighbors queries, the situation is in principle quite similar. By setting the distance to the k-th nearest neighbor as the search radius, we can transform the nearest neighbor query into a range query. In this case, the radius will not be known in advance, but as [Hjaltason and Samet, 1999] detail, good nearest neighbor search strategies only access subsets whose regions overlap with the region of the query response. In order to achieve this, a queue of candidate regions PR is maintained, and the regions are accessed starting with the most promising, that is, with the region nearest to the query region.

6.2 Incremental Similarity Search

An incremental similarity search can provide objects in order of decreasing similarity without explicitly specifying the number of nearest neighbors in advance. This is especially important in interactive database applications, as it makes it possible to display partial query results early. The incremental aspect also provides significant benefits in situations where the number of desired neighbors is unknown beforehand, for example when complex similarity queries are processed. In the following, we outline an algorithm proposed by [Hjaltason and Samet, 2000].

The incremental nearest neighbor algorithm is applicable whenever the search space is structured in a hierarchical manner such as one we have defined above. However, the authors use a different approach to define the hierarchy. The chief difference lies in defining specialized distance functions instead of covering regions, which allows a more straightforward explanation of the incremental search algorithm.

For a query object q the algorithm operates on a file X organized by a structure T as follows: The search hierarchy is composed of elements e_t of several different types $t = 0, \ldots, t_{\max}$. Each element represents a subset of X, with an element e_0 of type 0 representing a single object in X. An element e_t of type t can give rise to one or more child elements of type 0 through $t-1$, thus the search problem for e_t is decomposed into several smaller sub-problems. Each element of type t has an associated distance function $d_t(q, e_t)$ which measures the distance from a query object q to elements of that type. For correctness, it is sufficient that $d_t(q, e_t) \leq d_0(q, e_0)$ for any object e_0 in the subset represented by e_t. In this way, the function d_t bounds the distances from q to the objects in the subtree of e_t from below. The general incremental algorithm for kNN queries is specified in Figure 1.7.

The algorithm starts off by initializing the queue of pending requests with the root of the search structure – since the order of entries in this queue is crucial, we refer to it as the *priority queue*. In the main loop, the element e_t closest to q is taken off the queue. If it is an object, we report it as the next nearest object. Otherwise, the child elements of e_t in the search hierarchy are inserted into the priority queue.

This algorithm can easily be adapted to take advantage of imposed distance bounds, as in a range query, as well as the maximum result size, as in a k-nearest

Incremental Nearest Neighbor Search Algorithm
Input: query object q, search hierarchy T.
Output: nearest neighbors in decreasing similarity.

$e_t \leftarrow$ root of the search hierarchy
queue $\leftarrow \emptyset$
ENQUEUE(**queue**, e_t, 0)
while queue $\neq \emptyset$ **do**
   $e_t \leftarrow$ DEQUEUE(**queue**)
   if $t = 0$ **then** (e_t is an object)
     Report e_t as the next nearest object.
   else
     foreach child element e_l of e_t **do**
       ENQUEUE(**queue**, e_l, $d_l(q, e_l)$)
     enddo
   endif
enddo

Figure 1.7. Incremental search algorithm for nearest neighbor queries.

neighbors query. In particular, given a maximum distance bound d^+, we only enqueue elements distant from q by less than or equal to d^+.

A useful extension of the algorithm is to find the *furthest neighbor* of a query object. This means defining another set of functions $\bar{d}_t(q, e_t)$ that bound the distances from q to the objects under e_t from above. By replacing $d_t(q, e_t)$ as a key for any element e_t on the priority queue with a negative function $-\bar{d}_t(q, e_t)$, we order the elements in the priority queue inversely. Thus, once an object has reached the front of the priority queue, we know there is no unreported object more distant from q.

7.   Policies for Avoiding Distance Computations

Since the performance of similarity search in metric spaces is not only I/O, but also CPU-bound, as discussed in Section 3.7, it is very important to limit the number of distance computations as much as possible. To this aim, pruning conditions must be applied not only to avoid accessing irrelevant sets of objects, but also to minimize the number of distances computed. The rationale behind such strategies is to use already-evaluated distances between some objects, while properly applying the metric space postulates – namely the triangle inequality, symmetry, and non-negativity – to determine bounds on distances between other objects.

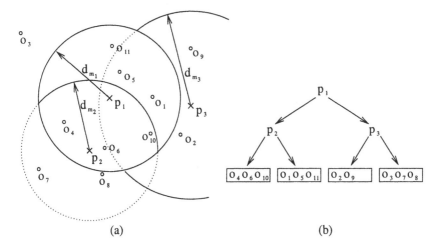

Figure 1.8. (a) Recursive ball partitioning of a metric space, (b) corresponding binary tree.

In this section, we describe several *bounding strategies*, originally proposed in [Hjaltason and Samet, 2000] and refined in [Hjaltason and Samet, 2003a]. These techniques represent general pruning rules that are employed, in a specific form, in practically all index structures for metric spaces. The following rules thus form the basic formal background. The individual techniques described differ as to the type of distance we have available, as well as what kind of distance computation we seek to avoid.

7.1 Explanatory Example

Consider a hypothetical index structure based on a recursive application of the ball partitioning procedure defined in Section 5. Figure 1.8a illustrates a recursively partitioned metric space of objects $o_1, \ldots, o_{11}$. The first level of the corresponding binary tree in Figure 1.8b is created by applying ball partitioning using the pivot p_1. The inner partition in Figure 1.8a (corresponding to the left subtree in Figure 1.8b) is divided using the same principle again, this time with the object p_2 as a pivot. As you can see from the figures, the ball partitioning has so far only split the inner partition at the first level. The outer area remains untouched. This is then itself divided using the pivot p_3.

In general, a search algorithm for range queries $R(q, r)$ works in top-down fashion. It starts at the root node where it decides which partitions must be visited and then descends the tree. Specifically, in each internal node, the algorithm computes distances $d(p_i, q)$ between the pivot p_i and the query object q. By respecting the median values d_{m_i} and the query radius r, the algorithm determines all subtrees which might contain qualifying data. In a leaf node, the query object q is compared with the data objects o_j and any objects satisfying

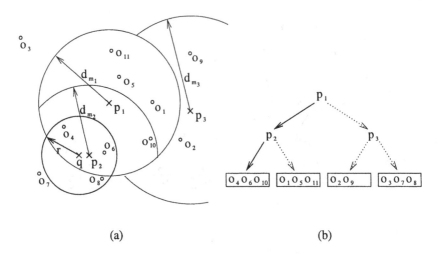

(a)   (b)

Figure 1.9. Range search for query $R(q, r)$: (a) from the geometric point of view, (b) algorithm accessing the left-most leaf node.

the range search constraint $d(q, o_j) \leq r$ are reported. However, in both types of nodes, we can apply some rules (bounding constraints) that would optimize the search procedure by avoiding (possibly expensive) distance computations. Such techniques are clarified in the following.

7.2 Object-Pivot Distance Constraint

The basic type of bounding constraint is the *object-pivot distance constraint*, so called because it is usually applied to leaf nodes containing the data, i.e., the metric objects of the searched collection. Figure 1.9 demonstrates a situation in which such a bounding constraint can be beneficial with respect to the trivial sequential scan computing distances to all objects. Assume a range query $R(q, r)$ is issued (see Figure 1.9a) and the search algorithm has reached the left-most leaf node as illustrated in Figure 1.9b. At this stage, the sequential scan would examine all objects in the leaf, i.e., compute the distances $d(q, o_4), d(q, o_6), d(q, o_{10})$, and decide qualifying objects. However, provided the distances $d(p_2, o_4), d(p_2, o_6), d(p_2, o_{10})$ are in memory (having been computed during insertion) and the distance from q to p_2 is $d(q, p_2)$, some distance evaluations can be omitted.

Figure 1.10a shows a detail view of the situation. The dashed lines represent distances we do not know and the solid lines, known distances. Suppose we need to estimate the distance between the query object q and the database object o_{10}. Given only an object and the distance from it to another object, the object's precise position in space cannot be determined. Knowledge of the distance alone is not enough. With respect to p_2, for example, the object o_{10} could lie anywhere

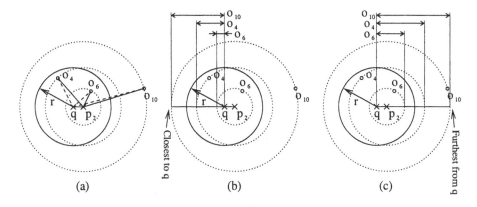

Figure 1.10. Illustration of the object-pivot constraint: (a) our model situation, (b) the lower bound, and (c) the upper bound.

along the dotted circle representing all equidistant positions. This also implies the existence of two extreme possible positions for o_{10} with respect to the query object q, a closest and furthest possible position. The former is depicted in Figure 1.10b while the latter is shown in Figure 1.10c. Systematically, the lower bound is computed as the absolute value of the difference between $d(q, p_2)$ and $d(p_2, o_{10})$, while the sum $d(q, p_2)$ and $d(p_2, o_{10})$ forms the upper bound on the distance $d(q, o_{10})$.

In our example, the lower bound on distance $d(q, o_{10})$ is greater than the query radius r, thus we are sure the object o_{10} cannot qualify the query and can skip it in the search process without actually computing the distance. If, on the contrary, we focus on the object o_6, it can be seen from Figure 1.10c that the upper bound on $d(q, o_6)$ is less than r. As a result, o_6 can be directly included in the query response set because the distance $d(q, o_6)$ cannot exceed r. In both cases described, one distance computation is omitted, speeding up the search process. Concerning the object o_4, we discover that the lower bound is less than the radius r and the upper bound is greater than r. That means o_4 must be compared directly against q using the distance function, i.e., $d(q, o_4)$ must be computed to decide whether o_4 is relevant to the query or not. We formally summarize the ideas described in Lemma 1.1.

LEMMA 1.1 *Given a metric space* $\mathcal{M} = (\mathcal{D}, d)$ *and three arbitrary objects* $q, p, o \in \mathcal{D}$*, it is always guaranteed:*

$$|d(q, p) - d(p, o)| \leq d(q, o) \leq d(q, p) + d(p, o).$$

Consequently, the distance $d(q, o)$ *can be bounded from below and above, provided the distances* $d(q, p)$ *and* $d(p, o)$ *are known.* □

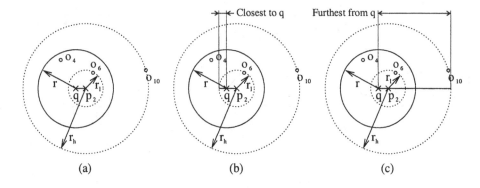

Figure 1.11. Illustration of the range-pivot constraint: (a) our model situation, (b) the lower bound, and (c) the upper bound.

7.3   Range-Pivot Distance Constraint

The object-pivot distance constraint described above assumes that all distances between the database objects o_i and the respective pivot p are known. However, some metric structures try to minimize the space needed to build the index, so storing such an amount of data is not acceptable. An alternative is to store only a range (a distance interval) in which the database objects occur with respect to p. Here, we can apply a weaker condition called the *range-pivot distance constraint*.

Consider Figure 1.9 with the range query $R(q, r)$ again and assume the search procedure is just about to enter the left-most leaf node of our sample tree. At this stage, a sophisticated search algorithm should decide if it is necessary to visit the leaf or not, i.e., whether any qualifying object can be found at this node. If we know the interval $[r_l, r_h]$ in which distances from the pivot p_2 to all objects o_4, o_6, o_{10} occur, it can be applied to solve the problem. A detail of such a situation is depicted in Figure 1.11a, where the dotted circles represent limits of the range and the known distance between the pivot and the query is emphasized by a solid line. The shortest distance from q to any object lying within the range is $r_l - d(q, p_2)$ (see Figure 1.11b). Obviously, no object can be closer to q, because it would be nearer p_2 than the threshold r_l otherwise. By analogy, we can define the upper bound as $r_h + d(q, p_2)$, see Figure 1.11c. In this way, we have two expressions which limit the distance between an object and the query q.

To reveal the usefulness of this, consider range queries again. If the lower bound is greater than the query radius r, we are sure that no qualifying object can be found and the node need not be accessed. On the other hand, if the upper bound is less than or equal to r, we can conclude that all objects qualify and directly include all descendant objects in the query response set – no further dis-

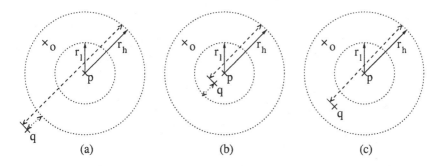

Figure 1.12. Illustration of Lemma 1.2 with three different positions of the query object: (a) above, (b) below and (c) within the range $[r_l, r_h]$.

tance computations are needed at all. Note that in the model situation depicted in Figure 1.11, we can neither directly include nor prune the node, so the node must be accessed and its individual objects examined instance by instance.

Up to now, we have only examined one possible position for the query and range, and stated two rules concerning the search radius r. Before we give a formal definition of the range-pivot constraint, we illustrate three different query positions in Figure 1.12, namely: above the range $[r_l, r_h]$ in (a), below the range in (b), and within the interval in (c). We can bound $d(q, o)$, provided $r_l \leq d(p, o) \leq r_h$ and the distance $d(q, p)$ is known. The dotted and dashed line segments denote the lower and upper bounds, respectively. At a general level, the problem can be formalized as follows:

LEMMA 1.2 *Given a metric space* $\mathcal{M} = (\mathcal{D}, d)$ *and objects* $o, p \in \mathcal{D}$ *such that* $r_l \leq d(o, p) \leq r_h$, *and given some* $q \in \mathcal{D}$ *and an associated distance* $d(q, p)$, *the distance* $d(q, o)$ *can be restricted by the range:*

$$\max\{d(q, p) - r_h, \ r_l - d(q, p), \ 0\} \leq d(q, o) \leq d(q, p) + r_h.$$

□

7.4 Pivot-Pivot Distance Constraint

We have just described two principles which lead to a performance boost in search algorithms. Now, we turn our attention to a third approach which, while weaker than the foregoing two, still provides some benefit. This is the *pivot-pivot distance constraint*, and to explain it we once again make use of the hypothetical index structure depicted in Figure 1.8. Consider a situation in which the range search algorithm has approached the internal node with pivot p_1 (the root node of the structure) and the distance $d(q, p_1)$ has been evaluated. Here, the algorithm can apply Lemma 1.2 to decide which subtrees to visit. The careful reader may object that the range of distances with respect to the pivot p_1 must be known separately for both left and right branches. But this

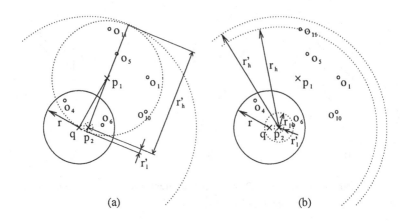

Figure 1.13. (a) The lower r'_l and upper r'_h bounds on distance $d(q, p_2)$, (b) the range $[r_l, r_h]$ on distances from p_2 and database objects – the range from (a) is also included.

is simple to achieve, because every object inserted into the structure must be compared with p_1. Thus, we can assume that the correct intervals are known. The specifics of applying Lemma 1.2 are left to the reader as an easy exercise.

Without loss of generality, we assume the algorithm has followed the left branch, reaching the node with pivot p_2. Now, the algorithm could compute the distance $d(q, p_2)$ and apply Lemma 1.2 again. But since we know the distance $d(q, p_1)$, then if we also know the distance between pivots p_1 and p_2, we can employ Lemma 1.1 to get an estimate of $d(q, p_2)$ without computing it, since $d(q, p_2) \in [r'_l, r'_h]$. In fact, we have now an interval on $d(q, p_2)$ and an interval on $d(p_2, o_i)$, where objects o_i are descendants of p_2. Specifically, we have $d(q, p_2) \in [r'_l, r'_h]$ and $d(p_2, o_i) \in [r_l, r_h]$. Figure 1.13 illustrates both intervals. Figure 1.13a depicts the range on $d(q, p_2)$ with the known distance $d(q, p_1)$ emphasized. In Figure 1.13b, the second interval on distances $d(p_2, o_i)$ is given in addition to the first interval, indicated by two dotted circles around the pivot p_2. The purpose of these ranges is to give bounds on distances between q and database objects o_i, leading to a faster qualification process that does not require evaluating distances between q and o_i, nor even computing $d(q, p_2)$. The figure shows both ranges intersect, which implies that the lower bound on $d(q, o_i)$ is zero. On the other hand, the sum $r_h + r'_h$ obviously forms the upper bound on the distances $d(q, o_i)$.

The example in Figure 1.13 only depicts the case when the ranges intersect. In Figure 1.14, we show what happens when the intervals do not coincide. In this case, the lower limit is equal to $r'_l - r_h$, which can be seen easily from Figure 1.14a. Figure 1.14b shows another view of the upper bound. The third possible position for the interval is opposite that depicted in Figure 1.14. This time, the intervals have been reversed, giving a lower limit of $r_l - r'_h$. The general formalization of this principle is as follows:

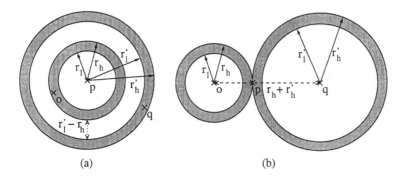

Figure 1.14. Illustration of Lemma 1.3: (a) the ranges $[r_l, r_h]$ and $[r'_l, r'_h]$ do not intersect, so the lower bound is $r'_l - r_h$; (b) the upper limit $r_h + r'_h$.

LEMMA 1.3 *Given a metric space $\mathcal{M} = (\mathcal{D}, d)$ and objects $o, p, q \in \mathcal{D}$ such that $r_l \leq d(p, o) \leq r_h$ and $r'_l \leq d(q, p) \leq r'_h$, the distance $d(q, o)$ can be bounded by the range:*

$$\max\{r'_l - r_h,\ r_l - r'_h,\ 0\} \leq d(q, o) \leq r_h + r'_h.$$

□

7.5   Double-Pivot Distance Constraint

The three previous approaches to speeding up the retrieval process in metric structures all use a single pivot, in keeping with the ball partitioning paradigm. Next we explore an alternate strategy based upon generalized hyperplane partitioning. As defined in Section 5, this technique employs two pivots to partition the metric space.

Figure 1.15a shows an example of generalized hyperplane partitioning in which pivots p_1, p_2 are used to divide the space into two subspaces – objects nearer p_1 belonging to the left subspace and objects nearer to p_2 to the right. The vertical dashed line represents points equidistant from both pivots. With this partitioning we cannot establish an upper bound on the distance from query object q to database objects o_i, because the database objects may be arbitrarily far away from the pivots. Thus only lower limits can be defined.

First, let us examine the case in which objects o and q are in the same subspace, not considered in Figure 1.15. Obviously the lower bound will equal zero, since it is possible some objects may be identical. Next, we consider the situation in Figure 1.15a, where the lower bound (depicted by a dotted line) is equal to $(d(q, p_1) - d(q, p_2))/2$. In Figure 1.15b, the hyperbolic curve represents all possible positions of the query object q with a constant value of $(d(q, p_1) - d(q, p_2))/2$. If we move the query object q up vertically while maintaining the distance to the dashed line, the expression $(d(q, p_1) - d(q, p_2))/2$

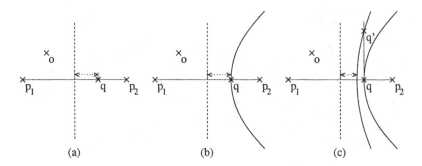

Figure 1.15. Illustration of Lemma 1.4: (a) the lower bound on $d(q, o)$, (b) the equidistant positions of q with respect to the lower bound, and (c) shrinking the lower bound.

decreases. For illustration, see Figure 1.15c, where q' represents the new position of the query object. Consequently, the expression $(d(q, p_1) - d(q, p_2))/2$ is indeed the lower bound on $d(q, o)$. The formal definition of this *double-pivot distance constraint* is given in Lemma 1.4.

LEMMA 1.4 *Assume a metric space* $\mathcal{M} = (\mathcal{D}, d)$ *and objects* $o, p_1, p_2 \in \mathcal{D}$ *such that* $d(o, p_1) \leq d(o, p_2)$. *Given a query object* $q \in \mathcal{D}$ *and the distances* $d(q, p_1)$ *and* $d(q, p_2)$, *the distance* $d(q, o)$ *is lower-bounded as follows:*

$$\max\left\{ \frac{d(q, p_1) - d(q, p_2)}{2}, 0 \right\} \leq d(q, o).$$

$\square$

We should point out this constraint does not employ any already-evaluated distance from a pivot to a database object. If we knew such distances to both pivots we would simply apply Lemma 1.1 twice, for each pivot separately. The concept of using known distances to several pivots is detailed in the following.

7.6   Pivot Filtering

Given a range query $R(q, r)$, we can eliminate database objects by applying Lemma 1.1, provided we know the distance between p and all database objects. This situation is demonstrated in Figure 1.16a, where the white area contains objects that cannot be eliminated under such a distance criterion. After elimination, the search algorithm would proceed by inspecting all remaining objects and comparing them against the query object using the original distance function, i.e., for all non-discarded objects o_i, verify the query condition $d(q, o_i) \leq r$.

To achieve a greater degree of pruning, several pivots can be combined into a single *pivot filtering* technique [Dohnal, 2004]. The underlying idea is shown in Figure 1.16b, where the reader can observe the improved filtering effect for two pivots. We formalize this concept in the following lemma.

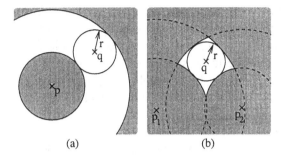

Figure 1.16. Illustration of filtering technique: (a) using a single pivot, (b) using a combination of pivots.

LEMMA 1.5 *Assume a metric space* $\mathcal{M} = (\mathcal{D}, d)$ *and a set of pivots* $P = \{p_1, \ldots, p_n\}$. *We define a mapping function* $\Psi \colon (\mathcal{D}, d) \to (\mathbb{R}^n, L_\infty)$ *as follows:*

$$\Psi(o) = (d(o, p_1), d(o, p_2), \ldots, d(o, p_n)).$$

Then, we can bound the distance $d(q, o)$ *from below:*

$$L_\infty(\Psi(q), \Psi(o)) \leq d(q, o).$$

$\square$

The mapping function $\Psi(\cdot)$ returns a vector of distances from an object o to all pivots in P. For a database object, the vector actually contains the pre-computed distances to pivots. On the other hand, the application of $\Psi(\cdot)$ on a query object q requires computation of distances from the query object to all pivots in P. Once we have the vectors $\Psi(q)$ and $\Psi(o)$, the lower bound criterion can be applied to eliminate the object o if $|d(q, p_i) - d(o, p_i)| > r$ for any $p_i \in P$. The white area in Figure 1.16b represents the objects that cannot be eliminated from the search using two pivots. These objects will still have to be tested directly against the query object q with the original metric function d.

The mapping $\Psi(\cdot)$ is *contractive*, that is the distance $L_\infty(\Psi(o_1), \Psi(o_2))$ is never greater than the distance $d(o_1, o_2)$ in the original metric space. The outcome of a range query performed in the projected space $(\mathbb{R}^n, L_\infty)$ may contain some spurious objects that do not qualify for the original query. To get the final result, the outcome has to be tested by the original distance function d. More details about the metric space transformations can be found in the next section.

8. Metric Space Transformations

It is intuitively clear that transforming one metric space into another actually means mapping all objects to a new domain so a different distance function can be used. In general, we change both the objects and the metric function, but, as we shall see, several applications of this concept may demand only the metric function or the domain be changed. The new domain allows a similarity query in the transformed space to be substituted for a query in the original metric space. The motivation may be to enable a less expensive computation, and in this case we talk about a *metric space embedding*, explained in Section 8.3. Otherwise, the transformation may be done to take *user-defined search functions* into account – see Section 8.2.

Obviously there must be additional restrictions in order to maintain a correlation between query results in the original and transformed metric space. These restrictions are formally defined in Section 8.1 using a concept labeled *lower-bounded metric functions*.

8.1   Metric Hierarchies

Before detailing specific techniques, we define the transformation of a metric space $\mathcal{M}_1 = (\mathcal{D}_1, d_1)$ into a metric space $\mathcal{M}_2 = (\mathcal{D}_2, d_2)$ as a function $f : \mathcal{D}_1 \rightarrow \mathcal{D}_2$, such that

$$\forall o_1, o_2 \in \mathcal{D}_1 : d_1(o_1, o_2) \approx d_2(f(o_1), f(o_2)).$$

Note that the distance in the transformed metric space may not exactly equal the original distance. For purposes of similarity search, it is necessary to define a relation between distances in the original and the transformed metric spaces.

We say that d_1 is a *lower-bounding distance function* of d_2 if d_1 is an underestimate of d_2, that is

$$\forall o_1, o_2 \in \mathcal{D}_1 : d_1(o_1, o_2) \leq d_2(f(o_1), f(o_2)).$$

Now assume instead that d_1 is not a lower-bounding distance function of d_2. We can define a new *scaled distance function* $d_{1s}(o_1, o_2) = s_{d_1 \rightarrow d_2} \cdot d_1(o_1, o_2)$ such that d_{1s} is a lower-bounding distance function of d_2, where $0 < s_{d_1 \rightarrow d_2} < 1$ is a real number called the *scaling factor*. Clearly, it is not always possible to define d_{1s} because a convenient scaling factor cannot be obtained for every pair of distance functions d_1, d_2. However, if $s_{d_1 \rightarrow d_2}$ exists, an infinite number of other values of the scaling factor can be found. Therefore, it is advisable to consider the maximum value, since it makes d_{1s} a tight lower bound of d_2. The maximum value of the scaling factor is termed the *optimal scaling factor*. For a complete explanation see [Ciaccia and Patella, 2002].

8.1.1   Lower-Bounding Functions

Having given a definition for lower-bounding distance functions, we provide the reader with examples of some of the most common ones. When necessary, a scaling factor is provided.

L_p **Norms.** Any L_p norm is a lower-bounding distance function for all $L_{p'}$ norms with $p' \geq p$. For example, let $V = \mathbb{R} \times \mathbb{R}$ be a 2-dimensional vector space. Given a pair of vectors $\vec{x}, \vec{y} \in V$, the L_2 and L_1, distances are defined as follows:

$$
\begin{aligned}
d_{L_2}(\vec{x}, \vec{y}) &= \sqrt{(x_1 - y_1)^2 + (x_2 - y_2)^2}\,, \\
d_{L_1}(\vec{x}, \vec{y}) &= |x_1 - y_1| + |x_2 - y_2|\,.
\end{aligned}
$$

It is apparent that the L_1 metric function will always be bigger than L_2 for the same pair of vectors given as arguments. Thus, L_2 forms a lower-bounding function on L_1.

For all other norms, i.e., $p' < p$, a lower-bounding scaled distance function L_{ps} can be defined. The optimal scaling factor is equal to $s = 1/n^{\frac{1}{p'} - \frac{1}{p}}$, where n is the dimensionality of the underlying vector space.

Quadratic Form Distance Functions. In [Hafner et al., 1995, Seidl and Kriegel, 1997] it is proved that a lower-bounding distance function for the class of quadratic form distance functions d_M (where M is the quadratic form matrix) is a scaled L_2 norm, denoted L_{2s}. The optimal scaling factor s is given by the square root of the minimum eigenvalue of M, $s = \sqrt{\min_j\{\lambda_j\}}$, where λ_js denote eigenvalues of M.

Weighted Edit Distances. Let γ be a weight function that assigns a non-negative cost to each replacement operation of edit distance d_{edit}. That is $\forall a, b \in \Sigma : \gamma(a \to b) \in \mathbb{R}^+$, where Σ is an alphabet over which strings are built. A weighted edit distance $d_{\gamma' edit}$ is then the lower-bounding function of $d_{\gamma edit}$ if and only if $\gamma'(a \to b) \leq \gamma(a \to b)$ for every replacement $a \to b$.

Otherwise, a scaling factor for $d_{\gamma' edit}$ must be provided. The optimal scaling factor is given by the minimum ratio between the cost of edit operations with γ' versus γ weight functions, that is, $s_{\gamma' \to \gamma} = \min_{a,b \in \Sigma, a \neq b}\{\gamma(a \to b)/\gamma'(a \to b)\}$. The idea behind this is to fix γ' below the function γ by multiplying the results of γ' with a value smaller than one (i.e., the scaling factor).

Multi-set Distance. Given a string x, let $ms(x)$ denote the multi-set (bag) of symbols in x. For instance, $ms(\text{"tree"}) = \{t, r, e, e\}$. The following can easily be proved to be a metric on multi-sets: $d_{ms}(x, y) = \max\{|ms(x) - ms(y)|, |ms(y) - ms(x)|\}$, where the difference has a bag semantics (e.g. $\{a, a, a, b\} - \{a, b, c, c\} = \{a, a\}$) and $|\cdot|$ counts the number of elements in a multi-set (e.g. $|\{a, a\}| = 2$). It is immediately apparent that $d_{ms}(x, y)$ is a lower-bounding distance for the unweighted edit distance: $\forall x, y \in \Sigma^\star$, $d_{ms}(x, y) \leq d_{edit}(x, y)$.

8.2   User-Defined Metric Functions

The notion of similarity, which ultimately determines the evaluation and the ranking of database objects, may vary from user to user. Thus, it should be made user-dependent to improve the effectiveness of similarity queries, so as to allow users sufficient flexibility in stating their preferences [Chomicki, 2002]. As an example, one user looking for a second-hand car on a trading site could be more interested in the car's price than its speed, whereas the opposite might hold true for another user.

Preferences on simple domains, such as in the example above, are easy to adjust. However, it might be difficult to specify user's preferences for complex domains such as color histograms, since it requires defining all the histogram values. There are applications with even more complex domains, like multimedia or data mining systems, where the preferences are simply beyond imagination of an ordinary user. In this respect, the tuning of the parameters may best be left to the system, which takes the burden of automatically "learning" preferences by monitoring the user's activity [Cetintemel et al., 2000] or exploiting feedback from previous queries [Ortega-Binderberger et al., 2002].

In a metric space, let us have an index structure built using a metric function d_b defined on a domain $\mathcal{D}$. Another metric function d_u on the same domain $\mathcal{D}$ is either explicitly specified by a user or automatically estimated by the system. The actual results of a user query must be computed according to d_u. To be able to exploit the index structure, the concept of lower-bound distance functions is used, as explained in the following.

8.2.1   Searching Using Lower-Bounding Functions

Because the user may specify a personalized function not constrained by the lower bounding concept, we define yet another metric function d_p on domain $\mathcal{D}$, such that d_p is the lower-bound of both the building function d_b and user's function d_u, i.e.

$$\forall o_1, o_2 \in \mathcal{D} : d_p(o_1, o_2) \leq d_b(o_1, o_2), d_p(o_1, o_2) \leq d_u(o_1, o_2).$$

Therefore, we can use d_p to search the index structure which has been built using d_b and retrieve only "promising" objects. Next, we use d_u to filter out irrelevant (false positive) matches.

More specifically, we retrieve a correct result-set for the user-specified query. Following the equations above, we can use d_p in a particular evaluation of a similarity query in the index structure, because every distance measured by d_p will always be less than or equal to d_b. Thus we will always have at least the results obtained for d_b. However, we may retrieve superfluous objects. The result will always contain all potential matches for the user-defined function d_u, but some false-positives may also have been added in. Again, this property is inherited from the fact that d_p is a lower-bounding function of d_u. The filtering phase ensures the results will not contain the irrelevant objects. A full proof along with modified algorithms for range and kNN queries can be found in [Ciaccia and Patella, 2002].

8.3 Embedding Metric Space

As stated earlier, some distance functions can be very expensive computationally. Therefore, it is desirable to substitute cheaper distance functions like the L_p metrics for these calculations. A common approach to achieving this is to map, or embed, the set of objects into points in a low-dimensional embedding vector space and conduct the search in that space. Intuitively, the rationale for performing such a mapping is that distances in the embedding space approximate the distances between objects in the original space but searching the embedding space is less expensive.

We have outlined the concept in Section 8.1. We use a transformation function f, such that the distances in the embedded vector space form lower bounds on the distances in the original metric space. The range query $R(q, r)$ evaluation process is modified as follows. (We focus on range queries only for the sake of simplicity, but other query types follow the same pattern.) The query object q is transformed using the function f into a vector $\vec{q} = f(q)$ in the embedded space. Next, the query $R(\vec{q}, r)$ is evaluated in the vector space and a result-set is obtained. However, this result contains some objects which do not qualify for the original query and we must filter out these false positives in the original space.

8.3.1 Embedding Examples

Lipschitz Embedding. A Lipschitz embedding is defined in terms of a set S of subsets of X, $S = \{S_1, S_2, ..., S_k\}$. The subsets S_i are termed the *reference sets* of the embedding. Let $d(o, S_i)$ be an extension of the distance function d to a subset $S_i \subset X$, such that $d(o, S_i) = \min_{x \in S_i}\{d(o, x)\}$. An embedding with respect to S is defined as a mapping f such that $f(o) = (d(o, S_1), d(o, S_2), \dots, d(o, S_k))$. In other words, what we are doing is defining a coordinate space where each axis corresponds to a subset S_i of the objects and the coordinate values of object o are the distances from o to the closest element in each S_i. Under this definition, the embedding is not suitable for similarity search due to its large computational cost. Thus, a method called SparseMap proposed in [Hjaltason and Samet, 2003b] applied a heuristics aimed at reducing the cost of producing this embedding.

Karhunen-Loeve transform. The Karhunen-Loeve transform (KLT) [Fukunaga, 1990] is a linear transformation that allows coordinate axes to be determined in such a way as to retain as much distance information as possible. It is essentially equivalent to Principal Component Analysis (PCA) [Dunteman,

1989]. In particular, for a database X of points in an n-dimensional Euclidean space, KLT identifies a new set of n coordinate axes, represented by an orthonormal set $V = \{\vec{v_1}, \vec{v_2}, \ldots, \vec{v_n}\}$ of basis vectors (i.e., each basis vector has a length of one and any two basis vectors are orthogonal). The set V is chosen such that the spread of points in X along an axis (represented by a vector from V) is maximal.

The transformation function $f_k(o)$ for an object $o \in X$ is then defined as the projection of the point o onto the first k basis vectors in V. It can be proven that $d_k(f_k(o_1), f_k(o_2))$ will preserve the distances as much as possible, in a mean-square sense, if d_k denotes the Euclidean distance in the transformed k-dimensional Euclidean space. In other words, KLT results in the transformation that minimizes $\sum_{o_1, o_2 \in X} (d_k(f_k(o_1), f_k(o_2)) - d(o_1, o_2))^2$. Inspired by this embedding, a FastMap method for similarity searching was defined in [Faloutsos and Lin, 1995].

MetricMap. The previous two examples define an embedding applicable only on vector spaces. The MetricMap [Wang et al., 2000] is a technique which embeds a generic metric space $\mathcal{M} = (\mathcal{D}, d)$ into a k-dimensional vector space. First, the metric space is transformed into an "imaginary" space using a subset $P \subset \mathcal{D}$ of size m, $P = \{p_1, p_2, \ldots, p_m\}$, where $m \geq k$. The authors suggest setting $m = 2k$ for best results. In the projected space, every object $o \in \mathcal{D}$ is identified using a vector $\Psi(o) = (d(p_1, o), d(p_2, o), \ldots, d(p_m, o))$. This imaginary space has a basis $(\Psi(p_1), \ldots, \Psi(p_m))$. As with the KLT technique, this basis is transformed to an orthonormal vector basis. The final k-dimensional space is then formed using first k dimensions of the imaginary space. Further refinements and a detailed explanation of properties of the MetricMap embedding can be found in [Hjaltason and Samet, 2003b].

8.3.2   Reducing Dimensionality

The embedding of metric space into vector space also offers the possibility of using other standard multidimensional vector space index structures, such as the R^*-tree [Beckmann et al., 1990] or SS-tree [White and Jain, 1996]. However, as dimensionality increases, query performance in index structures degrades. Moreover, some embedding techniques may result in a very high-dimensional embedding space. Both problems may be solved for specific cases by reducing the dimensionality of the vector space.

Such dimensionality reduction techniques assume that a few dimensions are sufficient to retain the salient information about the data objects represented, allowing other dimensions to simply be ignored. Typically, linear-algebraic methods such as the Karhunen-Loeve Transformation [Fukunaga, 1990], Discrete Fourier Transform [Oppenheim et al., 1999], Discrete Cosine Transform [Kailath, 1985], Discrete Wavelet Transform [Castelman, 1996] or

Singular Value Decomposition [Wall et al., 2003] are used to transform the original vectors into a new vector space where the distances are conveniently retained.

From a metric-space perspective (since any vector space is a subspecies of metric space), we can see dimensionality reduction as a means of transforming the space in such a way that the distance function stays the same while the domain is changed from a high-dimensional vector space to a lower-dimensional one. For a more exhaustive explanation see [Carreira-Perpinan, 1997].

9. Approximate Similarity Search

Similarity search in metric spaces is generally expensive and state-of-the art access methods still do not provide an acceptable response time for highly interactive applications. Fortunately, in many applications it is sufficient to perform an *approximate similarity search* where an inaccurate result-set is obtained. The attractiveness of this approach is emphasized by the fact that the approximate search is typically performed much faster. In the following, we set down the principles of approximate similarity search, describe generic algorithms to implement approximate range and the nearest neighbor search strategies, and finally discuss measures for assessing the performance of approximate similarity search algorithms. Whenever confusion might occur, we use the term *precise* or *exact* similarity search for the non-approximate version.

9.1 Principles

Approximate similarity search techniques offer greatly improved efficiency vis à vis precise similarity search, at a price of some imprecision in results. The general idea of approximation algorithms is to relax some constraints on the "precise" similarity search to reduce search costs, as measured by disk accesses and/or the number of distance computations. This obviously means *false hits* or *false dismissals* might occur.

The use of the approximate similarity search is mainly justified by the following observations:

- Similarity between objects is often subjective, thus very difficult to express by a unique rigorous function. For example, consider an image database. Given a query image and a set of candidate result images, different persons would make different choices as to which image is most similar to the query. But when the intuitive notion of similarity is formally defined by a mathematical formula (the distance function), subjectivity is not taken into account. Controlled imprecision which results in a faster similarity search might be tolerated by users.

- Similarity search processes are intrinsically iterative. Users typically issue several similarity queries to the search system, possibly reusing previous query results to express new ones. For instance, a user may start searching by using an initial image to find similar images. Not being satisfied with the result, the user may issue another similarity search query using one of the previously returned images as the reference. With such an approach, an efficient execution of elementary queries is important and users may accept some imprecision in the temporary results, provided query execution is fast.

Approaches to approximate similarity search can be broadly classified into two categories [Ferhatosmanoglu et al., 2001]:

1 Approaches which exploit transformation of the metric space;

2 Approaches which reduce the subset of data to be examined.

In the first category, approximation is achieved by changing the object representation and/or distance function with the objective of reducing search cost. In the second category, strategies are used which omit parts of the dataset not likely to contain qualifying objects.

Transformation techniques for metric spaces are thoroughly discussed in Section 8. As a typical example, consider dimensionality reduction in vector spaces. Good transformations are distance-preserving and satisfy the lower bounding property: distances in the transformed space are smaller than those computed in the original space. This implies that superfluous data, i.e., "false hits", may inhabit the result-set when a similarity search is executed in the transformed space. These false hits can be easily eliminated in a subsequent filtering step executed in the original metric space. However, if this second step is not applied, the search algorithm is approximate: the approximate similarity search is faster at the cost of false hits in the result.

On the other hand, techniques that reduce the amount of data examined aim at improving performance by accessing and analyzing less data than is technically needed. In this book, we focus more on this class of approaches than metric space transformation techniques, which find their chief use in vector spaces. There are two basic approximation strategies that employ data reduction:

- *Early termination strategies* stop the similarity search algorithm before its natural (precise) end. Similarity search algorithms are iterative processes in which the current result-set can be improved at each step. The precise algorithm stops when it detects that no further improvements are possible. Approximation algorithms, on the other hand, use a *stop condition* to decide the early termination of the algorithm. The algorithm terminates when it detects there is little chance significantly better results will be obtained. Here the hypothesis is that a good approximation can be had after some initial steps of the search iteration, while further iterations would only marginally improve the result-set and consume most of the total search costs.

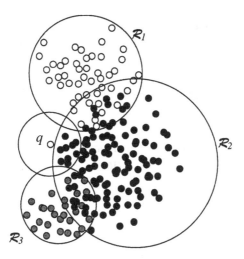

Figure 1.17. A relaxed branching strategy might decide not to access regions $\mathcal{R}_1$ and $\mathcal{R}_3$, which do not share objects with the query region, even if they overlap the query region.

- *Relaxed branching strategies* avoid accessing data regions that are not likely to contain objects belonging to the result-set. Precise similarity search algorithms access all data regions overlapping the query region and discard others. Relaxed branching strategies are based on the definition of an approximate *pruning condition* to decide the rejection of regions overlapping the query region. Data regions are discarded when the condition detects a low likelihood for objects to occur in the space shared with the query region. Relaxed branching strategies are particularly useful for access methods based on a hierarchical decomposition of the space.

Various approximation strategies can be implemented with specific definitions of stop and pruning conditions. Chapter 4 presents some of the most relevant in detail. To get some flavor of them, a trivial early termination strategy may involve simply stopping the similarity search algorithm after a certain percentage of the dataset has been accessed, or after a specified time has elapsed. In either case, some qualifying objects may obviously escape detection. A relaxed branching strategy, by contrast, is illustrated in Figure 1.17. The dataset is divided into three subsets, distinguished by the white, black, and gray points bounded by regions $\mathcal{R}_1$, $\mathcal{R}_2$, and $\mathcal{R}_3$. In the example, the query region overlaps all three data regions, so all of them are accessed by the precise similarity search algorithm. But regions $\mathcal{R}_1$, and $\mathcal{R}_3$ share no objects with the query region. A good relaxed branching technique should detect such situations and decide not to access these unpromising regions.

Approximate Range Search Algorithm
Input: query region $\mathcal{R}(Q)$, approximation parameters x_s and x_p.
Output: response set response.

Enter information about an available entry into PR.
response ← ∅
while PR ≠ ∅ **do**
  Extract entry $N = (G, \mathcal{R}(G))$ from PR.
  foreach object entry $o_j \in G$ **do**
    if $d(q, o_j) \leq r$ **then**
      $o_j \rightarrow$ response
  enddo
  if $Stop($response$, x_s)$ **then**
    exit
  foreach non-object entry $N' = (G', \mathcal{R}(G')) \in G$ **do**
    if $\neg Prune(\mathcal{R}(G'), \mathcal{R}(Q), x_p)$ **then**
      Insert the entry N' into PR.
  enddo
enddo

Figure 1.18. Approximate search algorithm for range queries.

9.2 Generic Algorithms

Algorithms for the approximate similarity search which exploit the early termination and relaxed branching strategies, can easily be obtained by modifying the generic similarity search algorithm discussed in Section 6.1. In Figures 1.18 and 1.19, we present pseudocode for the approximate similarity range and the nearest neighbor search, respectively.

The only difference from the exact versions shown in Section 6.1 is that the overlap test for regions is replaced by the pruning condition $Prune$, and the $Stop$ condition is used to decide premature termination. Note that if the $Prune$ function is a simple region overlap test and the $Stop$ function is always false, the algorithms perform the precise similarity search.

The generic stop condition $Stop($response$, x_s)$ takes as its arguments the current result-set response (the set of qualifying objects found up to the current iteration) and the approximation parameter x_s. It returns true when the stop strategy determines the approximation requirements have been satisfied, respecting the approximation parameter x_s. The argument response is passed to the stop condition to emphasize the possibility of defining strategies that

---

Approximate Nearest neighbor Search Algorithm
Input: query object q, number of neighbors k,
        approximation parameters x_s and x_p.
Output: response set `response` of cardinality k.

Enter information about an available entry into PR.
Fill `response` with k (random) objects from X.
Adjust $\mathcal{R}(Q)$ according to the maximum distance in the `response`
   from q designated as r.
Sort entries in PR with decreasing region proximity to $\mathcal{R}(Q)$.
while PR $\neq \emptyset$ **do**
  Extract the first entry $N = (G, \mathcal{R}(G))$ from PR.
  if $\neg Prune(\mathcal{R}(G), \mathcal{R}(Q), x_p)$ **then**
    foreach object entry $o_j \in G$ **do**
      if $d(q, o_j) \leq r$ **then**
        Update the `response`, r, and $\mathcal{R}(Q)$ by inserting o_j and
          removing the most distant object from q.
        Remove all entries $N' = (G', \mathcal{R}(G'))$ from PR
          which no longer intersects $\mathcal{R}(Q)$.
      endif
    enddo
    if $Stop(\text{response}, x_s)$ **then**
      exit
    foreach non-object entry $N' = (G', \mathcal{R}(G')) \in G$ **do**
      if $\neg Prune(\mathcal{R}(G'), \mathcal{R}(Q), x_p)$ **then**
        Insert the entry N' into PR.
    enddo
    Sort entries in PR with decreasing region proximity to $\mathcal{R}(Q)$.
  endif
enddo

Figure 1.19. Approximate search algorithm for nearest neighbor queries.

analyze the current response set to estimate the quality of the current approximation.

The generic pruning condition $Prune(\mathcal{R}(G), \mathcal{R}(Q), x_p)$ takes as arguments the query region $\mathcal{R}(Q)$, the bounding region $\mathcal{R}(G)$ of entry N, and the approximation parameter x_p. It returns true when the pruning strategy determines that the entry covered by the data region can be discarded according to the approximation parameter x_p. It is important to point out that the region $\mathcal{R}(G)$

is obtained without accessing the entry N itself. Information on the region is in fact maintained in the already accessed parent entry of N.

The approximation parameters x_s and x_p are used to tune the trade-off between efficiency and accuracy. Values corresponding to high performance offer low accuracy, because more qualifying objects may be dismissed. Values that give very good approximations correspond to more expensive query execution, because few entry accesses are avoided. Of course, the specific meaning of these two parameters and their use depend strictly on specific techniques employed to implement the stop and pruning conditions. Chapter 4 presents some of these techniques and defines their pruning and stop conditions.

9.3   Measures of Performance

Performance assessments of approximate similarity search algorithms focus on improvements in the efficiency and accuracy of approximate results. This is due to the natural tradeoff between the two – high improvements in efficiency vis à vis a precise similarity search are typically obtained at the cost of accuracy in the results. To compare different approximate similarity search algorithms, it is important to know the relationship between the two measures. Good approximate similarity search algorithms should demonstrate high efficiency, while still guaranteeing high accuracy of results. In the following, we define one measure of improvement in efficiency and several possibilities for assessing the accuracy of approximation. We also discuss the pros and cons of their possible application.

9.3.1   Improvement in Efficiency

The *improvement in efficiency*, IE, of an approximate search algorithm with respect to a precise algorithm is expressed as the cost ratio of the precise to approximate query execution. Formally, it is defined as

$$IE = \frac{cost(Q)}{cost^A(Q)},$$

where $cost$ and $cost^A$ denote the number of disk accesses for the precise and approximate execution of the query Q, respectively, which will be either $R(q, r)$ or $kNN(q)$. For example, an efficiency improvement of $IE = 10$ means approximate execution is ten times faster than precise execution. Search costs could alternatively be measured by the number of distance computations, but experiments demonstrate that the two values are strongly correlated.

9.3.2   Precision and Recall

Provided query response sets are not empty, there are two well-known measures from the field of Information Retrieval that can be used to quantify approximation quality. *Precision* measures the ratio of qualifying retrieved objects to the total of objects retrieved. *Recall* compares qualifying objects retrieved with the total number of qualifying objects which exist. Let S represent the result-set of a similarity search query and S^A be the result-set returned by the approximation query. Precision, P, and recall, R, can be formally defined as:

$$P = \frac{|S \cap S^A|}{|S^A|}$$

and

$$R = \frac{|S \cap S^A|}{|S|}.$$

Precision and recall are intuitive measures but their interpretation is not always obvious and may even be misleading. If an approximation algorithm for range queries has only false dismissals, i.e., it does not contain any false hits, the expression $S^A \subseteq S$ holds. This implies the precision is always one, so such a measure gives no useful information. Note that the approximate range search algorithm presented in Section 9.2 can only have false dismissals. On the other hand, given the fixed cardinalities of the precise and approximate response sets in the nearest neighbor queries, the recall and precision measures always return identical values. In addition, the measures do not consider response sets as ranked lists, so every element in the result-set is of equal importance. To clarify the last point, consider the following examples:

Example 1 We search for one nearest neighbor and the approximation algorithm retrieves the second actual nearest neighbor instead of the first one.

Example 2 We search for one nearest neighbor and the approximation algorithm retrieves the 10,000th actual nearest neighbor instead of the first one.

Example 3 We search for ten nearest neighbors and the approximation algorithm only misses the first actual nearest neighbor. Thus, the second actual nearest neighbor is in the first position, the third in second, etc. The eleventh nearest neighbor is in position ten.

Example 4 We search for ten nearest neighbors and the approximate algorithm misses only the tenth actual nearest neighbor. Thus, the first actual nearest neighbor is in first position, the second in second, etc. The eleventh nearest neighbor is in position ten.

In Examples 1 and 2, precision and recall evaluate to zero, no matter which object is found as the approximate nearest neighbor. However, an approximation in which the second, rather than the 10,000th, actual nearest neighbor is found should be rated as preferable. Only one object is skipped in the first case, while in the second 9,999 better objects are ignored.

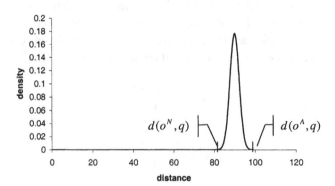

Figure 1.20. The relative distance error is not a reliable measure of approximation accuracy. Even though the relative distance error is small, almost all objects are missed by the approximate search algorithm.

In both Examples 3 and 4, precision and recall are equal to 0.9. However, the result in Example 4 should be considered a better approximation because the error appears only in the last position, while in Example 3, the best object is missing and all other objects are shifted by one position. Observe that objects can only be shifted in such a way as to place them in better positions. These inconveniences are tackled in the following.

9.3.3   Relative Error on Distances

Another measurement to asses the quality of approximate nearest neighbor searches is the *relative error on distances*, proposed in [Arya et al., 1998]. The relative error on distances, ED, is defined as

$$ED = \frac{d(o^A, q) - d(o^N, q)}{d(o^N, q)} = \frac{d(o^A, q)}{d(o^N, q)} - 1,$$

where o^A is the approximate nearest neighbor and o^N is the actual nearest neighbor. The relative error on distances measures the quality of approximation by comparing the distance of the approximate nearest neighbor to that of the actual nearest neighbor from the query object. This can be easily generalized to the case of the j-th nearest neighbor as follows:

$$ED_j = \frac{d(o_j^A, q)}{d(o_j^N, q)} - 1.$$

The relative error on distances has a drawback in that it does not take into account the actual distribution of distances in the object domain – see Section 10.1.2 for the definition of distance distribution and its usage in similarity searching in metric spaces. In the following, we discuss some consequences such an approach may entail.

The relative error on distances does not give an indication of the number of objects missed by the approximation algorithm. Specifically, suppose the distance between the first and the second actual nearest neighbor is large. Further suppose the approximation algorithm misses the first nearest neighbor o^N, and the first approximate nearest neighbor o^A is actually the second nearest neighbor. In this case the relative error on distances is high even if just one object is missed. And vice versa – suppose the relative error on distances is small, but the distance distribution is such that almost all objects have a distance smaller than o^A. In this case, many objects are missed even if the error is small.

The situation in Figure 1.20 depicts the extreme case in which o^A has a distance larger than almost all remaining objects, even though still *relatively* close in distance to o^N from the query object q. When the distances are distributed in a very small interval close to the upper bound of possible distances, as shown in Figure 1.20, the relative error on distances always assumes small values. In fact, the distance of the object furthest from the query object is not very different from that of the object nearest to it. Moreover, errors on distances measured in different datasets cannot be compared. A specific value of the relative error on distances might have different interpretations in different datasets depending upon the distribution and range of distances. A particular relative error value which would be large in the context of one dataset might be negligible in another with a larger range or lesser density of measured distances.

9.3.4 Position Error

An alternate way of assessing the accuracy of approximate similarity search algorithms is to measure the discrepancy between the approximate ordered list and the exact ordered list, as discussed extensively in [Diaconis, 1988, Dwork et al., 2001, Narasimhalu et al., 1997, Critchlow, 1985]. A measure to assess the difference between two ordered (ranked) lists is the *Sperman footrule distance* (see e.g., [Diaconis, 1988]). Suppose we have two ordered lists S_1 and S_2 containing all elements of a database X. The correlation between S_1 and S_2 is the sum of absolute differences between positions of each element in the two orderings. Given an ordered list S, we denote the position of the object o in S by $S(o)$, $o \in S$. The Sperman footrule distance is then given formally by

$$SFD = \sum_{i=1}^{|X|} |S_1(o_i) - S_2(o_i)|.$$

This can be normalized by dividing it by the maximum value possible, which is $|X|^2/2$.

Consider a result-set S^A returned by an approximate similarity search query, ordered with respect to the distance of objects from the query q. Let OX be the ordered list containing all elements of X, ordered by increasing distance from q. The previous measure cannot be used to assess the quality of S^A because it assumes the elements in both sets are identical. In our case, the ordered list S^A is a subset of OX. However, the Sperman footrule distance can be generalized to deal with partial lists resulting in the so-called *induced footrule distance* as follows:

$$IFD = \sum_{i=1}^{|S^A|} |OX(o_i^A) - S^A(o_i^A)|.$$

Observe that the ordering of objects in OX is always preserved in the approximate result S^A. That is, given $o_i^A, o_j^A \in S^A$ with $OX(o_i^A) < OX(o_j^A)$, it will also be true that $S^A(o_i^A) < S^A(o_j^A)$. This is due to the fact that, even though an approximation algorithm can retrieve a different set of objects, both use the same distance function. As a consequence, the position of an object in S^A is never higher than its position in OX, i.e., $S^A(o_i^A) \leq OX(o_i^A)$, so the absolute value operator can be omitted. In addition, the measure can be normalized by the factor $|S^A| \cdot |X|$. We use EP, *error on the position*, to denote the resulting measure:

$$EP = \frac{\sum_{i=1}^{|S^A|}(OX(o_i^A) - S^A(o_i^A))}{|S^A| \cdot |X|}.$$

Let us evaluate the accuracy of the four examples given in Section 9.3.2 using EP and suppose the cardinality of the dataset is $n = 10,000$. In Example 1, we have $EP = (2 - 1)/n = 1/10,000 = 0.0001$, while in Example 2, we have $EP = (10,000 - 1)/n = 9,999/10,000 = 0.9999$. Obviously, EP reflects the trivial fact that the approximation in Example 1 is much better than in Example 2. In Example 3, $EP = 10/(10 \cdot 10,000) = 0.0001$, while in Example 4, $EP = 1/(10 \cdot 10,000) = 0.00001$. The result-set of Example 4 is ten times better than that of Example 3.

10.   Advanced Issues

The design and implementation of any search structure depends upon a number of models, theories, and specific feature data, which help in selecting optimum strategies for specific data and search requirements. Due to the novel principles which underlie metric data searching, such tools are also unique. In this section, we start with a specification of statistics on metric datasets based exclusively on distances and their distributions. Next, we concentrate on approaches for measuring the proximity of ball regions, because such regions typically bound subsets of searched data. We also survey performance prediction methods, including approaches for estimating the quality of metric data trees. Finally, we elaborate on strategies for selecting reference objects, called pivots.

10.1 Statistics on Metric Datasets

The statistical characteristics of datasets have always been important in the performance optimization of database systems. Statistical information forms the basis for cost models of query optimizers. It is also used to tune access structure configurations in the physical database design. Statistical information employed in commercial systems is typically based on histograms of frequency values for the records in a database, or, if the data can be represented in a vector space, on the data distribution.

This type of information, though, cannot be used in generic metric spaces. Due to the lack of coordinates, the data distribution cannot be determined. Consequently, the statistical information used to characterize metric datasets must rely exclusively on the *distance density* and the *distance distribution* functions. In the following, we first introduce probabilistic notions of density and distribution functions. Then we discuss how these concepts apply to our scenario.

10.1.1 Distribution and Density Functions

Suppose V is a *continuous random variable* [Hoel et al., 1971], that is a real-valued function defined on a probability space, which depends upon an event occurring with zero probability.

The *distribution function* F_V of the random variable V is the following probability:

$$F_V(v) = \Pr\{V \le v\}.$$

For instance, suppose V is a continuous random variable associated with the distance between two objects in a metric space. Then $F_V(v)$ is the probability that two objects exist with distance smaller than v. Note that in a continuous space the probability that the distance is exactly equal to v is zero.

The *density function* f_V of a random variable V is a function such that

$$F_V(v) = \int_{-\infty}^{v} f_V(x)dx.$$

Of course, the following always holds

$$\int_{-\infty}^{+\infty} f_V(x)dx = 1.$$

If there are two random variables V_1 and V_2, we talk about the *joint distribution* $F_{V_1 V_2}(v_1, v_2)$ and the *joint density* $f_{V_1 V_2}(v_1, v_2)$. The joint distribution is defined as

$$F_{V_1 V_2}(v_1, v_2) = \Pr\{V_1 \le v_1 \wedge V_2 \le v_2\}$$

and the joint density $f_{V_1 V_2}(x_1, x_2)$ is a function such that

$$F_{V_1 V_2}(v_1, v_2) = \int_{-\infty}^{v_2} \int_{-\infty}^{v_1} f_{V_1 V_2}(x_1, x_2) dx_1 dx_2.$$

As before, the following equation holds

$$\int_{-\infty}^{+\infty} \int_{-\infty}^{+\infty} f_{V_1 V_2}(x_1, x_2) dx_1 dx_2 = 1.$$

This can easily be extended to an arbitrary number of random variables.

10.1.2   Distance Distribution and Density

A useful property that characterizes datasets represented in vector spaces is the *data distribution* and the corresponding *data density*. Figure 1.21 shows the data density function, say $f_{X_1 X_2}(x_1, x_2)$, in a two dimensional vector space, where X_1 and X_2 are continuous random variables corresponding to the coordinates x_1 and x_2 of vectors. In the figure, dark areas correspond to high values of $f_{X_1 X_2}(x_1, x_2)$, while light areas correspond to low values. For example, the data distribution can be used for an arbitrary region of the space to determine the probability that a random object belongs to this region. Various cost models of access methods for data represented in vector spaces are based on the data distribution, for example [Berchtold et al., 1997, Faloutsos and Kamel, 1994, Kamel and Faloutsos, 1993, Papadopulos and Manolopoulos, 1997, Theodoridis and Sellis, 1996].

In generic metric spaces, data distributions cannot be obtained because an object does not have an identifiable position and the only quantifiable property is the distance between objects. [Ciaccia et al., 1998a] have proposed a way of characterizing metric datasets by using the *distance distribution*. The distance distribution with respect to an object p (pivot) indicates the number of objects whose distance from p does not exceed a certain value or, in probabilistic terms, determines the probability that a random object has a distance from p smaller than or maximally equal to a certain value. In other words, the distribution of distances from p indicates how the other objects in the dataset are distributed around p. To give an intuitive idea of this statistical information, Figure 1.22 depicts such a situation for a two-dimensional vector space. Note that the distance density does not provide information on the really "dense" zones of the space, because an object whose distance from p is x may be placed in any position on the circumference with center p and radius x.

Formally, the distribution of distances with respect to a given object is defined as follows:

DEFINITION 1.6 *Let D_p be a continuous random variable corresponding to the distance $d(p, o)$, where o is a random object. The distance distribution*

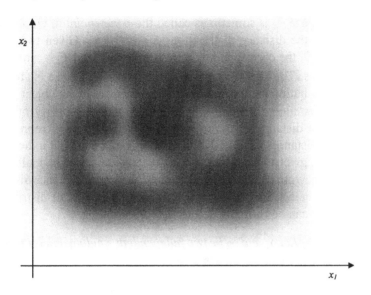

Figure 1.21. Density of data in a two dimensional vector space

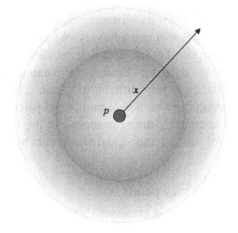

Figure 1.22. Density of distances from the object p

$F_{D_p}(x)$ *with respect to object p is defined as*

$$F_{D_p}(x) = \Pr\{D_p \le x\} = \Pr\{d(p,o) \le x\}.$$

$\square$

The distance density $f_{D_p}(x)$ from the object p can be obtained as the derivative of the distance distribution $F_{D_p}(x)$.

The distribution F_{D_p} is sometimes called the p *viewpoint* to emphasize the fact that it gives the distance distribution as seen by p. Given two different objects $p_i, p_j \in \mathcal{D}$, the corresponding viewpoints $F_{D_{p_i}}$ and $F_{D_{p_j}}$ are typically different functions. To simplify notation, in the following we use F_{p_i} to indicate the distance distribution (or the viewpoint) with respect to the object p_i.

The *overall distance distribution* is a global (unique) property of a metric dataset. Given a distance x, the overall distance distribution represents the probability that distances smaller than x exist. In other words, it indicates what the probability is, given two random objects, that their distance is smaller than x. Contrary to the viewpoints of individual objects, the overall distance distribution is a single characterization of the entire dataset. The overall distribution of distances over $\mathcal{D}$ can be formally defined as follows:

DEFINITION 1.7 *Let o_1 and o_2 be two independent random objects taken from $\mathcal{D}$. The overall distance distribution $F(x)$ on $\mathcal{D}$ is*

$$F(x) = \text{Pr}\{d(o_1, o_2) \leq x\}.$$

$\square$

Obviously, maintaining the overall distance distribution is much easier than maintaining the individual viewpoint of every object in the dataset. In fact, a single function is adequate for the updating process, instead of one function for every object in the database. From a computational point of view, the overall distance distribution is very difficult to obtain. However, it can easily be approximated by sampling a sufficient number of pairs of objects from the available dataset and computing their distances. In the following, we examine the possibility of substituting individual viewpoints by the overall distance distribution.

10.1.3   Homogeneity of Viewpoints

In [Ciaccia et al., 1998a], it is shown that the overall distance distribution can be substituted for the viewpoints, provided the dataset is probabilistically *homogeneous*, i.e., that there is no significant *discrepancy* between the various viewpoints. Assuming discrete distance functions, the discrepancy between two viewpoints is formally defined as

$$\delta(F_{p_i}, F_{p_j}) = \underset{x \in [0, d^+]}{\text{avg}} \left| F_{p_i}(x) - F_{p_j}(x) \right|,$$

where d^+ is the maximum distance between two objects of the dataset. The discrepancy between two viewpoints is the average difference of distance distribution values, across all values of x. By analogy, the discrepancy for continuous distance functions can be defined [Ciaccia et al., 1998a]. Then, the *index of homogeneity of viewpoints, HV,* is defined for the metric space $\mathcal{M}$ as

$$HV(\mathcal{M}) = 1 - \operatorname*{avg}_{p_1,p_2\in\mathcal{D}} \delta(F_{p_1}, F_{p_2}),$$

where p_1 and p_2 are random objects of $\mathcal{D}$. When $HV(\mathcal{M}) \approx 1$, two viewpoints are very likely to give the same probability for a given distance. That is, distances are distributed in almost the same way with respect to an arbitrary object, and any viewpoint can be chosen in place of any other. In addition, given the overall distance distribution as the average of all viewpoints, the overall distance distribution $F(x)$ itself can be used as a representative of any F_{p_i} – the overall distance distribution $F(x)$ also has characteristics similar to any of the distributions F_{p_i}.

As reported in [Ciaccia et al., 1998a], datasets used in real similarity search applications are typically highly homogeneous. Therefore in practice, the overall distance distribution $F(x)$ can be reliably applied to characterize a metric dataset.

10.2 Proximity of Ball Regions

There are several data management operations for which it is interesting to have an estimate of the number of objects in the intersection of ball regions. For example:

region splitting, where ball regions obtained by splitting a larger region should share as few objects as possible. Otherwise, queries, which typically follow the distance distribution of searched datasets, would frequently access both sets;

disk allocation, where ball regions sharing many objects need to be placed in consecutive (or nearby) blocks of a disk, because they have a high probability of being accessed together;

approximate search, where ball regions are only accessed when the chance of an object appearing in the intersection with the query region exceeds a certain threshold.

The number of data objects contained in the intersection of two ball regions depends on the distribution of data objects. Intuitively, there may be regions with a large intersection and few objects in common, but also regions with a small intersection and many objects in common, such as happens when the intersection covers a dense area of data space. The estimated count of objects actually shared by two ball regions is referred to as the *proximity of ball regions*. In [Amato et al., 2003] this proximity is formally defined as follows:

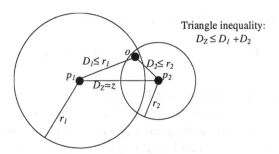

Figure 1.23. The overall proximity can be computed as the probability that an object is in the intersection of two regions of radii r_1 and r_2, given that the distance between their centers is z.

DEFINITION 1.8 *Let* $\mathcal{R}_1 = (p_1, r_1), \mathcal{R}_2 = (p_1, r_2)$ *be two ball regions with centers* p_1, p_2 *and radii* r_1, r_2, *respectively. The proximity* $prox(\mathcal{R}_1, \mathcal{R}_2)$ *of ball regions* $\mathcal{R}_1$, $\mathcal{R}_2$ *is the probability that a randomly chosen object* o *over the same metric space* $\mathcal{M}$ *appears in both regions. That is:*

$$prox(\mathcal{R}_1, \mathcal{R}_2) = \Pr\{d(p_1, o) \leq r_1 \wedge d(p_2, o) \leq r_2\}.$$

$\square$

To precisely compute proximity according to Definition 1.8, knowledge of distance distributions with respect to the regions' centers is needed. Since any object from $\mathcal{D}$ can become a region's center, such knowledge is very difficult to obtain. However, when the dataset is homogeneous (see Section 10.1.3), we can assume the distribution depends on the distance between the regions' centers, while remaining (practically) independent of the centers themselves. This also implies that all pairs of regions with the same radii and constant distance between centers have on average the same proximity, no matter their actual centers. Consequently, the proximity $prox(\mathcal{R}_1, \mathcal{R}_2)$ can be reliably estimated by the *overall proximity* of pairs of regions $prox_z(r_1, r_2)$ having radii r_1 and r_2, with distance between their centers z. Specifically:

DEFINITION 1.9 *Let* p_1, p_2 *and* o *be random objects from* $\mathcal{D}$*. Let* D_1, D_2 *and* D_Z *be continuous random variables corresponding, respectively, to distances* $d(p_1, o)$, $d(p_2, o)$, *and* $d(p_1, p_2)$. *The overall proximity* $prox_z(r_1, r_2)$ *of any two ball regions with radii* r_1 *and* r_2 *and distance between centers* z *is*

$$prox_z(r_1, r_2) = \Pr\{D_1 \leq r_1 \wedge D_2 \leq r_2 \mid D_Z = z\}.$$

$\square$

A graphical representation that helps intuitively understand the definition of overall proximity in terms of random variables D_1, D_2, and D_Z, is given in

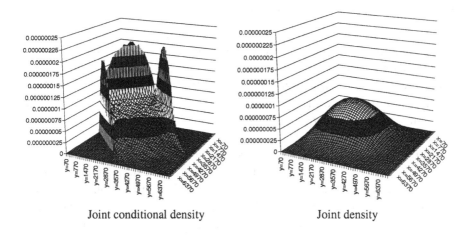

Joint conditional density   Joint density

Figure 1.24. Comparison between $f_{D_1,D_2|D_Z}(x,y|z)$ and $f_{D_1 D_2}(x,y)$, with a fixed z

Figure 1.23. Overall proximity can be computed by using the *joint conditional density* $f_{D_1,D_2|D_Z}(x,y|z)$ as follows:

$$prox_z(r_1,r_2) = \int_0^{r_1} \int_0^{r_2} f_{D_1,D_2|D_Z}(x,y|z)dydx.$$

Unfortunately, no generic analytic expression for $f_{D_1,D_2|D_Z}(x,y|z)$ is known. In [Amato et al., 2003], precise heuristics to approximate it using the joint density $f_{D_1 D_2}(x,y)$ are proposed, analyzed and validated. The heuristics are based on the observation that, as shown in Figure 1.24, $f_{D_1,D_2|D_Z}(x,y|z)$ is zero if x, y, and z do not satisfy the triangle inequality, because such distances in metric spaces simply cannot exist. However, $f_{D_1 D_2}(x,y)$ is not restricted by such a constraint, and any pair of distances x and y is possible for any z. Visually it seems the joint conditional density can be obtained by collecting the values of the joint density outside the bounds of the triangle inequality, and dragging them to places where they are satisfied. A detailed description of the heuristics can be found in [Amato et al., 2003, Amato, 2002]. The main motivation is that the joint density $f_{D_1 D_2}(x,y)$ is simple to obtain. In fact, D_1 and D_2 are independent random variables, so $f_{D_1 D_2}(x,y) = f_{D_1}(x) \cdot f_{D_2}(y)$. Given the definition of the random variables D_1 and D_2, it is also easy to show that $f_{D_1}(x) = f_{D_2}(x) = f(x)$, where $f(x)$ is the overall distance density (please refer to Section 10.1.2). Therefore, the joint density is $f_{D_1 D_2}(x,y) = f(x)f(y)$. The computational complexity needed to obtain the proximity using these heuristics is $O(n)$, where n is the size of the histogram representing $f(x)$. In this case, the storage overhead for maintaining such a histogram is entirely acceptable even for large values of n.

10.3   Performance Prediction

The problem of estimating CPU costs (mainly incurred by distance computations) and the I/O costs for processing range and nearest neighbor queries on distance data has been studied in [Ciaccia et al., 1998a]. Unlike the specific case of vector spaces, where information on data distribution can be exploited for predicting the performance of multi-dimensional access methods, no such possibility exists in generic metric spaces. This makes for a different problem that demands a novel approach.

Suppose we have a dataset partitioned into m subsets bounded by ball regions $\mathcal{R}_i(p_i, r_i)$, $1 \leq i \leq m$. Given a range query $R(q, r_q)$, the content of the i-th subset is accessed by the query if the corresponding ball region $\mathcal{R}_i$ intersects the query region, i.e., if $d(q, p_i) \leq r_i + r_q$. Let $\mathcal{R}^r = (p, r)$ be a ball region with random center p and radius r, bounding a subset. The probability of a decision to access the subset as $R(q, r_q)$ is processed can be estimated as:

$$\Pr\{d(q, p) \leq r + r_q\} = F_q(r + r_q) \approx F(r + r_q).$$

This is clearly true if the homogeneity of viewpoints in the dataset is high.

Suppose that for each subset we know the radius r_i of the corresponding bounding ball region. We are now able to estimate the expected number of accessed subsets for a range query by summing the probabilities of accessing each of them as follows:

$$subsets(R(q, r_q)) \approx \sum_{i=1}^{m} F(r_i + r_q). \tag{1.1}$$

Note that this does not take into account the cost of locating the position of a subset in the disk, which depends on the specific data structure used to organize the subsets. For example, in the case of a hierarchical organization of ball regions as exemplified in Section 6.1, the cost of locating subsets is already included in the cost of accessing the parent subset.

As stated in Section 3, the evaluation of the distance between two objects can be expensive. Accordingly, the possibility of estimating the number of distance computations needed to execute a range query is very important. This can be obtained as

$$distances(R(q, r_q)) \approx \sum_{i=1}^{m} |\mathcal{R}_i| F(r_i + r_q),$$

where $|\mathcal{R}_i|$ is the number of objects contained in the subset bounded by the ball region $\mathcal{R}_i$. In fact, unless specific techniques are used to reduce the number of distance computations (see Section 7) , distances must be evaluated from the query object to all objects of the accessed subsets.

Finally, the following formula estimates the expected number of retrieved objects as

$$objects(R(q, r_q)) \approx nF(r_q),$$

where n is the total number of objects in the dataset.

The expected execution cost of a nearest neighbor query is more complex to determine. Suppose a query $kNN(q)$ returning o_k as the k-th nearest neighbor. The optimal nearest neighbor search algorithm, as discussed in Section 6.1, accesses just those regions intersecting the query ball region $\mathcal{R}(q, d(q, o_k))$. Therefore, the costs of the $kNN(q)$ query are the same as the costs of the range query $R(q, d(q, o_k))$. Unfortunately, the object o_k and consequently the distance $d(q, o_k)$ are not known a priori. A way to solve this problem is to use the distance density of the k-th nearest neighbor as follows: Let $DNN_{q,k}$ be the continuous random variable corresponding to the distance of the k-th nearest neighbor from the query object q and let $f_{DNN_{q,k}}$ be the corresponding density function.

According to [Ciaccia et al., 1998a], the density function $f_{DNN_{q,k}}$ can be obtained first by computing the distribution of $DNN_{q,k}$ as follows:

$$
\begin{aligned}
F_{DNN_{q,k}}(x) &= \Pr\{DNN_{q,k} < x\} \\
&= \sum_{i=k}^{n} \binom{n}{i} \Pr\{d(q, o) \le x\}^{i} \Pr\{d(q, o) > x\}^{n-i} \\
&= 1 - \sum_{i=0}^{k-1} \binom{n}{i} \Pr\{d(q, o) \le x\}^{i} \Pr\{d(q, o) > x\}^{n-i} \\
&= 1 - \sum_{i=0}^{k-1} \binom{n}{i} F(x)^{i} (1 - F(x))^{n-i}.
\end{aligned}
$$

Notice that o denotes a random object. Then the density can be obtained as the derivative:

$$f_{DNN_{q,k}}(x) = \sum_{i=0}^{k-1} \binom{n}{i} F(x)^{i-1} f(x)(1 - F(x))^{n-i-1}(nF(x) - i).$$

Now, the number of subsets accessed by a nearest neighbor search is obtained by integrating Equation 1.1 over the entire range of possible distances multiplied by the density of the distance to the k-th nearest neighbor:

$$subsets(kNN(q)) \approx \int_{0}^{d^{+}} subsets(R(q, r)) f_{DNN_{q,k}}(r) dr.$$

By analogy, the number of distance computations is given by the following formula:

$$distances(kNN(q)) \approx \int_{0}^{d^{+}} distances(R(q, r)) f_{DNN_{q,k}}(r) dr.$$

In order to compute these cost prediction functions, statistics related to all subsets of the partitioned dataset should be kept. Since the number of subsets typically increases linearly with the size of the dataset, the amount of information can become unacceptable. Depending on the specific data organization, the statistical information can be reduced while still maintaining a high degree of reliability for results. For example, consider a tree-based organization of ball regions as outlined in Section 7.1. In this case, we can maintain statistical information for each level instead of for each subset. Specifically, for each level l we store only the number of subsets M_l and the average covering radius $\overline{r}_l$ of ball regions at this level. The cost function for range queries can now be modified as follows:

$$subsets(R(q, r_q)) \approx \sum_{l=1}^{L} M_l F(\overline{r}_l + r_q)$$

and

$$distances(R(q, r_q)) \approx \sum_{l=1}^{L} M_{l+1} F(\overline{r}_l + r_q),$$

where L is the number of tree levels, and M_{L+1} is the total number of objects in the dataset. The level-based cost function for nearest neighbor queries can be obtained analogously.

In [Ciaccia et al., 1999], this approach was extended to deal with datasets where the homogeneity hypothesis is not satisfied. The extension consists in maintaining several distance distributions with respect to different objects called *witnesses*. Special algorithms are proposed to choose witnesses and decide which distribution to use for a specific query. An extension of this approach is also proposed in [Amato et al., 2003] to derive a cost model for approximate range search queries in metric spaces. Another approach to performance prediction has been proposed by [Traina, Jr. et al., 1999, Traina, Jr. et al., 2000a].

10.4   Tree Quality Measures

As we will see in Chapter 2, many index structures for metric spaces are trees. For the moment, we can consider the hypothetical metric tree defined in Section 7.1. Given a tree, we would like to know whether the tree structure built over a dataset can be improved or not. We might also be interested in comparing two different trees to decide which of them is more efficient or optimal. Methods for such estimates are often based on a definition of the overlap between ball metric regions which cover individual nodes of the tree.

When analyzing the theoretical search costs of a metric tree structure in terms of the number of distance computations or the number of I/O operations, it is typically assumed that the tree is "good" [Faloutsos and Kamel, 1994].

However, in real situations, this is not necessarily true. The problem, nicely formulated by [Traina, Jr. et al., 2000b], is as follows:

Given n objects organized in a metric tree structure, how can we express its 'goodness' or 'fitness' with a single number?

To this aim, [Traina, Jr. et al., 2002] propose another concept of computing the overlap between two metric regions, based again on the number of objects covered by both regions. Specifically, the authors define a measure as follows: the overlap of two ball regions $\mathcal{R}_1$ and $\mathcal{R}_2$ is the number of objects in the corresponding subsets which are covered by both regions, divided by the total number of objects in these subsets. Notice that the quantified overlap is a real number between zero and one. Also observe the difference from the measure discussed in Section 10.2, where the overlap is related to the total number of objects in the dataset.

The measure of "goodness" of a metric tree is strictly related to the definition of the overlap. The authors claim a good tree has very little and ideally no overlap between metric regions of individual nodes. The definition of the *absolute fat-factor* follows this strategy.

DEFINITION 1.10 *Let T be a metric tree with height h and $m \geq 1$ nodes which organize n objects. The* absolute fat-factor *of T is*

$$fat(T) = \frac{I_C - nh}{n} \cdot \frac{1}{(m - h)},$$

where I_C denotes the total number of node accesses required to answer point queries for all n objects stored in the metric tree. □

The ideal metric tree requires accessing exactly one node per level and yields an absolute fat-factor of zero. By contrast, the worst tree visits all nodes regardless what point query is issued and the absolute fat-factor is equal to one. Using these two boundary examples, we can state the lower and upper limits on the value of I_C, i.e., the total number of accessed nodes for all n point queries. Accordingly, the lower bound is hn and the upper bound mn.

The absolute fat-factor is based on the following two assumptions:

- only range queries are taken into account; this is not very restrictive since a nearest neighbor query can be viewed as a special case of the range query;

- the distribution of point queries follows the distribution of data objects; in general, this is quite reasonable because we expect that queries are most likely to be issued in dense regions of the metric space.

To aid in understanding the absolute fat-factor, we provide the reader with an example of two trees organizing the same dataset (see Figure 1.25). The

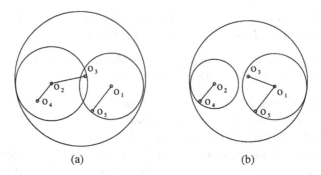

Figure 1.25. An example of two tree structures with different absolute fat-factors: (a) $fat(T) = 0.2$, and (b) $fat(T) = 0.0$.

connecting lines are drawn only to emphasize the relationships of objects with their corresponding representatives. Both trees organize the same five objects and consist of two levels and three nodes, i.e., $n = 5$, $h = 2$ and $m = 3$, respectively. By issuing five point queries, we get $I_C = 11$ for the tree in Figure 1.25a. In this case, the absolute fat-factor is 0.2. For the tree in Figure 1.25b, $I_C = 10$, and the absolute fat-factor is zero.

The notion of absolute fat-factor concentrates exclusively on the ratio of objects lying in overlapping regions. The main disadvantage to this approach is that it does not consider the number of nodes in trees, so a big tree with a low fat-factor is always better than a small tree with the fat-factor a bit higher. The *relative fat-factor* by [Traina, Jr. et al., 2002] assigns penalties to trees that use more than the minimum number of nodes. Such an approach does not consider the height and number of nodes of the actual tree, instead uses the respective characteristics of the minimum tree. Formally, the relative fat-factor is defined as follows.

DEFINITION 1.11 *Let T be a metric tree with more than one node organizing n data objects. The* relative fat-factor *of T is*

$$rfat(T) = \frac{I_C - nh_{min}}{n} \cdot \frac{1}{(m_{min} - h_{min})},$$

where the minimum height is $h_{min} = \lceil \log_C n \rceil$ and the minimum number of nodes is $m_{min} = \sum_{i=1}^{h_{min}} \lceil n/C^i \rceil$, with C representing the node capacity expressed as the number of objects. □

The value of the relative fat-factor may vary from zero to a positive number that can be greater than one.

In summary, the absolute fat-factor measures how satisfactory a tree is with respect to the number of objects in overlaps of regions on the same level, disregarding any possible waste of disk space due to under-occupied nodes. The

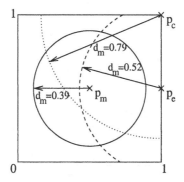

Figure 1.26. Different choices for pivot *p* to divide the unit square.

relative fat-factor extends this conception to compare trees with respect to both overlaps and the efficient occupation of nodes.

10.5 Choosing Reference Points

The problem of choosing reference objects (pivots) is important for any metric search technique, because all such structures need, directly or indirectly, "anchors" for partitioning and search pruning (see Sections 5 and 7.6). It is well-known that a specific selection of pivots can affect the performance of search algorithms. This has been recognized and demonstrated by several researchers, e.g. [Yianilos, 1993, Bozkaya and Özsoyoglu, 1999, Shapiro, 1977]. Roughly speaking, the higher and more narrowly-focused the distance density is with respect to a pivot, the greater the chance a query object will be located at the most frequent distance from that pivot. For example, if the distance d_m of a ball partitioning is the most frequent, and if all other distances are not very different, both resulting subsets are likely to be accessed for any given query, a very undesirable situation. Due to the complexity of the problem, pivots are often chosen at random. Obviously, random choice is the most trivial technique and does nothing to optimize pivot selection. Perhaps it is surprising, then, that many implementations use this approach with reasonable success.

For Euclidean spaces, [Yianilos, 1993] explains why some elements of the space may be better pivots than the others. To illustrate, consider Figure 1.26, which presents a unit square with uniform data distribution. To divide the space using ball partitioning, we have to pick a pivot and conveniently set the radius d_m. There are three natural choices for pivots: the midpoint p_m, the midpoint of an edge p_e, and a corner point p_c. To choose among these possibilities, note that the probability of entering both regions is proportional to the length of the partitioning boundary in the square. Thus, we aim at minimizing the boundary length. From this perspective, the most promising choice is the corner point p_c, with the object p_e as second choice since it is still better than the central point

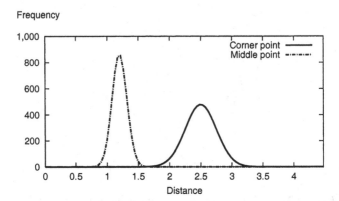

Figure 1.27. Distance densities for two pivots. One is the center while the other is a corner object, in the unit cube of a 20-dimensional Euclidean space.

p_m. It is interesting that from a clustering point of view, p_m is the center of a cluster but, as we have shown, it is the worst possible choice for partitioning. This observation can even be generalized by saying that a good pivot should be an *outlier*, that is an object located far away from the others, or one lying near the boundary of the space. Because of the generic metric, however, it's not always possible to define such an object.

The heuristics that selects pivots from corners of the space can be used in applications where we have some idea of the geometry of the space, which is not often true in metric spaces. In [Bozkaya and Özsoyoglu, 1999], a different reason is given why corner pivots may be better than the others, i.e., why they provide better partitioning. Succinctly, the distance density for a corner point is flatter than the density for a central point. Figure 1.27 illustrates this for uniformly distributed points in a 20-dimensional Euclidean data space. As we can easily see, the distance density with respect to the central object is sharper and thinner. Setting the ball-partitioning radius to the peak value leads to a higher concentration of objects near the boundary and, as a consequence, a higher probability of visiting both regions. This does not apply, by contrast, to the corner point because the distance density is much flatter. Thus the search would involve more trimming. A simple heuristics which tries to respect these observations is as follows:

- choose a random object,

- compute distances from this object to all others,

- select the furthest object as pivot.

This simple procedure cannot guarantee choosing the best possible pivot but it can help choose a better pivot than would be got randomly. The authors have verified this by experiment, with performance gains due to the heuristics varying between 5% and 10%.

When several reference points are used for partitioning, the problem gets even more complicated. Intuitively, they should be fairly far apart, but the problem of finding k furthest objects is very time-consuming. An approach suggested in [Brin, 1995] works as follows: Given a set of n points from which $m > 1$ objects are to be chosen as pivots, we choose $3m$ objects at random to form a candidate set – the number three is an empirical suggestion by the author. From this candidate set, an object is picked and the furthest candidate object from this one is selected as the first pivot. Next, another candidate object furthest from the first pivot is promoted to the second pivot. Up to this point, the algorithm follows the approach previously proposed in [Bozkaya and Özsoyoglu, 1999]. The succeeding pivot is picked as the furthest object from the previous two pivots. By furthest, we mean that the minimum of distances is maximized. Specifically, the third pivot is such a candidate object whose minimum of distances to the previous pivots is maximal. The procedure described is repeated until all m pivots are found. A simple dynamic algorithm can do this in $O(3m \cdot m)$ time. For small values of m, the process can be repeated several times with a different initial set of (random) candidate points, and the best setting of reference points is used.

Recently, the problem has been systematically studied in [Bustos et al., 2001], where several strategies for selecting pivots were proposed and tested. The authors suggest an *efficiency criterion* that compares two sets of pivots and designates the better of the two. It uses the mean distance between every pair of objects in $\mathcal{D}$, denoted by $\mu_{\mathcal{D}}$. Given two sets of pivots $P_1 = \{p_1, p_2, \dots, p_t\}$ and $P_2 = \{p'_1, p'_2, \dots, p'_t\}$ we call P_1 better than P_2 if

$$\mu_{\mathcal{D}_{P_1}} > \mu_{\mathcal{D}_{P_2}}.$$

However, the problem is how to find the mean for a given set P of pivots. An estimate of such a quantity is computed as follows:

- at random, choose l pairs of objects $\{(o_1, o'_1), (o_2, o'_2), \dots, (o_l, o'_l)\}$ from the given database $X \subseteq \mathcal{D}$;

- all pairs are mapped into the feature space associated with the set of pivots P using the mapping function $\Psi(\cdot)$ (refer to Section 7.6);

- for every pair (o_i, o'_i), compute the distance between o_i and o'_i in the feature space, that is, $d_i = L_\infty(\Psi(o_i), \Psi(o'_i))$;

- compute $\mu_{\mathcal{D}_P}$ as the mean of these distances, i.e., $\mu_{\mathcal{D}_P} = \frac{1}{l} \sum_{1 \le i \le l} d_i$.

As the most suitable strategy for real world metric spaces, the authors propose *incremental selection*. The advantage of this algorithm is that it is capable of selecting pivots incrementally, depending on the need for new pivots. The strategy works as follows: First choose a set $P_1 = \{p_1\}$ of one element from a sample of m database objects, such that the pivot p_1 has the maximum $\mu_{\mathcal{D}_{P_1}}$ value. Then choose a second pivot p_2 from another sample of m objects of the database, creating a new set $P_2 = \{p_1, p_2\}$ for fixed p_1, maximizing $\mu_{\mathcal{D}_{P_2}}$. The third pivot p_3 is chosen by analogy, creating another set $P_3 = \{p_1, p_2, p_3\}$ for fixed p_1, p_2, maximizing $\mu_{\mathcal{D}_{P_3}}$. This process is repeated until the desired number of pivots is determined. If all distances needed to estimate $\mu_{\mathcal{D}_P}$ are retained, only $2ml$ distances must be computed to estimate the new value of $\mu_{\mathcal{D}}$ whenever a new pivot is being added. The total cost for selecting k pivots is $2lmk$ distance evaluations.

The efficiency criterion presented above also tries to select pivots far away from each other. However, the key difference between this approach and the previous technique is that the criterion maximizes the mean of distances in the projected space and not in the original metric space. Specifically, it tries to spread the projected objects as much as possible according to the selected pivots. Note that these two procedures do not always go together.

Rough guidelines from current experience can be summarized as follows:

- good pivots should be *far away* from other objects in the metric space,

- good pivots should be *far away* from each other.

Finally, we would like to point out the dark side of the strategy of selecting pivots as outliers. Such an approach will not necessarily work in all possible situations. Consider a metric space with sets as data objects and the Jaccard's coefficient (see Section 3.5) as the distance measure. The outlier principle would select a pivot which is far away from the other objects. In the limit case, the selected pivot p would be completely different from the other objects, resulting in distance $d(p, o) = 1$ for any o in the database. Such an anchor is useless from the partitioning point of view, leaving the search unable to filter any single object.

Chapter 2

SURVEY OF EXISTING APPROACHES

In this chapter, we give an overview of existing indexes for metric spaces. Other relevant surveys on indexing techniques in metric spaces can be found in [Chávez et al., 2001b] or [Hjaltason and Samet, 2003a]. In the interests of a systematic presentation, we have divided the individual techniques into four groups. In addition we also present some techniques for approximate similarity search. Specifically, techniques which make use of ball partitioning will be found in Section 1, while Section 2 describes indexing approaches based on generalized hyperplane partitioning. A significant group of indexing methods computes distances to characteristic objects and then uses these results to organize the data. Such methods are reported in Section 3. In order to maximize performance, many approaches synergically combine several of the basic principles into a single index. The most important of these hybrid approaches are reported in Section 4. Finally, Section 5 treats the important topic of approximate similarity search, which trades some precision in search results for significant improvements in performance.

1. Ball Partitioning Methods

The advantage of ball partitioning is that it requires only one pivot and, provided the median distance d_m is known, the resulting subsets contain the same amount of data. Such a simple concept has naturally attracted a lot of attention and resulted in numerous indexing approaches being defined. In the following, we survey the most important of them. The first three structures assume discrete metric functions with a relatively small domain of values. The other methods can also be applied for continuous functions.

1.1   Burkhard-Keller Tree

Probably the first solution to support searching in metric spaces was that presented in [Burkhard and Keller, 1973]. It is called the Burkhard-Keller Tree, BKT. The tree assumes a discrete distance function and is built recursively in the following manner: From an indexed dataset X, an arbitrary object $p \in X$ is selected as the root node of the tree. For each distance $i \geq 0$, subsets $X_i = \{o \in X, d(o, p) = i\}$ are defined as groups of all objects at distance i from the root p. A child node of root p is built for every non-empty set X_i. All child nodes can be recursively repartitioned until it is no longer possible to create a new child node. When a child node is being divided, some object o_j from the set X_i is chosen as a representative of the set. A leaf node is created for every set X_i provided X_i is not repartitioned again. A set X_i is no longer split if it contains only a single object. Objects chosen as roots of subtrees (stored in internal nodes) are called pivots.

The algorithm for range queries is simple. The range search for query $R(q, r)$ starts at the root node of the tree and it compares its object p with the query object q. If p satisfies the query, that is if $d(p, q) \leq r$, the object p is returned. Subsequently, the algorithm enters all child nodes o_i such that

$$max\{d(q, p) - r, 0\} \leq i \leq d(q, p) + r \qquad (2.1)$$

and proceeds recursively downward. Observe that Equation 2.1 cuts out some branches of the tree. The inequality is a direct consequence of the lower bounds provided by Lemma 1.2 (pg. 31). In particular, by applying the lemma with $r_l = i$ and $r_h = i$, we find that the distance from q to an object o in the inspected tree branch is at least $max\{d(q, p) - i, i - d(q, p), 0\}$. Thus, we visit the branch i if and only if $max\{d(q, p) - i, i - d(q, p), 0\} \leq r$.

Figure 2.1b shows an example where the BKT is constructed from objects of the space illustrated in Figure 2.1a. Objects p, o_1, and o_4 are selected as roots of subtrees, so-called pivots. The range query is given by the object q and radius $r = 2$. The search algorithm discards some branches and the accessed branches are emphasized in the figure. Obviously, if the radius of range query grows the number of accessed subtrees (branches) increases. This leads to higher search costs, which are usually measured in terms of the number of distance computations. During the range query evaluation, the algorithm traverses the tree and determines distances to pivots in internal nodes. Thus, the increasing number of accessed subtrees leads to a growing number of distance computations because pivots in individual nodes are different.

BKTs are linear in space $\mathcal{O}(n)$ and the construction complexity measured in terms of the number of distance computations is $\mathcal{O}(n \log n)$. Search time complexity, also measured in terms of distance computations, is $\mathcal{O}(n^\alpha)$, where α is a real number satisfying $0 < \alpha < 1$ which depends on the search radius and the structure of the tree, see [Chávez et al., 2001b].

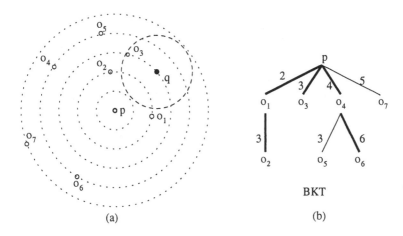

Figure 2.1. (a) An example of a metric space and a range query, (b) BKT built over the sample space.

1.2 Fixed Queries Tree

The Fixed Queries Tree, FQT, originally presented in [Baeza-Yates et al., 1994], is a modification of the BKT. In contrast to BKTs, where pivots on individual levels are different, Fixed Queries Trees use a single pivot for all nodes at the same level (see Figures 2.1b and 2.2a). All objects in a given dataset X are stored in leaves and internal nodes are used for navigation during the search (or insertion). The range search algorithm is the same as for the BKT. The advantage of this structure is a reduced number of distance computations, because even if more than one subtree has to be accessed to evaluate a query, only one distance computation between the query object and a specific pivot per level is computed. The experiments presented in [Baeza-Yates et al., 1994] confirm that FQTs need fewer distance computations than BKTs.

Figure 2.2a shows an example of an FQT built over the data of Figure 2.1a with objects p and o_4 as pivots on corresponding levels. Observe that all objects are stored in leaves, including the objects selected as pivots. The branches highlighted represent the process that evaluates the query $R(q, 2)$.

The space complexity is superlinear because the objects selected as pivots are duplicated, so the complexity varies from $\mathcal{O}(n)$ to $\mathcal{O}(n \log n)$. The number of distance computations required to build the tree is $\mathcal{O}(n \log n)$. The search complexity is $\mathcal{O}(n^\alpha)$, where α in the range $0 < \alpha < 1$ depends on the query radius and the object distribution in the metric space.

A variant of the FQT, called the Fixed-Height Fixed Queries Tree, FHFQT, is proposed in [Baeza-Yates et al., 1994, Baeza-Yates, 1997]. This structure has all its leaf nodes at the same level, i.e., leaves are at the same depth h. In other words, shorter paths are extended by additional paths. The enlargement of the

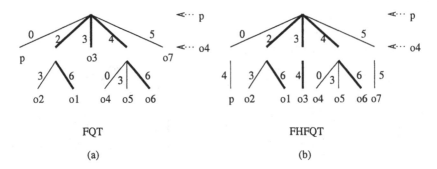

FQT

(a)

FHFQT

(b)

Figure 2.2. Examples of (a) FQT and (b) FHFQT built over objects of the data space depicted in Figure 2.1a.

tree can actually improve search performance, because the search process in the extended paths can be stopped before reaching the leaf. Note the distance computation to pivots for the extended paths does not typically imply extra costs, because such distances are computed due to the search needs of other (non-extended) paths. If we increase the height of the tree by thirty, we only add thirty more distance computations for the entire similarity search. We may introduce many new node traversals, but these are very cheap operations. However, thirty pivots filter out many objects, so the final candidate set is much smaller. This approach to filtering is explained in Section 7.6 of Chapter 1. For convenience, see Figure 2.2b where an example of the FHFQT is provided.

The space complexity of the FHFQT is superlinear and lies somewhere between $\mathcal{O}(n)$ and $\mathcal{O}(nh)$, where h is the height of the tree. The FHFQT is constructed with $\mathcal{O}(nh)$ distance computations. Search complexity is claimed to be constant $\mathcal{O}(h)$, that is the number of distance evaluations computed to h pivots. The extra CPU time is proportional to the number of traversed nodes and remains $\mathcal{O}(n^{\alpha})$, where $0 < \alpha < 1$ depends upon the query radius and the indexed space. The extra CPU time is spent on comparing distance values (integers) and in traversing the tree. In practice, the optimal tree height $h = \log n$ cannot always be achieved due to the space limitations.

1.3   Fixed Queries Array

The Fixed Queries Array, FQA, is presented in [Chávez et al., 2001a, Chávez et al., 1999b]. Though the structure of FQA is strongly related to the FHFQT, it is not a tree structure. First, the FHFQT with height h is built on a given dataset X. If the root-to-leaf paths of the FHFQT are traversed in order from left to right and placed in an array, the result is the FQA. Each column consists of h numbers representing distances to every pivot utilized in the FHFQT. In fact, the sequence of h numbers is the path from the root of FHFQT to its leaf. The FQA structure simply stores the database objects lexicographically sorted

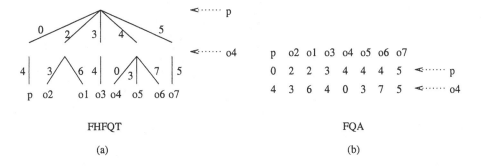

Figure 2.3. (a) An example of the FHFQT tree, (b) FQA built from the FHFQT.

by this sequence of distances. Specifically, the objects are initially sorted with respect to the first pivot and those at the same distance are sorted with respect to the second pivot and so on. For illustration, Figure 2.3b shows the FQA array constructed from the FHFQT in Figure 2.3a.

The range search algorithm is inherited from the FHFQT. Each internal node of the FHFQT corresponds to a range of elements in the FQA. Child nodes have a range of elements which is a subrange of their parents' range in the array. Naturally, there is a similarity between the FQA approach, the suffix trees, and the suffix arrays [Frakes and Baeza-Yates, 1992]. Navigation in the tree algorithm of the FHFQT is simulated by the binary search through the new range inside the current one.

The FQA is able to use more pivots than the FHFQT, which improves efficiency and search pruning. The authors of [Chávez et al., 2001a] show that the FQA outperforms the FHFQT. The space requirements are $n \cdot h \cdot b$ bits, where b is the number of bits used to store one distance. The number of distance computations evaluated during the search is $\mathcal{O}(h)$. As proved in [Baeza-Yates and Navarro, 1998], the extra CPU complexity of the FHFQT is $\mathcal{O}(n^\alpha)$. The FQA has $\mathcal{O}(n^\alpha \log n)$ extra complexity, where $0 < \alpha < 1$. The extra CPU time is due to the binary search of the array.

All the search structures presented above (BKT, FQT, FHFQT, and FQA) were designed for discrete metric functions, since a separate child is needed for any specific distance value. If we apply them to the continuous case, the tree degenerates to a flat tree of height one, and the search algorithm in effect performs a sequential scan.

In order to properly transform the continuous case to the discrete, we must segment the domain of potential distance values into a small set of subranges. Two discretizing schemata for the FQA have been proposed in [Chávez et al., 1999b, Chávez et al., 2001a]. The former divides the range of possible values into slices of identical width, the result being labeled a Fixed Slices Fixed

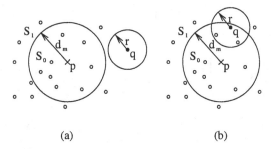

(a)   (b)

Figure 2.4. Examples of range queries: (a) S_0 is not accessed, (b) both subsets must be visited.

Queries Array. Such partitioning may lead to empty slices where no database object is accommodated. This, then, has motivated a more recent approach in which the entire range is divided into slices, each containing the same number of database objects. In other words, the domain is divided into fixed quantiles. The resulting FQA is called the Fixed Quantiles Fixed Queries Array.

1.4   Vantage Point Tree

The Vantage Point Tree (VPT) [Yianilos, 1993] is expressly designed for continuous distance functions, but discrete distance functions are also supported with virtually no modifications. It is based on the ball partitioning principle described in Section 5 of Chapter 1, which divides a set S into subsets S_1 and S_2 based upon a chosen object p called a vantage point or pivot, and the median distance d_m from p to the objects in S. Starting with the whole set of objects X and recursively applying this partitioning procedure leads to a balanced binary tree. Applying the median to divide a dataset into two subsets can be replaced by a strategy which instead employs the *mean* of distances from p to all objects in $X \setminus \{p\}$. This method, called the *middle point* in [Chávez et al., 2001b], may yield better performance for high-dimensional vector data. A disadvantage of the middle point strategy is that it may produce an unbalanced tree, impacting negatively on search algorithm efficiency.

The search algorithm for a range query $R(q, r)$ traverses the VPT from root to leaves. For each internal node, it evaluates the distance $d(q, p)$ between the pivot p and the query object q. If $d(q, p) \leq r$, the pivot p is reported to output. For internal nodes, the algorithm must also decide which subtrees to access. Doing so requires establishing lower bounds on the distances from q to objects in the left and right subtrees. If the query radius r is less than the lower bound, the algorithm does not visit the corresponding subtree. Figure 2.4a provides an example of a situation in which the inner ball region need not be accessed, whereas Figure 2.4b shows an example in which both subtrees must be checked. The lower bounds are established using Lemma 1.2 (pg. 31). More precisely, applying the equation and setting $r_l = 0$ and $r_h = d_m$, we have that the distance

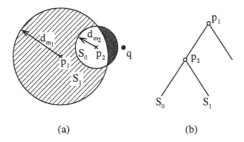

Figure 2.5. An example of VPT with two pivots p_1 and p_2: (a) the 2-D overview and (b) the corresponding tree representation.

from q to any object in the left branch is at least $max\{d(q,p)-d_m,0\}$. Likewise, setting $r_l = d_m$ and $r_h = \infty$ we get that the distance from q to an object in the right subtree is at least $max\{d_m - d(q,p),0\}$. Thus, we enter the left branch if $max\{d(q,p) - d_m,0\} \leq r$ and the right branch if $max\{d_m - d(q,p),0\} \leq r$. Note both subtrees can be visited simultaneously.

The ball partitioning principle applied in VPTs does not guarantee that the ball region around pivot p_2 will be completely inside the ball region around pivot p_1, which is the parent of p_2. For convenience, see Figure 2.5 where the situation is depicted for a query object q. In general, it is possible that the lower bound from q to a child node is smaller than the lower bound from q to the child's parent node, that is

$$max\{d(q,p_2) - d_{m_2},0\} < max\{d(q,p_1) - d_{m_1},0\}.$$

But this will not affect the behavior or correctness of the search algorithm – objects rooted in the subtree of p_2 are not closer than $max\{d(q,p_1) - d_{m_1},0\}$, even though the lower bounds may claim the opposite. In other words, objects in the left subtree of p_2 (the set S_0) are somewhere in the white area inside the ball region of p_2 and not in the shaded region (see Figure 2.5). On the other hand, objects in the right branch (the set S_1) must be in the hatch-marked area and not outside the ball region around p_1.

In constructing the VPT, many distance computations between pivots and objects are evaluated. For every object o in a leaf, distances are computed to each pivot p on the path from root to leaf. This information can be used to construct a more efficient search algorithm. The idea is employed in so-called VP^s trees, which are variants of VPTs proposed in [Yianilos, 1993]. Distances computed during insertion of objects are remembered and stored in the structure of the VP^s tree. They are then used in the range search algorithm as follows:

- if $|d(q,p) - d(p,o)| > r$ holds, we discard the object o without actually computing the distance $d(q,o)$,

- if $(d(q,p) + d(p,o)) \leq r$ holds, we directly include the object o in the query response set, again without computing the distance $d(q,o)$.

Given the distances $d(q,p)$ and $d(p,o)$, Lemma 1.1 (pg. 29) forms the lower and upper bounds of the actual distance between q and o:

$$|d(q,p) - d(p,o)| \leq d(q,o) \leq d(q,p) + d(p,o).$$

Thus the previous two pruning conditions are in fact direct consequences of Lemma 1.1.

Another variant of the VPT, also proposed in [Yianilos, 1993], is called the VP^{sb} tree. This tree is a further extension of the VP^s tree, where each leaf node is conceived as a bucket, that is, a unit of storage able to accommodate more than one object.

1.4.1 Multi-Way Vantage Point Tree

Figure 2.4b shows an elementary situation in which the search algorithm of the VPT must enter both subtrees and examine all objects. If such a situation occurs in many tree nodes, the global efficiency of the search deteriorates. In [Bozkaya and Özsoyoglu, 1997], the authors have tried to approach this problem by extending the binary VPT to a k-ary tree, with $k > 2$. The tree uses $k-1$ thresholds (percentiles) $d_{m_1}, \cdots, d_{m_{k-1}}$ in place of the single median d_m to partition the dataset into k subsets via spherical cuts. The modified tree is called the Multi-Way Vantage Point Tree, mw-VPT. Unfortunately, experiments reveal the performance of mw-VPTs is not always better because the spherical cuts become too thin. Take, for example, the case of high-dimensional domains where distances between any pair of objects are practically the same. The search algorithm leads to more branches of the tree being accessed during query execution. If i of k children of a node have to be searched then i distance computations are evaluated at the next level because all distances between the query object q and each pivot of the accessed children have to be determined – the VPT keeps a different pivot for each internal node at the same level.

Another extension of the VPT is called the Optimistic Vantage Point Tree, presented in [Chiueh, 1994]. This paper formulates algorithms for nearest neighbor queries and reports exhaustive performance tests on a database of image features.

These VPTs require $\mathcal{O}(n)$ space, the construction time for a balanced tree is $\mathcal{O}(n \log n)$, and search time complexity is $\mathcal{O}(\log n)$. The author of [Yianilos, 1993] claims this is only valid for very small query radii – too small to be interesting. The construction time of mw-VPT is $\mathcal{O}(n \log_k n)$ in terms of distance computations. The space complexity is the same, i.e., $\mathcal{O}(n)$. Likewise search time complexity is $\mathcal{O}(\log_k n)$.

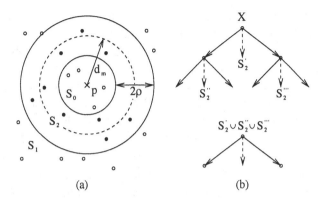

Figure 2.6. (a) An example of bp_ρ function with excluded points emphasized, (b) the VPF consisting of two trees.

1.5   Excluded Middle Vantage Point Forest

The Excluded Middle Vantage Point Forest, VPF, presented in [Yianilos, 1999], is another structure based on the ball partitioning principle. The motivation for the VPF comes from the following observation: Though the search time of the VPT [Yianilos, 1993] is sublinear, its performance depends upon not only the dataset, that is the distance distribution in X, but also on the choice of specific query object q. The VPF structure supports the worst-case sublinear search time for queries with a fixed radius up to the maximum ρ, so performance does not depend on the query object distribution. The VPF introduces a new concept of excluding objects at *middle distances* by modifying the ball partitioning technique. This principle has already been described in Section 5 of Chapter 1. For convenience, we repeat the key formula below.

$$bp_\rho(o) = \begin{cases} 0 \; if \; d(o,p) \leq d_m - \rho \\ 1 \; if \; d(o,p) > d_m + \rho \\ 2 \; otherwise \end{cases} \qquad (2.2)$$

Figure 2.6a depicts an example of the bp_ρ function, in which a dataset has been divided into two sets S_0, S_1, with the exclusion set S_2 containing objects excluded from the partitioning process. A binary tree is built recursively by repartitioning S_0 and S_1. The resulting exclusion sets S_2 are used to create another binary tree via the same principle. This procedure is repeated, and a forest of VPTs is produced. Figure 2.6b provides an example of the VPF. The first tree is built on the dataset X. All exclusion sets of the first tree, i.e., $\{S_2', S_2'', S_2'''\}$, are organized in the second tree. This process continues until the exclusion sets are not empty.

Excluding objects at distances near the threshold d_m has the outcome that no more than one branch of any internal node must be followed if the query radius is less than or equal to ρ. The following tree is searched if and only if the excluded area must be visited. It is correct to have the search algorithm enter only a single subtree (left or right) because every pair of objects (x, y) such that x belongs to the left subtree and y belongs to the right, must be at a distance greater than 2ρ, that is, $d(x, y) > 2\rho$. To prove this, consider the definition of the bp_ρ function in Equation 2.2. This implies $d(x, p) \leq d_m - \rho$ and $d(y, p) > d_m + \rho$. Since the triangle inequality holds between x, y, p, we get $d(x, y) + d(x, p) \geq d(y, p)$. Combining these inequalities and simplifying, we arrive at the desired formula, $d(x, y) > 2\rho$.

The VPF is linear in $\mathcal{O}(n)$ space, with a construction time of $\mathcal{O}(n^{2-\alpha})$, where $\mathcal{O}(n^{1-\alpha})$ is the number of trees in the VPF. Similarity queries are answered in $\mathcal{O}(n^{1-\alpha} \log n)$ distance computations. In a parallel environment with $\mathcal{O}(n^{1-\alpha})$ processors, search complexity is logarithmic, $\mathcal{O}(\log n)$. The parameter $0 < \alpha < 1$ depends on ρ, the dataset, and the distance function. Unfortunately, to achieve a greater value of α, the ρ parameter must be quite small.

2. Generalized Hyperplane Partitioning Approaches

In this section, we survey methods based on an approach which is orthogonal to ball partitioning. Specifically, we focus on Bisector trees and variants on them called the Monotonous Bisector Trees and Voronoi Trees. Next, we discuss properties of Generalized Hyperplane Trees. All these techniques share a common architecture based upon generalized hyperplane partitioning.

2.1 Bisector Tree

Probably the first indexing structure to use generalized hyperplane partitioning was the Bisector Tree (BST), proposed in [Kalantari and McDonald, 1983]. The BST is a binary tree built recursively over a dataset X as follows: Two pivots p_1, p_2 are selected at each node and a hyperplane partition is applied. Objects nearer the pivot p_1 than p_2 form the left subtree, while the objects closer to p_2 create the right subtree. For each of the pivots, *covering radii* are established and stored in respective nodes. The covering radius is the maximum distance between the pivot and any object in its subtree. The search algorithm for range query $R(q, r)$ enters a subtree if $d(q, p_i) - r$ is not greater than the covering radius r_i^c of p_i. Thus, we can prune a branch if the query does not intersect the ball centered at p_i with covering radius r_i^c. The pruning condition $d(q, p_i) - r \leq r_i^c$ is correct because its modification $d(q, p_i) - r_i^c \leq r$ is a direct consequence of the lower bound of Lemma 1.2 (pg. 31) with substitutions $r_l = 0$ and $r_h = r_i^c$. From the definition of the range query, $d(q, o)$ is upper-bounded by the query radius r.

A variant of the BST, called the Monotonous Bisector Tree (MBT), has been proposed in [Noltemeier et al., 1992b, Noltemeier et al., 1992a]. The idea

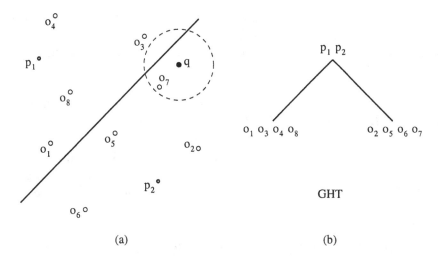

Figure 2.7. Generalized Hyperplane Tree (GHT): (a) a range query requiring access to both subsets of the hyperplane partition, (b) the corresponding structure of the tree.

behind this structure is that one of the pivots of each internal node other than the root node is inherited from its parent node. Specifically, pivots representing the left and the right subtrees are copied to the corresponding child internal nodes, respectively. This technique results in a structure with fewer pivots, and thus fewer distance computations are needed to execute a query.

BSTs are linear in space $\mathcal{O}(n)$ and require $\mathcal{O}(n \log n)$ distance computations to construct the tree. Search complexity is not analyzed by the authors.

An improvement on the BST called the Voronoi Tree (VT) is proposed in [Dehne and Noltemeier, 1987]. The VT uses two or three pivots in each internal node and also has the property that the covering radii are reduced as we move downwards in the tree. This provides better packing of objects in subtrees. The author of [Noltemeier, 1989] shows that balanced VTs can be obtained using an insertion algorithm similar to that of B-trees [Comer, 1979].

2.2 Generalized Hyperplane Tree

The Generalized Hyperplane Tree (GHT) proposed in [Uhlmann, 1991] is very similar to the BST in that both partition the dataset recursively via the generalized hyperplane principle. The difference is that the GHT does not use covering radii as a pruning criterion during the search operation. Instead, the GHT uses the hyperplane between pivots p_1 and p_2 to decide which subtrees to visit. Figure 2.7 depicts an example of the GHT. In (a), the partitioning is indicated and a range query specified. The corresponding tree structure can be seen in (b). At search time, we traverse the left subtree if $d(q, p_1) - r \leq d(q, p_2) + r$. The right subtree is visited if $d(q, p_1) + r \geq d(q, p_2) - r$ holds.

Again, note that it is possible to enter both subtrees. Observe also that the first inequality comes from Lemma 1.4 (pg. 34) and from the fact that $d(q, o) \leq r$, i.e., from the constraint given in the query specification. The second inequality is based on the same prerequisites, however, Lemma 1.4 is used in reverse, that is, the assumption about the position of o is $d(o, p_1) \geq d(o, p_2)$. A modification of the GHT that adopts the idea of reusing one pivot from the parent node, applied in MBTs, is presented in [Bugnion et al., 1993].

The space complexity of GHTs is $\mathcal{O}(n)$ and $\mathcal{O}(n \log n)$ distance computations are needed to construct the tree, the same as with BSTs. Unfortunately, search complexity was not analyzed by the authors. [Uhlmann, 1991] argues that GHTs should work better than VPTs in high-dimensional vector spaces, but no proof is provided.

3.   Exploiting Pre-Computed Distances

When distance computations become expensive, a sound objective is to reduce their number to a minimum. To give efficient answers to similarity search queries, [Shasha and Wang, 1990] have suggested using pre-computed distances between data objects. For a datafile of n objects, a table of size $n \times n$ is used to store distances between data objects once computed. Pairwise distances which are not stored are estimated as intervals using the pre-computed distances. Distances unknown in advance will be, e.g., those from a query object to database objects. This technique of storing and using pre-computed distances may be effective for datasets of small cardinality. But space requirements and search complexity become overwhelming for larger files.

In this section, we discuss other techniques based on a matrix of distances between objects in a metric space. Specifically, we present the Approximating and Eliminating Search Algorithm and its linear variant. We also briefly mention other modifications or improvements, such as TLAESA, ROAESA, and Spaghettis.

3.1   AESA

The Approximating and Eliminating Search Algorithm (AESA), presented in [Vidal, 1986, Vidal, 1994], uses a matrix of distances between database objects which have been computed during the creation of the AESA structure. The structure is simply an $n \times n$ matrix holding the distances between all pairs of n database objects. Due to the symmetry property of metric functions only that half of the matrix lying below the diagonal need to be stored, resulting in $n(n - 1)/2$ distances. Unlike the methods of previous sections, every object in the AESA plays the role of pivot.

The search operation for a range query $R(q, r)$ (and similarly for nearest neighbor queries) picks an object p at random and uses it as a pivot. The distance from q to p is evaluated and used for pruning some objects. An object o can be pruned if $|d(q,p) - d(p,o)| > r$, i.e., if the lower bound from Lemma 1.1 on page 29 is greater than the query radius r. Note again that this pruning condition only utilizes distances which have already been evaluated. The algorithm then chooses another pivot from among the still remaining objects. The choice of pivot is influenced by the lower bound $|d(q,p) - d(p,o)|$. Since we want to maximize the pruning effect, we must maximize the lower bound resulting in the choice of the closest object p to q [Vidal, 1986]. The new pivot is used in the pruning condition to further eliminate some non-discarded objects. The process is repeated until the set of non-discarded objects is small enough. Finally, the remaining objects are checked directly with q, i.e., distances $d(q, o)$ are evaluated and objects satisfying $d(q, o) \leq r$ are returned.

According to experiments presented in [Vidal, 1994], AESA performs an order of magnitude better than competing methods and it is argued that it has a constant query time with respect to the size of database ($\mathcal{O}(1)$). This superior performance is obtained at the expense of quadratic space complexity $\mathcal{O}(n^2)$ and quadratic construction complexity. The extra CPU time is spent scanning the matrix, and ranges from $\mathcal{O}(n)$ up to $\mathcal{O}(n^2)$. However, we should note that one distance computation is much more expensive than one scan through the matrix. Although its performance is promising, AESA is applicable only for small datasets. If, by contrast, range queries with large radii, or nearest neighbor queries with high k are specified, AESA tends to require $\mathcal{O}(n)$ distance computations, the same as a trivial linear scan.

3.2   Linear AESA

The main drawback of the AESA approach being quadratic in space is solved in the Linear AESA (LAESA) structure [Micó et al., 1992, Micó et al., 1994]. This works around the problem by storing distances from objects to only a fixed number m of pivots. Thus, the distance matrix is $n \times m$ rather than the $n(n-1)$ entries used in the AESA. However, this has its price: a new problem arises in choosing appropriate pivots. In [Micó et al., 1994], the pivot selection algorithm attempts to choose pivots that are as far away from each other as possible, in keeping with the observations noted in Section 10.5 of Chapter 1.

The search procedure is nearly the same as in the AESA, except for the fact that some objects will not be the pivots. Thus, we cannot choose the next pivot from non-discarded objects up to now, because we might have eliminated some pivots. First, the search algorithm eliminates objects using all pivots. Then, all remaining objects are directly compared with the query object q. More details can be found in [Hjaltason and Samet, 2000], which also provides a description of the nearest neighbor search algorithm.

The space complexity and construction time of LAESA are $\mathcal{O}(mn)$, while search complexity is $m + \mathcal{O}(1)$. The extra CPU time can be reduced by a modification called Tree LAESA (TLAESA), proposed in [Micó et al., 1996]. TLAESA builds a GHT-like structure using the same m pivots, with the extra CPU time being between $\mathcal{O}(\log n)$ and $\mathcal{O}(mn)$. The AESA and LAESA approaches are compared in [Rico-Juan and Micó, 2003].

3.3   Other Methods

A structure similar to the LAESA is proposed in [Shapiro, 1977]. It also stores mn distances in a matrix $n \times m$. However, the search procedure for $R(q, r)$ queries is slightly different. Database objects $(o_1, \ldots o_n)$ are sorted according to their distance from the first pivot p_1. The search starts with the object o_i such that $|d(p_1, o_i) - d(p_1, q)|$ is minimized, for $i = 1, \ldots, n$. Note that this is the lower bound on $d(q, o_i)$ defined by Lemma 1.1. In other words, we start with an object potentially closest to q. The object o_i is checked against all pivots p_j $(j = 1, \ldots, m)$ and if $|d(p_j, o_i) - d(q, p_j)| > r$ is true for any p_j, then o_i cannot qualify for $R(q, r)$. Observe that distances $d(p_j, o_i)$ are stored in the matrix and the distances $d(q, p_j)$ are computed only once at the beginning of the query evaluation. If o_i is not eliminated by this condition, the distance $d(q, o_i)$ must be computed to decide whether o_i qualifies or not. The search continues with objects $o_{i+1}, o_{i-1}, o_{i+2}, o_{i-2}, \ldots$ until the pruning conditions $|d(p_1, o_{i+c}) - d(q, p_1)| > r$ and $|d(p_1, o_{i-c}) - d(q, p_1)| > r$ are valid.

Another improvement on LAESA is a method called Spaghettis, introduced in [Chávez et al., 1999a]. This approach also stores mn distances, organized in m arrays of length n. Each array of distances to a pivot is sorted according to the distances it contains. The order of any two objects o_i, o_j may be inconsistent from one array to another, since distances to the corresponding pivots may differ e.g. $d(p_1, o_i) < d(p_1, o_j)$ and $d(p_2, o_i) > d(p_2, o_j)$. Thus, permutations of objects must be stored with respect to the preceding array. During the range search, m intervals are defined on individual arrays, $[d(q, p_1) - r, d(q, p_1) + r], \ldots, [d(q, p_m) - r, d(q, p_m) + r]$. All objects that qualify for the query will belong to the intersection of all these intervals. Each object in the first interval is checked to see whether it is a member of all other intervals – the stored permutations are used for traversing through arrays of distances. Finally, the non-discarded objects are compared with the query object for qualification. The extra CPU time is reduced to $\mathcal{O}(m \log n)$.

Both AESA and LAESA have an overhead of $\mathcal{O}(n)$, measured in terms of computations other than distance evaluations (i.e., searching the matrix). The Reduced Overhead AESA (ROAESA) from [Vilar, 1995] applies heuristics to eliminate unneeded traversals of the matrix. However, this technique is only applicable to nearest neighbor queries, and the range search algorithm is not accelerated. A variant of LAESA, designated the Approximating k-LAESA (Ak-LAESA), is presented in [Moreno-Seco et al., 2003]. This variant provides a faster algorithm for kNN queries particularly designed for classification purposes.

4. Hybrid Indexing Approaches

Indexing methods which employ pre-computed distances provide promising performance boosts in terms of computational costs. Their disadvantage lies in their enormous space requirements. A straightforward remedy is to combine both the partitioning principle and the pre-computed distances technique into a single index structure. Basically this entails having search algorithms take advantage of stored pre-computed distances while traversing a hierarchy-like structure built using partitioning principles.

Such an approach is applied to Multi Vantage Point Trees, presented later in this section. We also tackle slightly different approaches based on Voronoi diagrams, namely the Geometric Near-neighbor Access Tree and the Spatial Approximation Tree. Finally, we also provide the reader with a short summary of the M-tree, a disk-based access structure which has become very popular. The M-tree and its variants are discussed in-depth in Chapter 3. In addition, we briefly mention the new concept of similarity hashing, which is again analyzed in greater depth in the next chapter.

4.1 Multi Vantage Point Tree

The Multi Vantage Point Tree (MVPT) [Bozkaya and Özsoyoglu, 1997, Bozkaya and Özsoyoglu, 1999] is an extension of the VPT. The motivation behind the MVPT is to cut down on the number of pivots used to construct a tree, since computing distances between a query object and pivots brings significant search costs. One source of motivation is the FQT described in Section 1.2. Another interesting approach to helping reduce distance computations is based on storing distances between pivots and objects in leaf nodes – such distances are computed in the course of tree construction. The extra information kept in leaves is then exploited by a sort of filtering algorithm, explained in detail in Section 7.6 of Chapter 1. The filtering algorithm dramatically decreases the number of distance computations needed to answer similarity queries.

The MVPT uses two pivots in each internal node, instead of one as in the VPT. Thus, each internal node can be considered to be two VPT levels collapsed into one node. There is one significant difference. While VPTs use different pivots at lower levels, MVPTs apply only one. Thus all children at the lower level employ the same pivot. This allows for fewer pivots while still preserving the fanout, or degree of branching. Figure 2.8 depicts a situation where a VPT is collapsed into an MVPT. Observe that some sets are partitioned using pivots that are not members of the sets. This never occurs in VPTs. In Figure 2.8b, so is the set around p_1 which is divided using p_2 and the radius d_{m_3}. In this

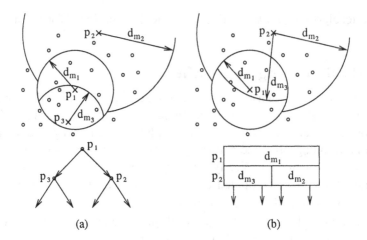

Figure 2.8. Comparison of the VPT and MVPT structures: (a) VPT with three pivots for partitioning to four sets, (b) MVPT using only two pivots.

case, each pivot leads to two subsets, which implies that the fanout of an MVPT node is 2^2. Since a pivot can generally partition data into m subsets, an internal node can root m^2 child nodes. In addition, MVPT can employ k pivots in each internal node, which implies a fanout of m^k. Moreover, each object in the leaf node is associated with a list of distances to the first l pivots, which are used for additional pruning at search time.

Since no objects are duplicated, space complexity is $\mathcal{O}(n)$ – objects chosen as pivots appear only in internal nodes. However, MVPTs need some extra space to keep l pre-computed distances for each object in leaves. Construction time complexity is $\mathcal{O}(nk \log_{m^k} n)$, where $\log_{m^k} n$ is the height of the balanced tree. Search complexity is $\mathcal{O}(k \log_{m^k} n)$, but is valid only for very small query radii. In the worst case, search complexity will be $\mathcal{O}(n)$. The authors of [Bozkaya and Özsoyoglu, 1999] show experimentally that MVPTs outperform VPTs, which they mainly attribute to the greater number of pivots in internal nodes rather than the increased fanout m. The largest performance boosts are achieved by storing more pre-computed distances in leaves.

4.2 Geometric Near-neighbor Access Tree

The Geometric Near-neighbor Access Tree (GNAT), proposed by [Brin, 1995], uses m pivots in each internal node. Specifically, a set of pivots $P = \{p_1, \ldots, p_m\}$ is chosen and the dataset X is split into $S_1, \ldots, S_m$ subsets, depending on the shortest distance to a pivot in P. In other words, for any object $o \in X - P$, o is a member of the set S_i if and only if $d(p_i, o) \leq d(p_j, o)$ for all $j = 1, \ldots, m$. Thus, applying this procedure recursively we build an m-ary tree. Figure 2.9 shows a simple example of the first level of a GNAT structure.

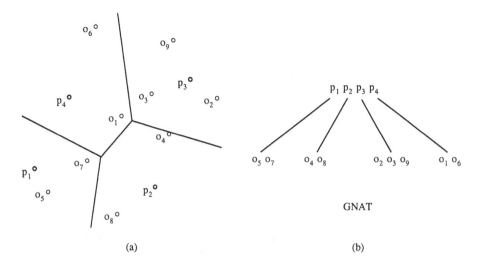

Figure 2.9. The Geometric Near-neighbor Access Tree: (a) an example of partitioning, (b) the corresponding tree.

Observe the close relationship between this idea and the Voronoi-like partitioning of vector spaces [Aurenhammer, 1991]. Each subset S_i corresponds to a cell in the Voronoi diagram – GNAT calls this cell the Dirichlet domain. The parameter m is adjusted according to the level of the tree. In fact, the number of children (i.e., the value of m) should be proportional to the number of data objects allocated in the node.

Besides applying the m-ary partitioning principle, the GNAT also retains objects' distances to their respective pivots. This enables additional pruning during the search, resulting in a range search algorithm quite different from the one used for the GHT. In each internal node, an $m \times m$ table consisting of distance ranges is stored. Specifically, the minimum and maximum distances between each pivot p_i and the objects of each subset S_j are stored. Formally, the range $[r_l^{ij}, r_h^{ij}]$, $i, j = 1, \ldots, m$, is defined as follows:

$$r_l^{ij} = \min_{o \in S_j \cup \{p_j\}} d(p_i, o),$$

$$r_h^{ij} = \max_{o \in S_j \cup \{p_j\}} d(p_i, o).$$

Note that the lower bound r_l^{ii} for pivot p_i itself is equal to zero, since the minimum is at distance $d(p_i, p_i) = 0$. Figure 2.10 illustrates two ranges. The first $[r_l^{ij}, r_h^{ij}]$ is defined for pivot p_i and set S_j around pivot p_j, while the second is $[r_l^{jj}, r_h^{jj}]$ for pivot p_j itself.

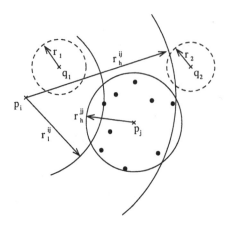

Figure 2.10. An example of the pruning effect of ranges in GNAT for two queries $R(q_1, r_1)$ and $R(q_2, r_2)$.

The range search algorithm for query $R(q, r)$ proceeds depth-first. In each internal node N, the distances between q and the pivots of N are computed and subtrees not containing qualifying objects are eliminated. After all distances from q to pivots have been computed, the algorithm visits all subtrees that remain. Starting with the set of pivots P, the procedure applied in each internal node is described in the following steps: First, pick one pivot p_i from P (repeatedly, but do not pick the same pivot twice) and compute the distance $d(p_i, q)$. If $d(p_i, q) \leq r$ holds, the pivot p_i is returned in the query result. Afterwards, for all $p_j \in P$ we remove p_j from P if $d(q, p_i) - r > r_h^{ij}$ or $d(q, p_i) + r < r_l^{ij}$. The inequalities are direct consequences of the lower bound $max\{d(q, p_i) - r_h^{ij}, r_l^{ij} - d(q, p_i)\} \leq r$ of Lemma 1.2 (pg. 31) with $d(q, o) \leq r$. When all pivots in P are examined, the subtrees of the node N corresponding to the remaining pivots in P are visited. Note that a pivot p_j can be discarded from P before its distance to q has been evaluated. Figure 2.10 depicts a situation in which two range queries $R(q_1, r_1)$ and $R(q_2, r_2)$ are given. In this example, only the range $[r_l^{ij}, r_h^{ij}]$ is sufficient for the query $R(q_1, r_1)$ to discard p_j. However, the other query requires the additional range $[r_l^{jj}, r_h^{jj}]$ to prune the subtree around p_j.

The space complexity of the GNAT index structure is $\mathcal{O}(nm^2)$, because tables consisting of m^2 elements are stored in each internal node. GNAT is built in $\mathcal{O}(nm \log_m n)$ time. The search complexity was not analyzed by the authors, but experiments in [Brin, 1995] reveal that the GNAT outperforms the GHT and VPT structures.

4.3   Spatial Approximation Tree

The indexes which have been described so far all use a partitioning principle to recursively divide the data space into subsets. For example, the GHT and GNAT are inspired by the Voronoi-like partitioning. In the following, we introduce the Spatial Approximation Tree, the sa-tree (SAT), proposed in [Navarro, 1999, Navarro, 2002]. The SAT is also based on the Voronoi diagrams, but in contrast to the GHT and GNAT it tries to approximate the structure of the *Delaunay graph*. Given a Voronoi diagram, a Delaunay graph, defined in [Navarro, 2002], is a graph where each node represents one cell of the Voronoi diagram and where nodes are connected with edges if the corresponding Voronoi cells are directly neighboring cells. In other words, the Delaunay graph is a representation of relations between cells in the Voronoi diagram. In the following, we use the term object for a node of the Delaunay graph and vice versa.

The search algorithm for the nearest neighbor of a query object q starts with an arbitrary object (node in the Delaunay graph) and proceeds to a neighboring object closer to q as long as it is possible. If we reach an object o where all neighbors of o are further from q than o, the object o is the nearest neighbor of q. The correctness of this simple algorithm is obvious. Unfortunately, it is possible to show that without more information about a given metric space $\mathcal{M} = (\mathcal{D}, d)$, knowledge of the distances between objects in a finite set $X \subseteq \mathcal{D}$ does not uniquely determine the Delaunay graph for X (for further details see [Navarro, 2002, Hjaltason and Samet, 2003a]). Thus, the only way to ensure the search procedure is correct is to use a complete graph, that is, the graph containing all edges between all pairs of objects in X. However, such a graph is not suitable for searching because the decision as to which edge should be traversed from the starting object requires computing distances from the query to all remaining objects in X. This boils down to a linear scan of all objects in the database and thus, from a searching point of view, is useless.

For a dataset X, the SAT is defined as follows: An arbitrary object p is selected as the root of the tree and the smallest possible set $N(p)$ of all its neighbors is determined so that:

$$o \in N(p) \Leftrightarrow \forall o' \in N(p) \setminus \{o\} : d(o, p) < d(o, o').$$

The intuition behind this definition is that for a valid set $N(p)$ (not necessarily the smallest), each object of $N(p)$ is closer to p than to any other object in $N(p)$ and all objects in $X \setminus N(p)$ are closer to an object in $N(p)$ than to p. Figure 2.11b shows an example of SAT built on a dataset depicted in Figure 2.11a. The object o_1 has been selected as the root node. The set of neighbors for o_1 is $N(o_1) = \{o_2, o_3, o_4, o_5\}$. Note that object o_7 cannot be included in $N(o_1)$ since o_7 is closer to o_3 than to o_1.

To build the tree, a child node is defined for every neighbor and the objects nearest the child are structured in the same way as defined above. The distance

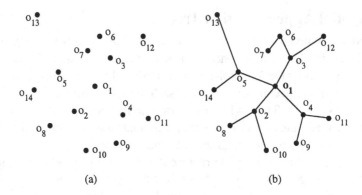

Figure 2.11. An example of SAT: (a) the dataset, (b) SAT structure with the root o_1.

to the furthest object o from p is also stored in each node, i.e., for the root node, $\max_{o \in X}\{d(p, o)\}$. In conventional terminology, it is the covering radius r^c.

As argued in [Navarro, 2002], the construction of $N(p)$ is NP-complete, so a heuristics is proposed which builds the set $N(p)$ in a way which may not be minimal. The method of selecting the set of neighbors influences the shape of the resulting tree. When the set is not minimal the fanout of the tree increases, which impacts upon search costs. The heuristics starts with an object p, a set $S = X \setminus \{p\}$, and initially empty set $N(p)$. We first sort the members of S with respect to their distance to p. Next, we pick an object o from S and add it to $N(p)$ if it is closer to p than any other object in $N(p)$. In this fashion, we incrementally construct a suitable set of neighbors.

The range search algorithm for the query $R(q, r)$ starts at the root node and traverses the tree, visiting all non-discardable subtrees. Recall that at the node p, we have the set of all neighbors $N(p)$. The algorithm first finds the closest object $o_c \in N(p) \cup \{p\}$ to q. Then, it discards all subtrees $o_d \in N(p)$ such that

$$d(q, o_d) > 2r + d(q, o_c). \tag{2.3}$$

Such a pruning criterion is correct and is a consequence of Lemma 1.4 (pg. 34) with substitutions $p_1 = o_d$ and $p_2 = o_c$. In particular, we get

$$\max\{\frac{d(q, o_d) - d(q, o_c)}{2}, 0\} \leq d(q, o).$$

Providing that $d(q, o) \leq r$ (the range query constraint) and q is closer to o_c than to o_d we get $(d(q, o_d) - d(q, o_c))/2 \leq r$. The branch o_d can easily be pruned if $(d(q, o_d) - d(q, o_c))/2 > r$, which is exactly what we desired.

The reason we select the closest object o_c to q is we want to maximize the lower bound of Lemma 1.4. When the current node is not the root of tree, we can even improve the pruning effect. Figure 2.12 depicts a sample SAT

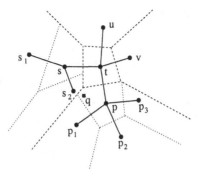

Figure 2.12. A sample of the SAT structure.

with root t, current node p (with neighbors p_1, p_2, p_3), and query object q. The dashed lines represent the boundaries between Voronoi cells of the first level of the SAT. The dotted lines depict the same for the second level. Assuming the current node is p, the algorithm presented above selects p among $\{p, p_1, p_2, p_3\}$ as the closest object to q, even though the object s_2 is closer. If we choose s_2 as the closest object, we further strengthen the pruning effect. However, this requires modifying the procedure for picking the closest object as follows: Select the closest object o_c from p's ancestor, including its neighbors and their associated neighbors, i.e., $o_c \in \bigcup_{o \in A(p)} (N(o) \cup \{o\})$. Here, $A(p)$ consists of the ancestors of p and its neighbors – in the figure, $A(p) = \{t, p, s, u, v\}$. Finally, the covering radius r^c of each node is used to further reduce search costs. We do not visit a node p if $d(q, p) > r^c + r$. This expression is derived from the lower bound in Lemma 1.2 (pg. 31) with $r_l = 0, r_h = r^c$ and from the fact that $d(q, o) \leq r$. The search algorithm is correct and returns all qualifying objects regardless of the strategy of selecting the closest object o_c. In other words, the strategy only influences the efficiency of pruning, see Equation 2.3.

The tree is built in $\mathcal{O}(n \log n / \log \log n)$ time, takes $\mathcal{O}(n)$ space and its search complexity is $\Theta(n^{1-\Theta(1/\log \log n)})$. The SAT is designed as a static structure. More details can be found in [Navarro, 1999, Hjaltason and Samet, 2003a, Navarro, 2002]. A dynamic version of SAT is presented in [Navarro and Reyes, 2002].

4.4 M-tree

A dynamic structure called the Metric Tree (M-tree) is proposed in [Ciaccia et al., 1997b]. It can handle data files that change size dynamically, which becomes an advantage when insertions and deletions of objects are frequent. In contrast to other metric trees, the M-tree is built bottom-up by splitting its fixed-size nodes. Each node is constrained by sphere-like (ball) regions of the metric space. A leaf node entry contains an identification of the data object, its feature value used as an argument for computing distances, and its distance from a routing object (pivot) that is kept in the parent node. Each internal node entry keeps a child node pointer, the covering radius of the ball region that bounds all objects indexed below, and its distance from the associated pivot. Obviously, the distance to the parent pivot has no meaning for the root. The pruning effect of search algorithms is achieved by using the covering radii and the distances from objects to their pivots in parent nodes.

Dynamic properties in storage structures are highly desirable but typically have a negative effect on performance. Furthermore, the insertion algorithm of the M-tree is not deterministic, i.e., inserting objects in different order results in different trees. That is why the *bulk-loading* algorithm has been proposed in [Ciaccia and Patella, 1998]. The basic idea of this algorithm works as follows: Given a set of objects, the initial clustering produces k sets of relatively close objects. This is done by choosing k distant objects from the set and making them representative samples. The remaining objects get assigned to the nearest sample. Then, the bulk-loading algorithm is invoked for each of these k sets, resulting in an unbalanced tree. Special refinement steps are applied to make the tree balanced.

The idea of M-trees was later extended by [Traina, Jr. et al., 2000b] in a metric tree structure called the Slim-tree. In order to get control over the overlap between metric regions, the fat-factor is defined and systematically used. The concept of fat-factor has been described in detail in Section 10.4 of Chapter 1. Slim-trees also use new insertion and split algorithms which result in improved performance. Slim-trees and many other variants of M-trees are described in Chapter 3.

4.5   Similarity Hashing

Similarity Hashing (SH), as proposed in [Gennaro et al., 2001] is built upon a completely different principle. It is a multi-tier hashing structure, consisting of search-separable sets on each tier, organized in buckets. The structure supports easy insertion and bounded search costs, because at most one bucket need to be accessed at each level for range queries up to a pre-defined value of the search radius. At the same time, the number of distance computations is always significantly reduced by the use of pre-computed distances obtained at insertion time. Buckets of static files can be arranged in such a way that I/O costs never exceed the cost of scanning a compressed sequential file. Experimental results demonstrate the performance of SH is superior to other available tree-based structures.

The similarity hashing approach is exploited in the so-called the D-index structure [Dohnal et al., 2003a]. The D-index applies excluded middle partitioning to hashed organizations. In contradistinction to VPF, navigation along the tree branches is unnecessary, and each storage bucket is directly accessible.

In principle, the concept of similarity hashing is not necessarily restricted to the excluded middle partitioning principle. [Dohnal et al., 2001] define another three ρ-split functions that are able to achieve the same effect, i.e., to produce sets separable up to a pre-defined distance radius ρ. Based on well-known geometric concepts, these methods are called the *elliptic*, *hyperbolic*, and *pseudo-elliptic* ρ-split functions. The second section of Chapter 3 deals with the D-Index and its variants suitable for similarity joins, and further extends the description of similarity hashing.

5. Approximate Similarity Search

Some applications can benefit from a very fast response to similarity queries even when it is obtained at the expense of precision in results. The fundamental concepts have already been discussed in Section 9 of Chapter 1. In the following, we survey some interesting approaches that have been proposed in the literature.

First, we briefly cover certain approximation techniques that exploit space transformations. Then we provide a more extensive presentation of techniques which reduce the subset of data that must be examined. Most of these techniques were originally applied to vector spaces, but some can also be used in generic metric spaces.

5.1 Exploiting Space Transformations

Space transformations are convenient to use for approximate similarity search. This has already been mentioned in Section 9 of Chapter 1. Obviously the transformations must satisfy the constraints described in Section 8 of Chapter 1. The general strategy is as follows: First, the original space is transformed. Then all search requests are executed in the projected space. Some false hits may be returned – but approximate similarity search algorithms do not apply the final cleansing phase which is necessary for obtaining exact results.

An approach to dimensionality reduction specifically designed for approximate similarity searching has been proposed in [Egecioglu and Ferhatosmanoglu, 2000]. The authors propose a dimensionality reduction technique that offers an easy way to compute the inner product between vectors approximately. Given a vector $\vec{z} = (z_1, \ldots, z_d)$, let $\psi_p(\vec{z})$ denote L_p norm to the p-th power. Then $\psi_p(\vec{z}) = (\| \vec{z} \|_p)^p = [L_p(\vec{z}, \vec{0})]^p$, where $\vec{0} = (0, \ldots, 0)$. The inner product of two vectors $< x, y >$ can be approximated with the estimate of its m-power as $< \vec{x}, \vec{y} >^m \approx b_1 \psi_1(\vec{x}) \psi_1(\vec{y}) + \ldots + b_m \psi_m(\vec{x}) \psi_m(\vec{y})$, where $m < d$ and $b_1, \ldots, b_m$ are parameters that should be tuned to obtain a good approximation. This technique saves disk space by storing the m-dimensional vector $(\psi_1(\vec{x}), \ldots, \psi_m(\vec{x}))$ instead of the d-dimensional vector $\vec{x}$, given that the approximate inner product can be computed using it. It also allows the

Euclidean distance $\| \vec{x} - \vec{y} \|_2$ to be also approximated, given that

$$\| \vec{x} - \vec{y} \|_2 = \sqrt{\psi_2(\vec{x}) + \psi_2(\vec{y}) - 2 < \vec{x}, \vec{y} >}.$$

In [Ogras and Ferhatosmanoglu, 2003], this approximation method is further refined as follows: The d-dimensional space is divided into orthogonal subspaces $S_1, \ldots, S_s$ each having l dimensions, $l = d/s$. Let xP_i be the projection of vector $\vec{x}$ in the subspace S_i. The Euclidean distance between $\vec{x}$ and $\vec{y}$ can be computed exactly as $\| \vec{x} - \vec{y} \|_2 = \| \vec{x}P_1 - \vec{y}P_1 \|_2 + \ldots + \| \vec{x}P_s - \vec{y}P_s \|_2$. If the individual $\| \vec{x}P_i - \vec{y}P_i \|_2$ are separately approximated using the approximate inner product technique, the approximation of the entire Euclidean distance which results is more precise. The authors note that the basic inner product approximation retains information on the magnitude of vectors only. A refined technique, also based on the space decomposition, is able to additionally retain information about the shape of approximated vectors, i.e., their direction.

A further approach to space transformation is presented in [Weber and Böhm, 2000], based on so-called Vector Approximation files, VA-files. The VA-file [Weber et al., 1998] reduces the size of multi-dimensional vectors by quantizing the original data objects. It demands a nearest neighbor search performed in two steps. Initially, the approximated vectors are scanned to identify candidate vectors. Then, in the second step, the candidate vectors are visited in order to find the actual nearest neighbors. The approximate search variant on this algorithm basically omits the second step of the exact search. A modification of the VA-files approach has been proposed in [Ferhatosmanoglu et al., 2000] in which the VA-file building procedure is improved by initially transforming the data into a more suitable domain using the Karhunen-Loeve transform, KLT. An approximate search algorithm based on the modified VA-file approach is proposed in [Ferhatosmanoglu et al., 2001]. The performance improvement offered by techniques based on VA-files is significant. However, they are applicable to vector spaces only.

A final approach which falls into this category is FastMap [Faloutsos and Lin, 1995]. This technique is also suitable for generic metric spaces, provided we have k feature-extraction functions which transform the metric space into a k-dimensional space. A similar technique which is, however, applicable directly to metric spaces is called MetricMap [Wang et al., 2000] and has already been discussed in Section 8.3 of Chapter 1.

5.2   Approximate Nearest Neighbors with BBD Trees

Suppose we have a query object q and a dataset X represented in a vector space whose distances are measured by Minkowski distance functions. Arya et al. [Arya et al., 1998] propose an approximate nearest neighbor algorithm which guarantees to find *(1+ε)-k-approximate-nearest-neighbors*. Specifically, it retrieves k objects whose distances from the query are at most $1 + \epsilon$ times

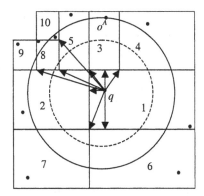

Figure 2.13. Overview of the approximate nearest neighbors search algorithm using BBD trees.

larger than that of the k-th actual nearest neighbor of q. The time complexity of this algorithm is $\mathcal{O}(k \log n)$, where n is the size of the dataset X. The parameter ϵ is used to control the tradeoff between the efficiency and quality of the approximation. The higher the value of ϵ, the higher the performance and error.

As its underlying indexing structure, the algorithm uses the *Balanced Box-Decomposition tree* (BBD) that is a variant of the Quad-tree [Samet, 1984] and is similar to other balanced structures based on box-decomposition [Bern et al., 1993, Bespamyatnikh, 1995, Callahan and Kosaraju, 1995]. A property of the BBD tree is that regions associated with nodes which have the same parent do not overlap. Node regions are recursively repartitioned until they contain only one object, thus every region associated with a leaf node contains just a single object. The tree has $\mathcal{O}(n)$ nodes and is built in $\mathcal{O}(dn \log n)$ time, where d is the number of dimensions of the vector space.

The nearest neighbor algorithm associated with this data structure proceeds as follows: Given a query object q, the tree is traversed and the unique leaf node associated with the region containing the query is found in $\mathcal{O}(\log n)$. At this point, a priority search is performed by enumerating leaf regions in increasing order of distance from the query object. The distance from an object o to a region is computed as the distance of o to the closest point that can be contained in the region. When a leaf region is visited, the distance of the associated object from q is measured and the k closest points seen so far are recorded. Let us call o_k^A the current k-th closest point. The algorithm terminates when the distance from q to the region of current leaf is larger than $d(q, o_k^A)$, that is, the current region cannot contain objects whose distance from the query object is shorter than that of o_k^A. Since all remaining leaf regions are more distant from the current region, the k objects retrieved so far are the k nearest neighbors to q.

In contrast, the approximate nearest neighbor algorithm uses a stop condition to terminate the search prematurely. Specifically, the algorithm stops as soon as the distance to the current leaf region exceeds $d(q, o_k^A)/(1 + \epsilon)$. It is easy to show that under these circumstances, o_k^A is the $(1 + \epsilon)$-k-th-approximate-nearest-neighbor. To clarify the behavior of the precise versus approximate nearest neighbor search algorithms, look at Figure 2.13, in which data objects are represented as black spots and a query $1NN(q)$ is posed. Each object is included in a rectangular region associated with a leaf node. Given a nearest neighbor query $1NN(q)$, every region is identified by a number assigned incrementally and based on the distance of the region to the query object q. Thus, the region containing q itself is assigned the value 1, while the region farthest away is labeled 10. The algorithm starts to search in Region 1 for a potential nearest object to q. The figure illustrates the situation in which Region 3 has been accessed in the current stage of execution, and the object o^A found as the current closest object. The circumference is indicated as having radius $d(q, o^A)$. The precise algorithm will continue accessing regions that overlap the circumference and stop only after accessing Region 10, which contains the actual nearest neighbor. The approximate algorithm, by contrast, accesses only those regions which overlap the dotted circumference whose radius is $d(q, o^A)/(1 + \epsilon)$. Therefore, it terminates after accessing Region 8, missing the actual nearest neighbor.

The priority search can be performed in $\mathcal{O}(m \log n)$, where m stands for the number of regions visited. The upper bound on m depends only on the dimensionality d, ϵ of the space and the number of nearest neighbors k, for any Minkowski metric, and is defined as $2k + \lceil 1 + 6d/\epsilon \rceil^d$. Provided that d and ϵ are fixed, the algorithm finds the $(1 + \epsilon)$-k-approximate-nearest-neighbors in $\mathcal{O}(k \log n)$ time.

Note that upper bound on m is independent of the dataset size n. However, it depends exponentially on d, so this algorithm is feasible only in low-dimensional vector spaces.

5.3   Angle Property Technique

Other two vector-space-only techniques for reducing the number of nodes accessed during nearest neighbor searches are proposed in [Pramanik et al., 1999a, Pramanik et al., 1999b]. The chief novelty of these techniques lies in their exploitation of angles formed by objects contained in a ball region, the center of this region and a query object (see Figure 2.14). These techniques have been successfully applied to SS-trees [White and Jain, 1996]. However, they are generally applicable to any access method for vector spaces which partitions the data space, restricts groups of objects with ball regions, and organizes regions hierarchically.

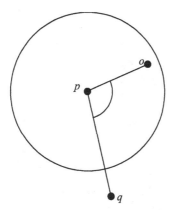

Figure 2.14. An angle between objects contained in a ball region and a query object q with respect to the center p of the ball region.

The heuristics employed in the search algorithm and proposed in [Pramanik et al., 1999a, Pramanik et al., 1999b] is justified by the following three properties of datasets in high-dimensional vector spaces:

- As dimensionality rises, the points in a ball region become almost equidistant from the region's center.

- With the increasing dimensionality, the radii of smaller child ball regions grow nearly as fast as the radius of the parent ball region, and thus their centers also tend to be close to each other.

- Given a query point and a set of points covered by a ball region, the angle between the query point and any point in the ball region will fall into an interval of angles around 90 degrees. As dimensionality grows, this interval will decrease.

Assuming regions are hierarchically structured, the algorithm uses an approximate pruning condition to decide whether a region should be accessed or not. In [Pramanik et al., 1999a], it is suggested that a region be inspected if at least one of the following conditions holds:

- The node corresponding to the region is an internal node.

- The center of the region's parent is contained in the ball region defined by the query object and the current candidate set of nearest neighbors.

- The region's center resides in the half of the parent's ball region closer to the query object, i.e., the angle between the center of the region and the query object with respect to the center of the parent's ball region is less than 90 degrees.

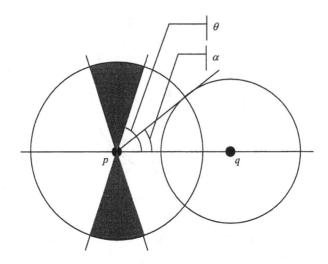

Figure 2.15. If the query region does not intersect promising portions of the data region, the region is discarded.

On reaching a leaf node, all objects of the leaf are examined and directly compared to the query object. If an object is closer to the query object than the current candidate for the k-th nearest neighbor, it is added to the response, superseding the k-th nearest neighbor.

This algorithm is, however, unable to trade performance with quality of results. In [Pramanik et al., 1999b], the algorithm is further improved by introducing a threshold angle θ to allow such a trade-off. Here is a brief sketch of how the improvement comes about:

According to the properties listed above, the area where qualifying objects are most likely to be found is close to the border of the ball region, forming an angle of about 90 degrees with the query object. Assume θ indicates the value of such an angle and the angle α is obtained by considering the query object q, the region's center p and the intersection of the query region and the region being examined (see Figure 2.15). If the angle α is greater than θ, the region is accessed, otherwise it is excluded – this is the situation depicted in the figure. Notice that if $\theta = 0$ all regions overlapping the query region are accessed and the query response-set is determined exactly.

5.4   Clustering for Indexing

The Clindex technique (Clustering for indexing) performs approximate similarity searches in high-dimensional vector spaces using an index structure supported by a clustering technique [Li et al., 2002]. The Clindex partitions the dataset into similar clusters, i.e., into clusters containing elements close to each other in the space. Each cluster is represented by a separate file and all files are sequentially stored on a disk.

The Clindex technique uses a new algorithm for building clusters of objects. The algorithm starts by dividing each dimension of the d-dimensional vector space into 2^n segments, so every segment can be identified using an n-bit number. This process forms $(2^n)^d$ cells in the data space. The clustering algorithm aggregates these cells into clusters as follows: Each cell is associated with the number of objects it contains. The algorithm starts with the cells containing the largest number of objects and checks to see if they are adjacent to other clusters. If a cell is not adjacent to any cluster it is used as the seed for a new cluster. If a cell is adjacent to just one cluster, it is attached to that cluster. Finally, if the cell neighbors more than one cluster a special heuristics is applied to decide whether the clusters should be merged or to which cluster the cell belongs. This process is iterated until the remaining cells contain fewer objects than a specified threshold. Underfilled or empty cells are grouped in an *outlier* cluster and stored separately.

Once the clusters are obtained, an indexing structure is built for speeding access to them. The index is a simple encoding scheme which maps an object to a cell and a cell to its corresponding cluster. The associations between clusters and disk files are also kept.

Approximate similarity search is processed by first identifying the cluster to which the query object belongs. This is obtained by determining the cell which covers the query object and then identifying the corresponding cluster. If the query's cell is empty, a cluster cannot be obtained, so a cluster having the centroid closest to the query object is located. Once a cluster is identified, the file corresponding to it is sequentially searched, and objects qualifying for the query are returned. Of course, this search algorithm is approximate, because only one cluster is examined. In fact, it might happen that objects in non-selected clusters might also qualify for the query, so these objects are falsely dismissed by the algorithm.

5.5 Vector Quantization Index

Another approach that uses a clustering technique to organize data and process similarity queries approximately is the Vector Quantization Index (VQ-index) [Tuncel et al., 2002]. The VQ-index is based on reducing both the dataset and the size of data objects at the same time. The basic idea is to organize the dataset into subsets which are not necessarily disjoint, and then reduce the size of data by compression. The approximate search algorithm first identifies the subset to be searched. Next, it goes through its compressed content and qualifying objects are reported.

The dataset is grouped into subsets by exploiting a query history in the following way: Queries from the record of requests posed in the past are divided into m clusters C_i $(i = 1, \ldots, m)$ using the k-means algorithm [MacQueen, 1967, Duda and Hart, 1973, Kaufman and Rousseeuw, 1990]. If the query history is too long, a sample is used instead. A subset S_i of the entire dataset corresponding to each cluster C_i is defined as follows:

$$S_i = \bigcup_{q \in C_i} kNN(q),$$

where $kNN(q)$ obviously represents the k objects of the dataset nearest to q. Each subset S_i contains elements of the dataset close to queries in the cluster C_i. Thus an element may belong to several different subsets. The overlap of subsets S_i versus index performance can be tuned by the choice of m and k.

The reduction in object size is obtained using the vector quantization technique [Gresho and Gray, 1992]. The objective of the vector quantization is to map an arbitrary vector from the original d-dimensional space into a reproduction vector. Reproduction vectors form a set of n representatives from the original space. The process of mapping can be decomposed into two modules – an encoder Enc and a decoder Dec. The encoder transforms the original space $\mathbb{R}^d$ into a set $\{1, \ldots, n\}$ of numbers, thus each vector $x \in \mathbb{R}^d$ gets assigned an integer $Enc(x) = c$ $(1 \le c \le n)$. The decoder, by contrast, maps the set $\{1, \ldots, n\}$ to the set of n reproduction vectors, so-called code-vectors, which in fact, approximate all possible vectors from $\mathbb{R}^d$, i.e., $Dec(c) = x$, $x \in \mathbb{R}^d$. For each subset S_i, a separate encoder Enc_i and decoder Dec_i is defined. S_i is compressed by representing it with the set $S_i^{enc} = \{Enc_i(x) | \forall x \in S_i\}$. The decoder function Dec_i is used to obtain the reproduction vectors corresponding to the elements in S_i^{enc}, i.e., the approximation of the original elements in S_i.

Here is an example: Having a fixed encoder Enc, several vectors can be mapped to a single number c. The best value for the corresponding code-vector is one minimizing its average distance to all vectors mapped to c. In this way, a suitable decoder function can be obtained. An approximate nearest neighbors query is processed by locating the cluster C_i nearest the query. Next, by applying the decoder function Dec_i on S_i^{enc}, the set S_i is reconstructed and sequentially searched for k nearest neighbors. A certain level of imprecision is present at both stages. In the first stage, it cannot be guaranteed that the selected subset S_i contains all objects which qualify for the given query. In the second stage, the vectors contained in the re-created set S_i might have distances to the query object significantly different from the distances of the original vectors. The approximation quality of the vector quantization technique depends on the number n of code-vectors. In practice, the number n is much smaller than the total number of vectors. Initially, the set of code-vectors is very small and huge collisions are solved by replacing the code-vector in question with two new vectors, improving the quality of the quantization. However, the experiments presented in [Tuncel et al., 2002] reveal the VQ-index is very competitive and outperforms other techniques based on linear quantization by factor of ten to twenty, while retaining the same precision in the response.

5.6 Buoy Indexing

Another approach to approximate nearest neighbor search which is based on clustering is presented in [Volmer, 2002]. In this proposal, the dataset is partitioned into disjoint clusters bounded by ball regions. A cluster is represented by an element called a *buoy*. Clusters are gradually built by assigning objects to the cluster with the closest buoy. Radii of ball regions are defined as the distance between the buoy of a cluster and the furthest element in that cluster. This iterative optimization procedure attempts to find buoys of clusters so that radii of ball regions of these clusters are minimized. However, any other clustering algorithm that organizes the space into disjoint clusters bounded by ball regions can be used with the approximate search algorithm described below.

Imagine a dataset X with clusters $C_1, \ldots, C_n \subset X$, where each C_i is bounded by a ball region $\mathcal{R}_i = (p_i, r_i)$ and p_i denotes the cluster's buoy. A precise k-nearest neighbors search algorithm accesses the clusters in the order determined by the distance between the query and the cluster's center, starting with the closest. The qualifying objects from every cluster visited are determined. This process is repeated until no better objects can be found in remaining clusters. The stop condition can be formalized as

$$\text{stop if } d(q, o_k) + r_j < d(q, p_j), \tag{2.4}$$

where q is the query object of a $kNN(q)$ query, o_k is the current k-th nearest neighbor, and p_j and r_j form a ball region $\mathcal{R}_j = (p_j, r_j)$ of a cluster to be accessed in the next step.

The proposed approximation strategy is to reduce the amount of data accessed by limiting the number of accessed clusters, i.e., modifying the stop condition. A parameter f $(0 < f \leq 1)$ is introduced which specifies the clusters to be accessed. Specifically, the approximate kNN search algorithm stops when either Equation 2.4 holds, or the ratio of clusters accessed exceeds f. This technique guarantees $\lceil f \cdot n \rceil$ clusters will be accessed at a maximum, where n stands for the total number of clusters.

The results of experiments reported in [Volmer, 2002] imply query execution may be about four times faster than a linear scan, with about 95% recall ratio. The advantage of this method is that it is not limited to vector spaces only but can be applied to metric spaces as well.

5.7 Hierarchical Decomposition of Metric Spaces

There are other techniques beyond those mentioned for approximate similarity searching which have been especially designed for metric spaces. In what follows, we briefly introduce the basics of these techniques. However, in view

of their prominent role in the field of approximate similarity search, they are
more extensively discussed in Chapter 4.

5.7.1   Relative Error Approximation

A technique employing a user-defined parameter as an upper bound on approximation error is presented in [Zezula et al., 1998a, Amato, 2002]. In particular, the parameter limits the relative error on distances from the query object
to objects in the approximate result-set with respect to the precise results. The
proposed technique can be used for both approximate nearest neighbor and
range searches in generic metric spaces. Assuming a dataset organized in a tree
structure, the approximate similarity search algorithm decides which nodes of
the tree can be pruned even if they overlap with the query region. At the same
time, it guarantees the relative error obtained on distances does not exceed
the specified threshold. On a similar basis, nearest neighbor queries retrieve
$(1+\epsilon)$-k-approximate-nearest-neighbors. Details of this technique are given in
Section 1 of Chapter 4.

5.7.2   Good Fraction Approximation

The technique presented in [Zezula et al., 1998a, Amato, 2002] retrieves k
approximate nearest neighbors of a query object by returning k objects that
statistically belong to the set of l ($l \geq k$) actual nearest neighbors of the query
object. The value l is specified by the user as a fraction of the whole dataset.
By using the overall distance distribution, the approximate similarity search
algorithm stops when it determines that k objects currently retrieved belong to
the specified fraction of objects nearest to the query. This method is discussed
in detail in Section 2 of Chapter 4.

5.7.3   Small Chance Improvement Approximation

An approximate nearest neighbor search strategy proposed in [Zezula et al.,
1998a] and later refined in [Amato, 2002] is based upon the pragmatic observation that similarity search algorithms for tree structures are defined as iterative
processes where the result-set is improved in each iteration until no further improvement can be made. As for k-nearest neighbors queries, algorithms refine
the response, which means that k objects retrieved in the current iteration will
be nearer than those in the previous one. This can be explicitly measured by the
distance between the current k-th object and the query object. Such a distance
decreases rapidly in first iterations and it gradually slows down and remains
almost stable for several iterations before the similarity search algorithm stops.
The approximate similarity search algorithm exploits this behavior and stops
the search algorithm when the reduction of distance to the current k-th object

slows down. A detailed description of this approach is given in Section 3 of Chapter 4.

5.7.4 Proximity-Based Approximation

A technique that uses a proximity measure to decide which tree nodes can be pruned even if their bounding regions overlap the query region is proposed in [Amato et al., 2003, Amato, 2002]. This has already been discussed in Section 10.2 of Chapter 1 from a theoretical point of view. When the proximity of a node's bounding region and the query region is small, the probability that qualifying objects will be found in their intersection is also small. A user-specified parameter is employed as a threshold to decide whether a node should be accessed or not. If the proximity value is below the specified threshold, the node is not promising from a search point of view, and thus not accessed. This method is defined for both nearest neighbor and range queries and is discussed in detail in Section 4 of Chapter 4.

5.7.5 PAC Nearest Neighbor Search

A technique called *Probably Approximately Correct* (PAC) nearest neighbor search in metric spaces is proposed in [Ciaccia and Patella, 2000b]. The approach searches for a $(1+\epsilon)$-approximate-nearest-neighbor with a user-specified confidence interval. The proposed algorithm stops execution prematurely when the probability that the current approximate nearest neighbor is not the $(1+\epsilon)$-approximate-nearest-neighbor falls below a user-defined threshold δ. Details of the approach are given in Section 5 of Chapter 4.

PART II

METRIC SEARCHING IN LARGE COLLECTIONS OF DATA

Overview

Database scalability is a topic which has been well-explored and much-debated, but there are still no easy answers. There are several ways to achieve higher scalability of a database, but which of them to choose depends greatly upon the unique needs of individual users.

Even creating a search index structure which scales to very large dimensions presents many challenges, and the task is becoming increasingly difficult as the amount of data grows. The most successful search engine capable of scaling all the way to the dimension of the Web is Google, but it can only manage text-like data.

At the same time, the term *large data* is relative: what was large ten years ago is small today. In this part of the book, we assume that an index for processing large data stores and accesses indexed features on a secondary memory, that is on a disk.

For this reason, we first concentrate on disk-oriented metric search indexes running on dedicated computers in Chapter 3. We provide enough detailed description of each of the structures to allow an understanding of their functionality. More specifics can then be found by following the citations to the respective original papers. We also report results from practical experiments which illustrate the capabilities of such single-computer implementations.

In Chapter 4, we report on the approximate similarity search. This enables scalability problems to be sidestepped by significantly increasing search performance, but with a tradeoff of reduced precision in search results.

Finally, we present the latest developments in distributed approaches to similarity searching in Chapter 5. We show how recent trends in network architectures, such as the GRID technology, the peer-to-peer communication paradigm and overlay networks can also be exploited to develop real scalable and distributed similarity search structures for arbitrary metric distance functions.

Chapter 3

CENTRALIZED INDEX STRUCTURES

Most existing search structures have been designed to run on a single computer. Let us call them centralized structures. They are built with different assumptions about type of distance function (discrete vs. continuous), form of query (range, nearest neighbor, etc.), and temporal properties (static or dynamic) of the data to be organized. Although many index structures have been proposed as main memory structures, there are several indexes which organize data using disk storage to allow the processing of a large volume of data. In what follows, we focus on two basic approaches which store objects in secondary memories. Specifically, we discuss tree-based structures and methods which employ hashing (i.e., the key-to-address transformation) principles.

1. M-tree Family

[Ciaccia et al., 1997b] have proposed a dynamic organization, called the M-tree, which can handle data files that vary dynamically in size, i.e., in cases when insertion and deletion of objects is frequent. In contrast to other metric tree-based structures, the M-tree is built bottom-up and maintains the same length for all tree paths because the tree is balanced. This paradigm has become very popular and many researches have developed extensions of the M-tree storage structure with a main objective of increasing search efficiency, sometimes conditioned by specific application requirements. We start with the original idea of the M-tree, then describe its most important extensions.

1.1 The M-tree

Most of the indexing methods described in Chapter 2 are either static, unbalanced, or both. They are not very suitable for dynamic environments where data is subject to permanent alteration, nor for large data repositories where disk-based techniques are necessary. The M-tree is, by nature, designed as a dynamic and balanced index structure capable of organizing data stored on a disk. By building the tree in a bottom-up fashion from its leaves to its root, the M-tree shares some similarities with R-trees [Guttman, 1984] and B-trees [Comer, 1979]. This concept results in a balanced tree structure independent of the number of insertions or deletions and has a positive impact on query execution.

In general, the M-tree behaves like the R-tree. All objects are stored in (or referenced from) leaf nodes while internal nodes keep pointers to nodes at the next level, together with additional information about their subtrees. Recall that R-trees store minimum bounding rectangles in non-leaf nodes that cover their subtrees. In general metric spaces, we cannot define such bounding rectangles because a coordinate system is lacking. Thus M-trees use an object called a *pivot*, and a *covering radius*, to form a bounding ball region. In the M-tree, pivots play a role similar to that in the GNAT access structure [Brin, 1995], but unlike in GNAT, all objects are stored in leaves. Because pre-selected objects are used, the same object may be present several times in the M-tree – once in a leaf node, and once or several times in internal nodes as a pivot.

Each node in the M-tree consists of a specific number of entries, m. Two types of nodes are presented in Figure 3.1. An internal node entry is a tuple

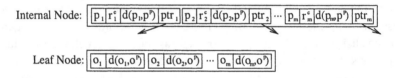

Figure 3.1. Graphical representation of the internal and leaf nodes of the M-tree.

$\langle p, r^c, d(p, p^p), ptr \rangle$, where p is a pivot and r^c is the corresponding covering radius around p. The parent pivot of p is denoted as p^p and $d(p, p^p)$ is the distance from p to the parent pivot. As we shall soon see, storing distances to parent objects enhances the pruning effect of search processes. Finally, ptr is a pointer to a child node. All objects o in the subtree rooted through ptr are within the distance r^c from p, i.e., $d(o, p) \leq r^c$. By analogy, a tuple $\langle o, d(o, o^p) \rangle$ forms one entry of a leaf node, where o is a database object (or its unique identifier) and $d(o, o^p)$ is the distance between o and its parent object, i.e., the pivot in the parent node.

Figure 3.2 depicts an M-tree with three levels, organizing a set of objects $o_1, \ldots, o_{11}$. Observe that some covering radii are not necessarily minimum values for their corresponding subtrees. Look, e.g., at the root node, where neither the covering radius for object o_1 nor that for o_2 is optimal. (The minimum radii are represented by dotted circles.) Obviously, using minimum values of covering radii would reduce the overlap of individual bounding ball regions, resulting in a more efficient search. For example, the overlapping balls of the

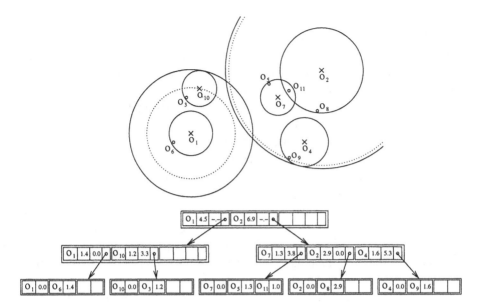

Figure 3.2. Example of an M-tree consisting of three levels. Above, a 2-D representation of partitioning. Pivots are denoted by crosses and the circles around pivots correspond to values of covering radii. The dotted circles represent the minimum values of covering radii.

root node in Figure 3.2 become disjoint when the minimum covering radii are applied. The original M-tree does not consider such optimization, but [Ciaccia and Patella, 1998] have proposed a *bulk-load algorithm* for building the tree which creates a structure that sets the covering radii to their minimum values. More details are reported in Section 1.2.

The M-tree is a dynamic structure, thus we can build the tree gradually as new data objects come in. The insertion algorithm looks for the best leaf node in which to insert a new object o_N and stores the object there if enough space is available. The heuristics for finding the most suitable leaf node proceeds as follows: The algorithm descends down through a subtree for which no enlargement of the covering radius r^c is needed, i.e., $d(o_N, p) \leq r^c$. If multiple subtrees exist with this property, the one for which object o_N is closest to its pivot is chosen. Such a heuristics supports the creation of compact subtrees and tries to minimize covering radii. Figure 3.2 depicts a situation in which object o_{11} could be inserted into the subtrees around pivots o_7 and o_2. Because o_{11} is closer to o_7 than to the pivot o_2, it is inserted into the subtree of o_7. If there is no pivot for which zero enlargement is needed, the algorithm's choice is to minimize the increase of the covering radius. In this way, we descend through the tree until we come to a leaf node where the new object is inserted. During the tree traversal phase, the covering radii of all affected nodes are adjusted.

Insertion into a leaf may cause the node to *overflow*. The overflow of a node N is resolved by allocating a new node N' at the same level and by redistributing the $m + 1$ entries between the node subject to overflow and the one newly created. This *node split* requires two new pivots to be selected and the corresponding covering radii adjusted to reflect the current membership of the two new nodes. Naturally, the overflow may propagate towards the root node and, if the root splits, a new root is created and the tree grows up one level. A number of alternative heuristics for splitting nodes is considered in [Ciaccia et al., 1997b]. Through experimental evaluation, a strategy called the *minimum maximal radius* mM_RAD_2 has been found to be the most efficient. This strategy optimizes the selection of new pivots so that the corresponding covering radii are as small as possible. Specifically, two objects $p_N, p_{N'}$ are used as new pivots for nodes N, N' if the maximum (i.e., the larger, $\max(r_N^c, r_{N'}^c)$) of corresponding radii is minimum. This process reduces overlap within node regions.

Starting at the root, the range search algorithm for $R(q, r)$ traverses the tree in a depth-first manner. During the search, all the stored distances to parent objects are brought into play. Assuming the current node N is an internal node, we consider all non-empty entries $\langle p, r^c, d(p, p^p), ptr \rangle$ of N as follows:

- If $|d(q, p^p) - d(p, p^p)| - r^c > r$, the subtree pointed to by *ptr* need not be visited and the entry is pruned. This pruning criterion is based on the fact that the expression $|d(q, p^p) - d(p, p^p)| - r^c$ forms the lower bound on the distance $d(q, o)$, where o is any object in the subtree *ptr*. Thus, if the lower bound is greater than the query radius r, the subtree need not be visited because no object in the subtree can qualify the range query.

- If $|d(q, p^p) - d(p, p^p)| - r^c \leq r$ holds, we cannot avoid computing the distance $d(q, p)$. Having the value of $d(q, p)$, we can still prune some branches via the criterion: $d(q, p) - r^c > r$. This pruning criterion is a direct consequence of the lower bound in Lemma 1.2 in Chapter 1 with substitutions $r_l = 0$ and $r_h = r^c$ (i.e., the lower and upper bounds on the distance $d(p, o)$).

- All non-pruned entries are searched recursively.

Leaf nodes are similarly processed. Each entry $\langle o, d(o, o^p) \rangle$ is examined using the pruning condition $|d(q, o^p) - d(o, o^p)| > r$. If it holds, the entry can be safely ignored. This pruning criterion is the lower bound in Lemma 1.1 in Chapter 1. If the entry cannot be discarded, the distance $d(q, o)$ is evaluated and the object o is reported if $d(q, o) \leq r$. Note that in all three steps where pruning criteria hold, we discard some entries without computing distances to the corresponding objects. In this way, the search process is made faster and more efficient.

The algorithm for k-nearest neighbors queries is based on the range search algorithm, but instead of the query radius r the distance to the k-th current nearest neighbor is used – for details see [Ciaccia et al., 1997b]. The general idea of an algorithm for kNN queries based on range queries is presented in Section 6.1 of Chapter 1.

From a theoretical point of view, the space complexity of the M-tree involves $\mathcal{O}(n+mm_N)$ distances, where n is the number of distances stored in leaf nodes, m_N is the number of internal nodes, and each node has a capacity of m entries. The construction complexity claimed is $\mathcal{O}(nm^2 \log_m n)$ distance computations. Search complexity was not analyzed in [Ciaccia et al., 1997b], but in [Ciaccia et al., 1998a] an analytic cost model for M-trees is presented.

In the following, we present the most important extensions of the original ideas applied in the M-tree.

1.2   Bulk-Loading Algorithm of M-tree

[Ciaccia and Patella, 1998] have proposed what was likely the first extension of the M-tree. They defined the so-called *bulk-loading* algorithm for insertion. Their technique is based on optimizations of the tree-building process, resulting in a non-trivial performance boost. But the procedure requires the entire indexed dataset to be given in advance to analyze the distribution of data objects and preprocess them so that the resulting M-tree is efficiently built.

Roughly speaking, the bulk-loading algorithm performs a clustering of n data objects in $X = \{o_1, \ldots, o_n\}$ and returns the M-tree. Given the database X, we randomly select l objects $p_1, \ldots, p_l$ where l is usually set to m, i.e., to the number of entries per node in the M-tree. The selected objects – call them pivots – form the sample set P. All objects of X are assigned to the nearest pivot, thus producing l subsets $P_1, \ldots, P_l$. Those subsets are used to recursively call the bulk-loading algorithm. In this fashion, we obtain l subtrees $T_1, \ldots, T_l$. By the recursion, we acquire leaf nodes with maximally l objects. Finally, the root node is created, all subtrees are connected to it, and the final tree T is obtained. In other words, the bulk-loading algorithm is invoked several times on the set of pivots P and the supertree T_{sup} is built. Each subtree T_i is appended to the leaf of T_{sup} corresponding to pivot p_i and the final T is completed.

The authors also discuss the problem of choosing the sample set P, because a pivot picked in a sparse region would produce a shallow subtree – when most objects are far away from a pivot, they get assigned to other pivots. If, on the other hand, the region is dense, any pivot selected will lead to a deep subtree, since many objects are closer to it than to the other pivots.

Figure 3.3 gives an example of objects in 2-dimensional space and the corresponding tree produced by the bulk-loading algorithm with $k = 3$. In the first step, the algorithm picks three objects o_1, o_2, o_3 as pivots at random and creates corresponding clusters. Clusters containing more than k objects are recursively processed and form subtrees. For example, in the cluster around o_1, three new pivots are selected (namely o_1, o_4, o_5), where the pivot o_1 is inherited from the

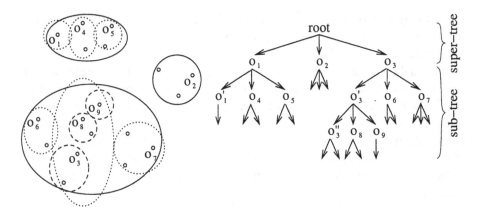

Figure 3.3. An example of the first phase of bulk-loading algorithm with the resulting tree.

upper level. Note the resulting tree confirms the above theory about sparse and dense regions: the individual subtrees are not of equal depth. Objects o_3, o_3', o_3'' are identical because pivots are inherited from upper levels.

The bulk-loading proceeds to the next phase if subtrees resulting from the first stage are of different heights, i.e., the tree is unbalanced. The following two techniques are applied to resolve such a problem:

- Underfilled nodes are reassigned to other subtrees and corresponding pivots deleted from the set P.

- Deeper subtrees are split into shallower ones and the newly obtained roots inserted into P to replace the original root nodes of deeper subtrees.

An underfilled node is one which contains fewer items than the minimum occupation, minimum occupation being the second parameter of the bulk-loading algorithm.

In the example shown in Figure 3.3, the first heuristics detects underfilled nodes under objects o_1' and o_9. These objects are deleted and reassigned to their closest pivots o_4 or o_8, respectively. The latter technique reveals different depths in tree branches. The subtrees rooted in nodes o_1 and o_3 are taller, thus they are split into new subtrees rooted in $o_4, o_5, o_3'', o_8, o_6$, and o_7. More specifically, the pivots o_1 and o_3 are replaced with $o_4, o_5, o_3'', o_8, o_6, o_7$ in the set P. Finally, the bulk-loading algorithm creates a supertree over the set P (see Figure 3.4). Note that the objects o_4, o_3, o_2 are selected as pivots in the supertree.

Experiments by [Ciaccia and Patella, 1998] reveal that the bulk-loading algorithm builds the M-tree with fewer distance computations than does the standard M-tree insertion procedure. I/O costs are also much lower with the bulk-loading

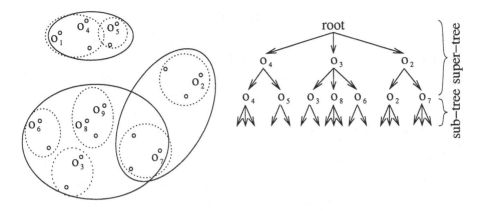

Figure 3.4. The example after the second phase of the bulk-loading algorithm.

procedure, mainly due to the massive use of internal memory. As for search efficiency, the M-tree built using the bulk-loading algorithm provides only slightly better performance than an M-tree built with traditional insertion.

In the following, we describe an optimization technique that further speeds the building process. The merit of this method, also proposed by [Ciaccia and Patella, 1998], lies in the way it uses pre-computed distances according to Lemma 1.1 in Chapter 1. After the initial phase of the bulk-loading algorithm, we have a set of pivots P and corresponding subsets $P_1, \ldots, P_k$. The algorithm is applied during the recursive call on each subset. Assume that the algorithm processes the subset P_1. At this point, we know all distances between the pivot p_1 and objects $o \in P_1$, because these distances have been computed during the initial clustering. In the next step, a new set of pivots is chosen and the other objects must be clustered, i.e., we have to find the nearest pivot for each $o \in P_1$. Suppose that $p_{1,N}$ is the nearest pivot for the object o_i obtained so far, and the distance from o_i to another pivot $p_{1,j}$ has to be evaluated. Since we know the distances $d(p_1, o_i)$ and $d(p_1, p_{1,j})$ (from the previous clustering), we can establish a lower bound on the distance $d(p_{1,j}, o_i)$ by following Lemma 1.1 (pg. 29):

$$|d(p_1, o_i) - d(p_1, p_{1,j})| \leq d(p_{1,j}, o_i).$$

If the distance to the current nearest pivot $d(p_{1,N}, o_i)$ is less than our lower bound, we can safely leave off computing $d(p_{1,j}, o_i)$, because in the worst case, it will equal $d(p_{1,N}, o_i)$ and cannot be less. This optimization cuts the number of distance computations in the bulk-loading algorithm by 11%. By exploiting pre-computed distances to multiple pivots, tests conducted by the same authors on clustered datasets showed an increased savings ranging up to 70%, with a mean value of 20%.

1.3   Multi-Way Insertion Algorithm

Another extension to M-tree insertion algorithms with the objective of building more compact trees was proposed in [Skopal et al., 2003]. The difference between the bulk-loading procedure and this approach is in their respective dynamic capabilities: The bulk-loading algorithm assumes static data collections while the *multi-way insertion algorithm* is able to deal with dynamically changing data and in this way is closer to the original insertion algorithm of the M-tree.

The original insertion algorithm of the M-tree can be seen as a single-path or "single-way" insertion, because it traverses the tree along exactly one branch. In this way, exactly h nodes are accessed, where h is the height of the tree. The single-way insertion heuristics is designed to keep building costs as low as possible, and within this limitation tries to select a leaf node for which the increase in covering radii is zero or minimum. However, [Skopal et al., 2003] point out that the technique behaves very locally and the leaf selected may not be the most convenient. Their priority is to choose the most convenient leaf node in every situation and they propose procedure we now describe.

Before inserting a new object o_N, a point query $R(o_N, 0)$ is issued. For all leaves visited, distances between o_N and the leaf's pivots are computed. The leaf node whose pivot is the closest to o_N is then chosen to store the new object. If no such leaf is found, single-way insertion is employed. This happens when no leaf node covers the area of o_N and the search algorithm terminates empty before reaching a leaf. The heuristics behaves more globally because it inspects more nodes, naturally increasing I/O costs.

Comparison experiments testing the single and multi-way insertion algorithms by [Skopal et al., 2003] show multi-way insertion requires about 25% more disk accesses than the single-way algorithm and nearly 40% more accesses than the bulk-loading algorithm. These higher I/O costs also lead to higher CPU costs as measured by distance computations. Because multi-way insertion descends the tree using multiple branches, more pivots are compared against the inserted object, and thus more distance computations must be performed. As for query performance, trees built by multi-way insertion execute queries with 15% fewer disk accesses on average. The number of distance computations is nearly the same for range queries, but multi-way insertion produces a tree needing about 10% fewer distance computations for nearest neighbor queries.

In summary, multi-way insertion supports higher utilization of nodes than single-way insertion, thus producing more compact trees with fewer nodes. The multi-way insertion algorithm is advantageous in applications where building costs are not very important in comparison with query execution performance. Since the savings are more significant for I/O than CPU costs, inexpensive metric functions are preferable.

1.4   The Slim Tree

The objective of the Slim tree, introduced in [Traina, Jr. et al., 2000b], is to reduce overlaps between node regions. In principle, the Slim tree is an extension of the M-tree that speeds up insertion and node splitting and at the same time it improves storage utilization. In particular, this technique is based on a new node-splitting algorithm and a special post-processing procedure which helps make the resulting trees more compact.

The structure of the Slim tree is the same as that of the M-tree, but the insertion algorithm is modified as follows: Starting at the root node, the algorithm tries to locate a suitable node to cover the incoming object. If none is found, the node whose pivot is nearest the new object is selected. This is the first point of difference from the M-tree which, in this situation, would select the node whose covering radius requires the smallest expansion, not necessarily the nearest pivot. When several nodes qualify, the Slim tree selects the one which occupies the minimum space. This tie-breaker technique is a second difference from the M-tree – M-trees choose the node whose pivot is closest to the new object. This modified insertion strategy tends to fill insufficiently occupied nodes first, and in this way defers splitting, boosts node utilization, and cuts the number of tree nodes needed to organize a dataset. Based on the same mM_RAD_2 splitting policy, an experimental comparison of M-trees and Slim trees confirms this hypothesis and the results exhibit lower I/O costs for Slim trees, while keeping the number of distance computations nearly the same for both the M-tree and the Slim tree. This observation applies not only to the tree building procedure but also to query execution.

The Slim tree also concentrates on reducing the relatively high building costs of M-trees, due mainly to their node-splitting strategy – the complexity of the mM_RAD_2 strategy is $\mathcal{O}(n^3)$, using $\mathcal{O}(n^2)$ distance computations. The split algorithm presented in the Slim tree is based on constructing a *minimum spanning tree* (MST) [Kruskal, 1956], which has been successfully used for clustering. This algorithm needs $\mathcal{O}(n^2)$ distance computations and the total execution time is $\mathcal{O}(n^2 \log n)$. The MST splitting algorithm assumes a fully connected graph consisting of n objects (acting as vertices) and $n(n-1)$ edges, where each edge is given a weight equal to the distance between a pair of connected objects. The algorithm proceeds according to the following steps:

1 Build the minimum spanning tree on the full graph;

2 Delete the longest edge;

3 The resulting two subgraphs determine the content of the new nodes;

4 Choose as a pivot for each group the object whose distance to all the other objects in the group is the shortest.

The disadvantage of this procedure is that it does not guarantee the minimal occupation of nodes, i.e., the split can be highly unbalanced. To obtain a more balanced split, the authors suggest choosing the most appropriate edge from among the longer edges in the MST. If no such edge is found, e.g., in the case of a star-shaped dataset, the unbalanced split is accepted and the longest edge is removed.

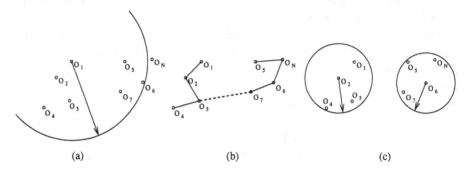

(a)   (b)   (c)

Figure 3.5. An example of a node split using the MST splitting algorithm.

Figure 3.5 shows the use of the MST splitting algorithm. In (a), a node that is to be split is presented in the 2-D vector space. The newly-arrived object causing the node to split is denoted by o_N and the pivot of this node is the object o_1. The MST is built in (b) and the longest edge connecting two components is represented by the dashed line. Finally, in (c), we show two resulting nodes and their new pivots o_2 and o_6.

Experiments in [Traina, Jr. et al., 2000b] compare the efficiency of the new MST splitting strategy with the original mM_RAD_2 strategy. The results show that tree building using the MST algorithm is at least forty times faster than the original, while query execution time remains practically the same. In this respect, the MST strategy is preferable, especially in highly dynamic environments requiring many splitting operations.

1.4.1   Slim-Down Algorithm

The second major contribution of [Traina, Jr. et al., 2000b] is the definition of the Slim-down algorithm, which is applied in the post-processing phase. This method attempts to minimize the overlap of balls of sibling nodes and, in the established terminology, tries to decrease the value of the *fat-factor* (see Section 10.4, Chapter 1) of the tree. The following example explains the idea. Given a point query (i.e., the range query with $r = 0$), the search procedure gradually enters all nodes whose regions contain the query object. By reducing the overlap between them (making the balls smaller), we decrease the probability that a point query hits several nodes at the same level. See Figure 3.6a, where we are searching for object o_3. In this example, the search must enter both the nodes, because o_3 is contained in their regions. If the nodes are grouped as seen in Figure 3.6b, the search algorithm looking for o_3 will visit only one node.

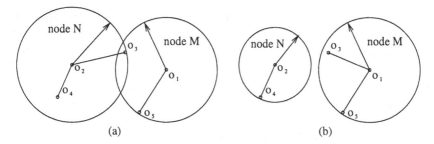

(a)   (b)

Figure 3.6. A Slim tree before slimming down in (a) and after in (b). The covering radii of nodes are denoted with arrows.

The Slim-down algorithm can be characterized using the following three steps (see Figure 3.6 for reference):

1 For each node N at a given level of the tree, locate the object furthest from the node's pivot. In the figure, this applies to the object o_3 vis à vis pivot o_2.

2 Search for a sibling node M that also covers o_3. If such a node M exists and if it is not fully occupied, move o_3 from node N to node M and update the covering radius of N.

3 Steps 1 and 2 are applied to all nodes at the given level. If a single object is relocated after a complete circuit using these two steps, the entire algorithm is executed again.

By applying this algorithm to the tree in Figure 3.6, we move the object o_3 from node N into node M. Since o_3 is the only object in N at distance $d(o_3, o_2)$ from the pivot o_2, the covering radius of N shrinks, and no other region is enlarged. As a result of the radius reduction, the object o_3 passes out of the intersection of the covering regions of nodes N and M and the search for o_3 no longer visits both nodes. From a terminological point of view, we have decreased the fat-factor of the tree.

As a result of the Slim-down algorithm, some nodes can become poorly occupied or even empty. The authors suggest objects in nearly empty nodes be reinserted into the tree and their nodes deleted. Experiments confirm that this strategy is effective and leads to more compact trees. Though the algorithm was only applied to the leaves of the tree in [Traina, Jr. et al., 2000b], it can also be used in principle on other levels. The idea of dynamic object relocation can also be applied to *defer splitting*. During the insertion of an object into a full node, a simple relocation of the furthest object from this node should be tried instead of executing a node split. This technique has already been studied in the area of spatial access methods (e.g. R-trees in [García et al., 1998]).

[Traina, Jr. et al., 2002] provide a thoroughgoing discussion of the properties of the Slim-down algorithm and describe a possible deadlock in the algorithm. In Step 3, we repeat the procedure when a single object is moved from one node to another. Figure 3.7 depicts a situation in which the algorithm gets stuck in an infinite loop. After the first full round, the objects o_4, o_5, o_6 move to their neighboring nodes, as indicated by the dashed lines. Because of this reorganization, the algorithm restarts and the same objects are reassigned back to the original nodes (see the solid lines). In this way, the algorithm mingles the three objects forever. To avoid such a situation, the authors suggest limiting the number of times the algorithm is called to a certain value.

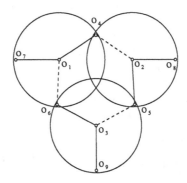

Figure 3.7. A cyclic move of object during the Slim-down algorithm elaboration. The covering radii cannot be reduced.

The advantage of the Slim-down algorithm is that it reduces the overlap between node regions, which helps improve total I/O costs. Trials on several datasets show the algorithm decreases the number of disk accesses by at least 10%. Such performance improvements were observed not only for the MST split strategy, but also for the original mM_RAD_2 strategy.

1.4.2   Generalized Slim-Down Algorithm

[Skopal et al., 2003] have modified the original Slim-down algorithm to run also on the non-leaf nodes of a tree. It starts from leaf nodes, where the algorithm follows the original Slim-down post-processing steps. Then index levels of the tree are considered consecutively, terminating in the root. For each pivot p in the non-leaf node N, the range query $R(p, r^c)$ is issued, where r^c is the covering radius attached with respect to the pivot p. The query determines a set of nodes whose regions entirely contain the query region. From this set, the algorithm chooses the node M whose parent pivot $pivot(M)$ is the closest to the currently inspected (query) pivot p. If the inspected pivot p is closer to

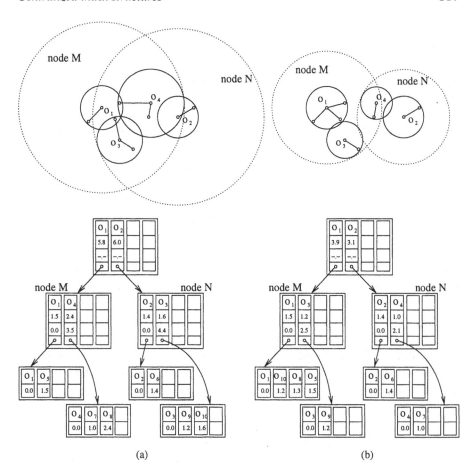

Figure 3.8. (a) An M-tree before slim-down optimization, (b) the resulting tree after applying the general slim-down.

$pivot(M)$ than to its original parent pivot $pivot(N)$, it is moved from node N to node M. If the entry containing pivot p determines the minimum bounding region (ball) of N, the covering radius of N is updated, i.e., reduced. This sequence of steps is repeated at a given level until an entry is reallocated. Then, the algorithm continues in the next upper level.

The generalized Slim-down algorithm reduces the covering radii of internal nodes as well as leaf nodes. The number of nodes per level is preserved, because node overflow (underflow) is not considered.

Figure 3.8a depicts a hypothetical M-tree structure and the corresponding 2-D representation of the indexed space. The root node contains two pivots for nodes M and N. Node M navigates to leaf nodes represented by pivots

o_1 and o_4. The remaining leaves are rooted in node N under pivots o_2 and o_3. Observe the large overlap between regions of nodes M and N, which furthermore completely covers the regions around pivots o_3 and o_4. The fact that eight of ten objects occur in the overlap results in a fat-factor of 0.8. After applying the generalized slim-down algorithm, the tree significantly slims down and the overlap of nodes M and N contains only two objects. The algorithm first optimizes the leaf level and o_{10}, the object furthest from pivot o_3, is reallocated to the node around o_1. The same applies to the object o_8. Note that the covering radius of node around o_1 has not been expanded and the original home nodes of o_8 and o_{10} have been able to shrink their covering radii because their most distant objects have been excised. Next, the upper level is reorganized and nodes around o_3 and o_4 swap owners, leading to smaller covering radii for nodes M and N.

The above example demonstrates very desirable behavior on the part of the generalized slim-down algorithm. Its validity has been confirmed by experiments. By applying this post-processing algorithm, tree building costs in terms of disk accesses grow by about three times compared to the original M-tree building procedure, and more than three times vis à vis the bulk-loading algorithm. Building costs in terms of distance evaluations were not provided by the authors. Even though tree building costs increase, the search for range queries is almost twice as fast, and about 3.5 times faster for nearest neighbor queries. Such improvements were observed for both disk accesses and distance computations.

In summary, the generalized slim-down post-processing technique is mainly suitable for applications where insertions are not so frequent, and where the search is the prevalent operation. This approach produces trees which are tighter and more efficient than the slim-down algorithm by [Traina, Jr. et al., 2002].

1.5   Pivoting M-tree

Very recently, [Skopal, 2004] has proposed an M-tree variant which combines the M-tree with principles of the LAESA approach (see Sections 3 and 4 of Chapter 2). In contrast to previously described extensions which minimize the volume covered by regions around pivots, the aim of this technique is to bound covering ball regions more tightly by additionally defining *ring regions*. A ring metric region is defined similarly to a ball region but uses two radii r_{min}, r_{max} and a pivot p. Such a ring region is restricted only to objects o within both radii, i.e., $r_{min} \le d(o, p) \le r_{max}$.

The classic M-tree uses a set of pivots for clustering the data space into ball regions and navigating the tree during search. In the PM-tree (Pivoting M-tree), another set P of pivots ($|P| = n_p$) is selected and a matrix of pre-computed distances is defined. The matrix is divided into one-dimensional arrays related to individual node entries. Specifically, a leaf node entry is defined as a tuple $\langle o, d(o, o^p), PD \rangle$. The additional member of the tuple PD stands for an array of n_{pd} pivot distances, where the l-th distance is $PD[l] = d(p_l, o)$. Intuitively, we store distances between database objects o and pivots $p_l \in P$. The value of n_{pd} is a parameter of the PM-tree access structure and must satisfy $n_{pd} \leq n_p$, because we simply do not have additional pivots. The entry of an internal node is likewise modified as $\langle p, r^c, d(p, p^p), ptr, HR \rangle$. However, HR is not an array of distances but an array of n_{hr} intervals defining ring regions. The value of n_{hr} is the next parameter of the structure and naturally $n_{hr} \leq n_p$ holds. The l-th ring region $HR[l]$ is defined as follows:

$$HR[l].min = min(\{d(o_j, p_l) | \forall o_j \in ptr\}),$$
$$HR[l].max = max(\{d(o_j, p_l) | \forall o_j \in ptr\}).$$

Each ring region stored in HR contains all objects indexed in the subtree determined by ptr. The intersection of all ring regions and the ball region defined by the covering radius forms a new metric region that bounds all the indexed objects. As a result, the PM-tree's regions are smaller than an M-tree's, a necessary condition for improving the search efficiency. Figure 3.9 illustrates the differences between the M-tree and the PM-tree. Observe that the range query posed no longer collides with the node's region in the PM-tree, thus the node is not visited during the search.

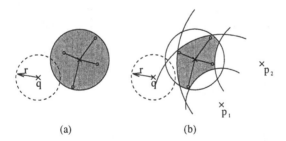

(a)   (b)

Figure 3.9. (a) A covering region of a node in an M-tree, (b) the same region trimmed by two ring regions in PM-tree.

Extending the structure using additional pivots requires modifying the insertion and search algorithms. During the insertion of a new object o_N, the HR array of each internal entry along the insertion path must be updated with values $d(o_N, p_l)$ for all pivots p_l, $l \leq n_{hr}$. When the new object is inserted into a leaf, a new leaf entry is created and the respective PD array is filled in with the values $d(o_N, p_l), \forall l \leq n_{pd}$. In this way, several levels of the tree are updated using distances $d(o_N, p_l)$. However this does not necessarily require reevaluation of these distances in descending levels, because, once computed, distances are remembered for later use.

This modification of the insertion procedure increases computational costs by $max(n_{hr}, n_{pd})$ distance function evaluations. Naturally, the node splitting also involves some maintenance of the corresponding HR or PD arrays. In the case of a leaf split, two new HR arrays of intervals are created by using all leaf entries of the corresponding leaf nodes – the $HR[l].min$ for the left node is simply the minimum of $PD[l]$ values of all objects in the left node. $HR[l].max$ is determined analogously, and the HR array for the right node is built. Splitting a leaf node can get relatively expensive when $n_{hr} \gg n_{pd}$, which means that we use more pivots in internal nodes than leaf nodes. This results in additional distance computations when constructing HR arrays for leaf nodes, because we do not remember all the necessary $PD[l]$ values ($l > n_{pd}$), so they must be evaluated again. Such obstacles are not connected with the splitting of internal nodes because all internal nodes use the same value of n_{hr}. After the split of an internal node, the HR arrays of the two resulting nodes are created simply by the union over all HR arrays of respective entries.

To fully exploit the additional information stored in the PM-tree, the search algorithms must also be modified. Before processing any similarity query, distances $d(q, p_l)$ for all pivots p_l such that $l \leq max(n_{hr}, n_{pd})$ are determined. Then the search procedure is started and the tree is traversed by considering nodes whose metric regions coincide with the query region. The relevant entries are determined not only by the standard ball-region test used in M-trees (see Equation 3.1) but also by a new ring-region check in Equation 3.2. In particular, the internal entry $\langle p, r^c, d(p, p^p), ptr, HR \rangle$ is considered to be relevant to a range query $R(q, r)$ if both the following expressions hold:

$$d(q, p) \leq r + r^c, \tag{3.1}$$

$$\bigwedge_{l=1}^{n_{hr}} (d(q, p_l) - r \leq HR[l].max \wedge d(q, p_l) + r \geq HR[l].min). \tag{3.2}$$

For a leaf node entry, the standard covering radius test takes the form:

$$\bigwedge_{l=1}^{n_{pd}} (|d(q, p_l) - PD[l]| \leq r).$$

Note that none of the previous checks employ any additional distance evaluations and only previously computed distances are used. Refer to Figure 3.9 again, where an example range query is given. In the M-tree, the standard covering radius check (see Equation 3.1) passes and the entry's subtree must be visited. In the PM-tree, however, the additional ring-region checks prevent the algorithm from entering the subtree. The ring region defined by pivot p_1 cannot eliminate the entry from processing but the second ring around p_2 does not intersect the query region. As a consequence, we regard this entry as irrelevant to the query. In other words, the query cannot find any qualifying object in the entry's subtree, because it does not intersect the filled area in Figure 3.9b.

The ring-region check above must be incorporated into original search procedures for range and nearest neighbor queries. For range queries, the adjustment is straightforward – the new condition is combined with the original ball-region check whenever applied. However, the search algorithm for nearest neighbor queries must be completely redesigned, due to the use of a priority queue. The specific modification to the kNN algorithm is described in [Skopal et al., 2005].

The authors compared their PM-tree access structure and the original M-tree in a number of experimental trials. They studied performance for various values of PM-tree parameters n_{hr} and n_{pd}. Considering the number of disk accesses, the most economical PM-tree structure uses $n_{pd} = 0$, which is quite intuitive because the space needed to store HR arrays of internal nodes is not so overwhelming compared to the filtering effectiveness gained. In this way, the PM-tree is able to save from 15% to 35% of disk accesses with respect to the M-tree. The PM-tree with $n_{pd} = n_{hr}/4$ needs about the same number of disk accesses as the M-tree. Trees with higher values of n_{pd} need more leaf nodes to store the objects (because they must save the PD arrays), thus the search is more expensive.

In contrast to the number of disk accesses, the increased number of distances stored in PD arrays positively impacts performance in terms of distance computations. With $n_{pd} = n_{hr}/4$, the PM-tree is up to 10 times faster than the M-tree. The most promising setting for disk costs is also more efficient than the M-tree with regard to distance computations, however improvements are marginal, averaging around 30%. A rule-of-thumb for parameter tuning in PM-trees is as follows: if disk costs need to be optimized, choose n_{pd} as small as possible; when, on the other hand, the distance function is expensive to compute, the value of n_{pd} should be higher. In any case, performance boosts for $n_{pd} > n_{hr}/4$ are not significant, thus the value of n_{pd} should not exceed $n_{hr}/4$.

1.6 The M$^+$-tree

A recent proposal by [Zhou et al., 2003] suggests improving the performance of M-trees by exploiting a concept called *key dimension*. The resulting structure, labeled an M$^+$-tree, inherits substantial properties from the M-tree – it is a balanced tree implemented on disk memory. Its important difference can be seen in a new partitioning strategy. The M$^+$-tree has a larger fanout, achieved by further partitioning each M-tree node into two subspaces called *twin-nodes*, using the key dimension. Unlike the M-tree, which is able to index any metric data, application of the M$^+$-tree is limited to vector datasets employing the L_p metric. In what follows, we briefly introduce the key dimension and discuss the general properties of M$^+$-trees.

The key dimension is defined as the dimension that most affects distances among indexed data objects, that is the dimension along which the data objects are most spread. For example, suppose data objects in a 2-D vector space are positioned at various locations along the x axis, but appear to be a single object from the vantage point of the y axis. In this case, the key dimension is the x axis. In general, the following expression holds for two vectors $(x_1, x_2, \ldots, x_n)$ and $(y_1, y_2, \ldots, y_n)$ and the key dimension D_{key}:

$$|x_{D_{key}} - y_{D_{key}}| \leq \sqrt{(x_1 - y_1)^2 + (x_2 - y_2)^2 + \cdots + (x_n - y_n)^2} \, .$$

On no account can the distance between any pair of objects computed using only the key dimension be greater than the distance which takes all dimensions into consideration. For convenience, we show the concept of key dimension for the Euclidean distance. The same applies to any L_p distance on vectors, but not to generic metric spaces.

The M$^+$-tree modifies the internal node structure so that each entry uses two pointers to twin-nodes instead of one – twin-nodes cover two disjoint subspaces according to the key dimension principle. These two subspaces are defined by two boundary values of the key dimension, the maximum value of the key dimension for the left twin space and the minimum value for the right. Such a partitioning improves filtering: the greater the gap between these two values of the key dimension, the more effective the filter. The structure of an internal node entry takes the form:

$$\langle p, r^c, d(p, p^p), D_{key}, ptr_{left-twin}, d_{lmax}, d_{rmin}, ptr_{right-twin} \rangle,$$

where p is a pivot and r^c is the corresponding covering radius around p. The expression $d(p, p^p)$ represents the distance from p to its parent pivot p^p. Finally, D_{key} is the number of the selected key dimension. The bounding values of the key dimension are d_{lmax} and d_{rmin} for the left and the right twin subspaces, respectively. The pointers navigate to roots of the corresponding twin subtrees.

Figure 3.10 illustrates differences between the M-tree and M$^+$-tree structures. In part (a) of the figure, the M-tree's subspace, containing 10 objects, is presented. A new object o_N must be stored in this node and the split procedure is executed. After the split, a new node is allocated and all objects including o_N are distributed between two nodes. Figure 3.10b, on the other hand, presents the same situation, but respecting the M$^+$-tree principles. Observe that the original M-tree's node region is further split by means of two parallel lines. These lines stand for the two values of the key dimension.

Now suppose a new object o_N arrives and the split is initiated. All objects of the affected node pair (twin nodes) plus the object o_N are considered a single set and the min-Max strategy (mM_RAD_2) is applied exactly as with the M-tree. For the two new resulting nodes (regions), key dimensions are selected and the

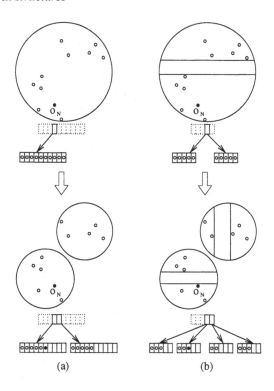

Figure 3.10. Comparison of (a) M-tree and (b) M^+-tree partitioning.

regions further partitioned. Finally, we get four nodes from the original two. Provided the same node capacity is used, an M^+-tree typically has fewer levels than the corresponding M-tree.

From a performance point of view, the M^+-tree is slightly more efficient than the M-tree. (See the performance evaluation in [Zhou et al., 2003]). The key dimension filtering strategy enables greater pruning effects for range queries with small query radii. For such queries, performance of M^+-trees is promising, however, for larger query radii, it becomes practically the same as for the M-tree. The performance boost for nearest neighbor queries is not clear-cut. In general, the advantage of lower CPU costs for range queries is difficult to exploit, because the search radius in nearest neighbor searches is initially high and decreases only slowly. The sole advantage over M-trees lies in the shorter priority queue, because the M^+-tree stores only one of the twin-nodes. Due to the larger fanout of the M^+-tree, the priority queue can be shorter, thus, some processing time can be saved for queue maintenance. In summary, this variation of the M-tree provides moderate performance improvements. At the same time, it restricts the application domain to vector datasets and L_p metric norms.

To make the list of M-tree-like structures more complete, we briefly mention a more efficient index structure called the BM^+-tree [Zhou et al., 2005]. The structure further extends the concept of single key dimension of M^+-trees to make use of two key dimensions, which define a binary hyperplane. This allows a better approximation of the direction in which high-dimensional objects are spread the most. The hypothesis behind is inherently the same: the more spread objects are, the higher probability of not accessing both the twin nodes during similarity queries evaluation. Despite the fact that BM^+-trees offer higher performance compared to M^+-trees, they are still limited to vector spaces only.

1.7   The M^2-tree

In contrast to previously presented members of the M-tree family, which try to improve performance of the M-tree in various respects and directions, this final variant has different objectives. Specifically, the M^2-tree is able to run complex similarity queries as defined in Section 4.6 of Chapter 1.

The first attempt to extend the M-tree to run complex similarity queries can be found in [Ciaccia et al., 1998b]. This approach supports the execution of queries with multiple predicates using the same distance function. The M^2-tree by [Ciaccia and Patella, 2000a] further extends this basic idea and accepts several distance functions. For example, consider the query: *Find images that contain a lion and the scenery around it like this.* Assuming we have an image database with keyword-annotated objects and color histograms, this query involves both features. Using a keyword search, it is able to locate images with lions and by comparing histograms it can find the required matching scenery. Qualifying objects are then identified by using a *scoring function* d_f, which takes as input distances to objects with respect to individual query predicates.

Figure 3.11 illustrates the difference between nodes in the M-tree and in the M^2-tree. Since each object o_i in the M^2-tree can be characterized by more than one feature value, e.g. $o_i[1]$ and $o_i[2]$, the leaf node structure is extended to contain all the object's features as well as distances to respective parents. Notice that every feature can use a different distance function. The internal nodes are expanded by analogy, but additionally use separate covering radii for each feature. In the figure, we also give a geometric illustration of the difference. In the M-tree, all objects of a subtree rooted in ptr are sorted according to the pivot and the covering radius is established. However, in the M^2-tree, we have multiple features for each object, so the transformation can be viewed as an n-dimensional space and the subtree's region turns out to be a hypercube.

When a range query $R(q, r)$ is executed in M-trees, the tree is traversed from its root, and branches are pruned by testing whether entries intersect the query region. To this end, the lower bounds on distances between the query and objects in the subtrees are computed. In the M^2-tree, the search procedure is very similar

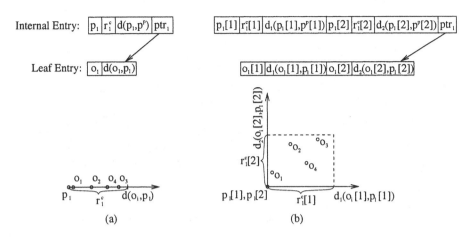

Figure 3.11. Node structure of (a) M-tree and (b) M²-tree. Below the representation of node's covering region.

and the lower bounds are assessed as follows: We compute the lower bound for every feature, specifically $\forall i, min(|d_i(q[i], p^p[i]) - d_i(p[i], p^p[i])| - r^c[i], 0)$. These lower bounds are then combined together using the scoring function d_f, and only those entries for which the scoring function is maximally r are visited. The algorithm for kNN queries uses an analogous strategy.

The authors compared the M²-tree with the sequential scan and Fagin's $\mathcal{A}_0$ algorithm, outlined in Section 4.6 of Chapter 1. An image collection containing two features, the image name and its color histogram, was chosen and several kNN queries executed. To implement Fagin's algorithm, two M-trees were built, one for each feature. The experiments revealed that the M²-tree is able to save about 20% in distance computations and 30% in I/Os compared to the $\mathcal{A}_0$ algorithm. Moreover, the performance of the $\mathcal{A}_0$ algorithm in terms of block accesses decreases for high values of k beyond the sequential scan. On the other hand, the M²-tree only reaches this sequential scan threshold.

2. Hash-based metric indexing

In tree-like indexing techniques, search algorithms traverse trees and visit nodes which reside within the query region. This represents logarithmic search costs in the best case. Indexes based on hashing, sometimes called key-to-address transformation paradigms, contrast by providing a direct access to searched regions with no additional traversals of the underlying structure. In this section, we focus on hash-based techniques. For example, AESA variants can be classified as hashing techniques, because they are capable of direct ac-

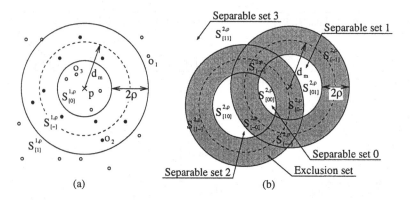

Figure 3.12. (a) The *bps* split function and (b) the combination of two *bps* functions.

cess. But they are restricted to main memory. In the following, we present an interesting hash-based index structure that supports disk storage.

2.1   The D-index

The Distance Index (D-index) is a multi-level metric structure, based on hashing objects into buckets which are *search-separable* on individual levels – see Section 5.3 in Chapter 1 for the concept of partitioning with exclusion. The structure supports easy insertion and bounded search costs because at most one bucket per level need to be accessed for range queries with a search radius up to some predefined value ρ. At the same time, the use of a *pivot-filtering strategy* described in Section 7.6 of Chapter 1 significantly cuts the number of distance computations in the accessed buckets. In what follows, we provide an overview of the D-index, which is fully specified in [Dohnal et al., 2003a]. A preliminary idea of this approach is available in [Gennaro et al., 2001].

Before presenting the structure, we provide more details on the partitioning principles employed by the technique, which are based on multiple definition of a mapping function called the ρ-split function. An example of a ρ-split function named *bps* (ball-partitioning split) is illustrated in Figure 3.12a. With respect to the parameter (distance) ρ, this function uses one pivot p and the median distance d_m to partition a dataset into three subsets. The result of the following *bps* function uniquely identifies the set to which an arbitrary object $o \in \mathcal{D}$ belongs:

$$bps^{1,\rho}(x) = \begin{cases} 0 & \text{if } d(o,p) \leq d_m - \rho \\ 1 & \text{if } d(o,p) > d_m + \rho \\ - & \text{otherwise} \end{cases} \tag{3.3}$$

In principle, this split function uses the excluded middle partitioning strategy described in Section 5.3 of Chapter 1. To illustrate, consider Figure 3.12 again. The split function *bps* returns zero for the object o_3, one for the object o_1 (it lies in the outer region), and '−' for the object o_2. The subset of objects characterized by the symbol '−' is called the *exclusion set*, while the subsets characterized by zero and one are *separable sets*. In Figure 3.12a, the separable sets are denoted by $S^{1,\rho}_{[0]}(\mathcal{D}), S^{1,\rho}_{[1]}(\mathcal{D})$ and the exclusion set by $S^{1,\rho}_{[-]}(\mathcal{D})$. Recall that $\mathcal{D}$ is the domain of a given metric space. Because this split function produces two separable sets, we call it a *binary bps* function. Objects of the exclusion set are retained for further processing. To emphasize the binary behavior, Equation 3.3 uses the superscript 1 which denotes the order of the split function. The same notation is retained for resulting sets.

Two sets are separable if any range query using a radius not greater than ρ fails to find qualifying objects in both sets. Specifically, for any pair of objects o_i and o_j such that $bps^{1,\rho}(o_i) = 0$ and $bps^{1,\rho}(o_j) = 1$, the distance between o_i and o_j is greater than 2ρ, i.e., $d(o_i, o_j) > 2\rho$. This is obvious from Figure 3.12a, however, it can also be easily proved using the definition of the bps function and applying the triangle inequality. We call such a property of ρ-split functions the *separable property*.

For most applications, partitioning into two separable sets is not sufficient, so we need split functions that are able to produce more separable sets. In the D-index, we compose higher order split functions by using several *binary bps* functions. An example of a system of two binary split functions is provided in Figure 3.12b. Observe that the resulting exclusion set is formed by the union of the exclusion sets of the original split functions. Furthermore, the new separable sets are obtained as the intersections of all possible pairs of the original separable sets. Formally, we have n binary $bps^{1,\rho}$ split functions, each of them returning a single value from the set $\{0, 1, -\}$. The joint n-order split function is denoted as $bps^{n,\rho}$ and the return value can be seen as a concatenated string of results of participating binary functions, that is, the string $b = (b_1, \ldots, b_n)$, where $b_i \in \{0, 1, -\}$. In order to obtain an addressing scheme, which is essential for any hashing technique, we need another function that transforms the string b into an integer. The following function $\langle b \rangle$ returns an integer value in the range $[0..2^n]$ for any string $b \in \{0, 1, -\}^n$:

$$\langle b \rangle = \begin{cases} [b_1, b_2, \ldots, b_n]_2 = \sum_{j=1}^{n} 2^{n-j} b_j, & \text{if } \forall j \; b_j \neq - \\ 2^n, & \text{otherwise} \end{cases}$$

When no string elements are equal to '−', the function $\langle b \rangle$ simply treats b as a binary number, which is always smaller than 2^n. Otherwise the function returns 2^n.

By means of ρ-split functions and the $\langle \cdot \rangle$ operator, we assign an integer number i ($0 \leq i \leq 2^n$) to each object $o \in \mathcal{D}$ and in this respect, group objects from $\mathcal{D}$ in $2^n + 1$ disjoint subsets. Considering again the illustration in Figure 3.12b, the sets denoted as $S^{2,\rho}_{[00]}, S^{2,\rho}_{[01]}, S^{2,\rho}_{[10]}, S^{2,\rho}_{[11]}$ are mapped to $S^{2,\rho}_{[0]}, S^{2,\rho}_{[1]}, S^{2,\rho}_{[2]}, S^{2,\rho}_{[3]}$ (i.e., four separable sets). The remaining combinations

$S^{2,\rho}_{[0-]}, S^{2,\rho}_{[1-]}, S^{2,\rho}_{[-0]}, S^{2,\rho}_{[-1]}, S^{2,\rho}_{[--]}$ are all interpreted as a single set $S^{2,\rho}_{[4]}$ (i.e., the exclusion set). Once again, the first 2^n sets are called separable sets and the exclusion set is formed by the set of objects o for which $\langle bps^{n,\rho}(o)\rangle$ evaluates to 2^n.

The most important fact is that the combination of split functions also satisfies the separable property. We say that such a disjoint separation of subsets, or partitioning, is *separable up to* 2ρ. This property is used during retrieval, because a range query with radius $r \leq \rho$ never requires accessing more than one of the separable sets and, possibly the exclusion set.

Naturally, the more separable sets we have, the larger the exclusion set is. For a large exclusion set, the D-index allows an additional level of splitting by applying a new set of split functions to the exclusion set of the previous level. This process is repeated until the exclusion set is conveniently small.

The storage architecture of the D-index is based on a two dimensional array of buckets used for storing data objects. On the first level, a *bps* function is applied to the whole dataset and a list of separable sets is obtained. Each separable set forms a separable bucket. In this respect, a bucket represents a metric region and organizes all objects from the metric domain falling into it. Specifically, on the first level, we get a one-dimensional array of buckets. The exclusion set is partitioned further at the next level, where another *bps* function is applied. Finally, the exclusion set on the final level, which will not be further partitioned, forms the exclusion bucket of the whole multi-level structure. Formally, a list of h split functions $(bps_1^{m_1,\rho}, bps_2^{m_2,\rho}, \ldots, bps_h^{m_h,\rho})$ forms $1 + \sum_{i=1}^{h} 2^{m_i}$ buckets as follows:

$$B_{1,0}, B_{1,1}, \ldots, B_{1,2^{m_1}-1}$$
$$B_{2,0}, B_{2,1}, \ldots, B_{2,2^{m_2}-1}$$
$$\vdots$$
$$B_{h,0}, B_{h,1}, \ldots, B_{h,2^{m_h}-1}, E_h .$$

In the structure, objects from all separable buckets are included, but only the E_h exclusion bucket is present because exclusion buckets $E_{i<h}$ are recursively repartitioned on levels $i + 1$. The *bps* functions of individual levels should be different but must employ the same ρ. Moreover, by using a different order of split functions (generally decreasing with the level), the D-index structure can have a different number of buckets at individual levels. To deal with overflow problems and file growth, buckets are implemented as *elastic buckets* and consist of the necessary number of fixed-size blocks (pages) – basic disk access units.

In Figure 3.13, we present an example of the D-index structure with a varying number of separable buckets per level. The structure consists of three levels. Exclusion buckets which are recursively repartitioned are shown as dashed rectangles. Obviously, the exclusion bucket of the third level forms the exclusion bucket of the whole structure. Observe that the object o_5 falls into the exclusion

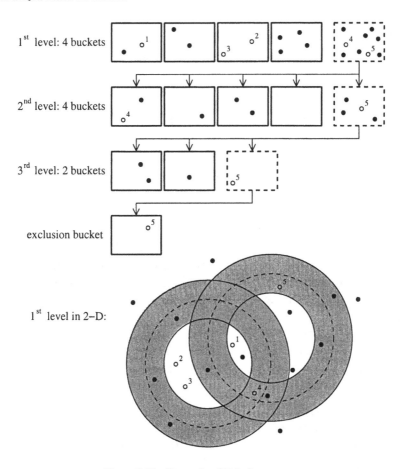

Figure 3.13. Example of D-index structure.

set several times and is finally accommodated in the global exclusion bucket. The object o_4 has also fallen into the exclusion bucket on the first level, but it is accommodated in a separable bucket on the second level. Below the structural view, there is an example of the partitioning applied to the first level.

2.1.1 Insertion and Search Strategies

In order to complete our description of the D-index, we present an insertion algorithm and a sketch of a simplified search algorithm. In Figure 3.14, the algorithm inserts a new object o_N into the D-index access structure specified as $DI^\rho(X, m_1, m_2, \ldots, m_h)$, where m_i denotes the order of the split function. Obviously, o_N belongs to the database X, which is a subset of the domain $\mathcal{D}$ of the metric space. Starting with the first level, the algorithm tries to accommodate o_N in a separable bucket. If a suitable bucket is found, the object is stored in it. If it fails for all levels, the object o_N is finally placed in the exclusion bucket

---

Insertion Algorithm
for $i = 1$ **to** h **do**
   if $\langle bps_i^{m_i,\rho}(o_N) \rangle < 2^{m_i}$ **then**
      $o_N \mapsto B_{i,\langle bps_i^{m_i,\rho}(o_N)\rangle}$
      exit
   endif
enddo
$o_N \mapsto E_h$

Figure 3.14. Insertion algorithm of the D-index.

E_h. In any case, the insertion algorithm selects exactly one bucket in which to store the object, and no other buckets are accessed. As for the number of distance computations, the D-index needs $\sum_{i=1}^{j} m_i$ distance computations to store a new object, assuming it is inserted into a separable bucket on the j-th level.

Given a range query $Q = R(q, r)$, where q is from the metric domain $\mathcal{D}$, $r \leq \rho$ and $\mathcal{R}(Q)$ denotes the query region, a simple algorithm can be used to execute the query as depicted in Figure 3.15. The function $\langle bps_i^{m_i,0}(q) \rangle$ always

---

Search Algorithm
for $i = 1$ **to** h **do**
   return all objects o such that $o \in \mathcal{R}(Q) \cap B_{i,\langle bps_i^{m_i,0}(q)\rangle}$
enddo
return all objects o such that $o \in \mathcal{R}(Q) \cap E_h$

Figure 3.15. Simple search algorithm for range queries.

gives a value smaller than 2^{m_i}, because the parameter ρ is set to zero in this function call. Consequently, exactly one separable bucket for each level i is determined. Objects of the query response set cannot be in any other separable bucket on level i, because the query radius r is not greater than ρ ($r \leq \rho$) and the buckets are separable up to 2ρ. However, some may be in the exclusion zone – the algorithm above assumes that exclusion buckets are always accessed. For that reason, all levels are considered, and the global exclusion bucket E_h is also accessed. The execution of this algorithm requires $h+1$ bucket accesses, which forms the upper bound of a more sophisticated algorithm described in [Dohnal et al., 2003a]. The advanced algorithm is also not limited by the size of the query radius, i.e., $r \leq \rho$. A detailed description of the general range search algorithm as well as its extension for nearest neighbor queries is available in [Dohnal et al., 2003a].

2.2 The eD-index

Up to now, we have only considered similarity range and nearest neighbor queries. Some work in the field of hash-based index structures has also been done for similarity joins. In the following, we describe indexing techniques which support similarity self-joins in metric spaces, as defined in Section 4.4 of Chapter 1. In principle, there are two types of algorithm for answering similarity joins. The first category concerns methods based on the range search, while the second category is formed by specialized algorithms.

Given a similarity self-join request $SJ(\mu)$, algorithms based on the range search strategy employ a metric access structure that supports range queries to retrieve qualified pairs of objects, i.e., pairs (o_i, o_j) such that $d(o_i, o_j) \leq \mu$. The idea is to perform n range queries, one for all objects in the database, using the same search radius $r = \mu$. As a result, it is quite straightforward to define a specific algorithm for any access structure presented in Chapter 2.

The bounded search costs and excellent performance for small similarity range queries of the D-index, confirmed by experiment, formed the chief motivation to employ this structure for similarity joins, as well – in typical applications, the join parameter μ is small. More details about experimental evaluation of the D-index are given in Section 3. The algorithm based on range queries is proposed in [Dohnal et al., 2002] and given in Figure 3.16.

The second category of similarity self-join algorithms is mainly comprised by specialized algorithms tailored to the specific needs of individual applications. For example, [Gravano et al., 2001] proposed a solution of similarity joins over string collections on top of a commercial database system. The core idea of such approaches is to transform the difficult problem of approximate string matching into some other search problem for which an efficient solution exists, e.g. query processing in a relational database system. [Dohnal et al., 2003b] have proposed a general solution, which is based, by contrast, only on the metric space postulates. The suggested structure, called an extended D-index (eD-index), is able to execute a similarity self-join over any data collection from a metric space domain.

As the titles suggest, the partitioning principles of the eD-index and D-index are very similar. The core idea behind the eD-index is to modify the original ρ-split function so that the similarity self-join can be executed independently in individual buckets. The exclusion set produced by the modified function overlaps with the corresponding separable sets by a predefined margin (distance) ϵ – see Figure 3.17 for illustration. Objects within the overlap are replicated, that is they belong to both the exclusion set and the corresponding separable set. This principle, called *exclusion set overloading*, ensures there is always

---

Range Query Join Algorithm
 # for every D-index level
for $i = 1$ **to** h **do**
  # for every separable bucket $B_{i,j}$ on the level i
  for $j = 0$ **to** $2^{m_i} - 1$ **do**
    # for every object q in the bucket $B_{i,j}$
    forall q **in** $B_{i,j}$ **do**
      execute $S = R(q, \mu)$
      $\forall o \in S$: add the pair (q, o) to the response set
    enddo
  enddo
enddo
 # access the exclusion bucket
 # for every object q in the bucket E_h
forall q **in** E_h **do**
  execute $S = R(q, \mu)$
  $\forall o \in S$: add the pair (q, o) to the response set
enddo

Figure 3.16. Algorithm for similarity self-join queries based on range queries.

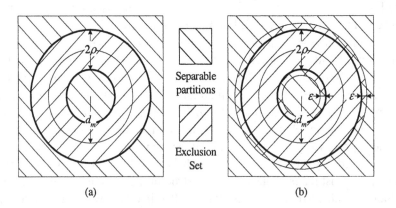

Figure 3.17. The modified *bps* split function: (a) original ρ-split function; (b) modified ρ-split function.

a bucket in which any qualifying pair (x, y) $(d(x, y) \leq \epsilon)$ can be found. In the eD-index, the overloading principle is implemented as a modified insertion algorithm of the D-index. In Figure 3.18, you can observe the adjustment which employs the original *bps* function. The only difference lies in the stop condition applied when the inserted object does not fall into the overlapping region of

---

eD-index Insertion Algorithm
  for $i = 1$ **to** h **do**
    if $\langle bps_i^{m_i,\rho}(o_N) \rangle < 2^{m_i}$ **then**
      $o_N \mapsto B_{i,\langle bps_i^{m_i,\rho}(o_N) \rangle}$
      if $\langle bps_i^{m_i,\rho+\epsilon}(o_N) \rangle < 2^{m_i}$ **then**
        exit
      endif
    endif
  enddo
  $o_N \mapsto E_h$

Figure 3.18. Insertion algorithm for the eD-index.

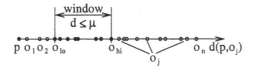

Figure 3.19. The Sliding Window algorithm.

the exclusion set and a separable set. Otherwise, the algorithm proceeds to the next level where the copy of the new object is stored. As explained later, a special algorithm is used to find these buckets efficiently and avoid retrieving duplicates. In this way, the eD-index speeds up the evaluation of similarity self-joins.

2.2.1 Similarity Self-Join Algorithm with eD-index

The basic strategy of the similarity self join with the eD-index can be characterized as follows: Execute the join query independently in every separable bucket on all levels of the eD-index and additionally on the exclusion bucket of the entire structure. This approach is correct due to the exclusion set overloading principle – every object of a separable set which can make a qualifying pair with an object of the exclusion set is copied into the exclusion set. Finally, the partial results are concatenated to form the answer.

The similarity self-join algorithm in individual buckets applies a *sliding window* approach – the idea is outlined in Figure 3.19. First, all objects of a bucket are ordered with respect to the pivot p. This pivot is one of the pivots used in a ρ-split function applied to partition the metric space into separable sets. Next, we define a sliding window of objects as an interval $[o_{lo}, o_{hi}]$. The algorithm moves the sliding window over the ordered list of objects from left to right until all objects are examined. All pairs of objects at each window position are considered and qualifying pairs are reported. The length of the window is limited to the distance μ, specifically $d(p, o_{hi}) - d(p, o_{lo}) \leq \mu$. The specification of the algorithm is given in the pseudocode in Figure 3.20. The pivot-based strategy, i.e., a strategy taking pre-computed distances to all other pivots into account, is also employed because it significantly cuts the number of distance computations. In the figure, it is characterized by the function *PivotFilter*.

Sliding Window Algorithm
```
response ← ∅
lo = 1
for hi = 2 to n do
    # move the lower boundary up to preserve window's width ≤ μ
    increment lo while d(o_hi, p) − d(o_lo, p) > μ
    # for all objects in the window
    for j = lo to hi − 1 do
        # apply the pivot-based strategy
        if not PivotFilter() then
            compute d(o_j, o_hi)
            if d(o_j, o_hi) ≤ μ then
                # add the pair to the result
                (o_j, o_hi) → response
            endif
        endif
    enddo
enddo
```

Figure 3.20. Sliding Window Algorithm.

Two important issues must be considered in the application of the exclusion set overloading principle. The first concerns the problem of possible duplicate pairs in the result of the join due to copies of objects reinserted into exclusion sets. Suppose, for example, that one of the separable buckets on the first level has a qualifying pair of objects. However these objects also fall into the overlap with the exclusion bucket. Consequently, they are both examined on the second level and may both fall once again into a common separable bucket. When such buckets are (independently) processed, identical pairs are reported several times. The authors propose a special "coloring" technique which marks duplicates of objects. Specifically, each level of the eD-index has a unique color assigned,

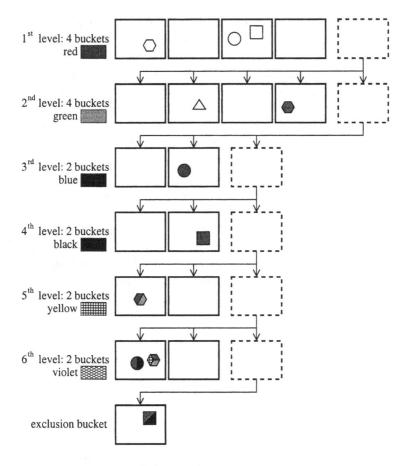

Figure 3.21. Coloring technique applied in the eD-index.

and every duplicate of an object receives all colors of preceding levels on which the replicated object is stored.

Figure 3.21 provides an example of an eD-index structure with 4 objects, represented by a circle, square, triangle, and hexagon. The circle, for example, is replicated and stored at levels one, three, and six. The circle at the first level has no color because it is the original, while the circle at the third level is red colored, because it has already been stored at the first (red) level. Furthermore, the circle at level six receives the red and blue colors, because it is stored at the corresponding levels. The other objects are analogously marked by their respective colors. Observe that the exclusion bucket has no specific color because no additional levels follow, so the objects accommodated there cannot be further duplicated.

Before the search algorithm examines a pair, it decides whether objects of the pair share a color. If they have at least one color in common, the pair is not considered. The concept of sharing a color by two objects means that these objects are also stored together at the same (previous) level, thus they have already been checked in a bucket of that level. Observe the circle and the hexagon stored in the same bucket on level six. Even though they form a qualifying pair, they are not reported because they share the color red. This is a consequence of the fact that both these objects are also stored at the first level. Thus, if they form a qualifying pair, they must have already been reported.

The second issue concerns the value of parameter ρ, which is constrained by $\epsilon \leq 2\rho$. If $\epsilon > 2\rho$ is true, some qualifying pairs cannot be examined by the algorithm, because the replication is not performed among separable sets. For example, assume objects o_i and o_j located in different separable sets – the separability property ensures that $d(o_i, o_j) > 2\rho$. However, the expression $\epsilon > 2\rho$ implies that a similarity join with $\mu > 2\rho$ can also be issued. The direct computation of distance between o_i, o_j reveals that $d(o_i, o_j) \leq \mu$. Unfortunately, the exclusion set overloading principle replicates objects in the overlap of the exclusion set and a separable set. As a result, the objects o_i, o_j cannot fall into the same bucket. Consequently, the separable sets are not contrasted enough to avoid omitting some of the qualifying pairs.

The limitation on the value of ϵ ($\epsilon \leq 2\rho$) seems to be the main drawback of the eD-index approach. However, the typical task of a similarity self-join is to find pairs of very close objects, which implies relatively small values for μ. Thus, in reality, this issue is not that restrictive.

3.   Performance Trials

In previous sections, we have surveyed various centralized (single computer) access structures, storing indexed data on a disk. In this section, we report our experience with two typical representatives of such methods in experimental trials, namely the M-tree and the D-index. To test the M-tree, we made use of the publicly available implementation [Ciaccia et al., 1997a]. For the D-index, we have used the implementation provided by D-index's authors. To render the results comparable, we used the same block size in both the M-tree and the D-index.

We undertook three independent sets of experimental trials, each motivated by its own research question. They involved:

1 a comparison of the M-tree with the D-index to highlight the advantages and disadvantages of tree-like versus hash-based approaches,

2 a study of the effect on search costs of processing different types of queries, and

3 a study of the applicability of centralized solutions to growing data archives, that is the problem of scalability.

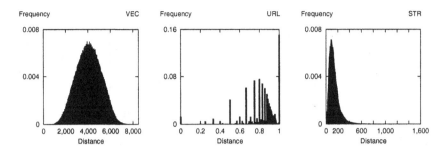

Figure 3.22. Distance densities for VEC, URL, and STR.

Additional details on the performance evaluation can be found in [Dohnal, 2004].

3.1 Datasets and Distance Measures

In order to make the experimental evaluation as objective as possible, we use three different datasets, each differing significantly in terms of its distance distribution. The specific datasets used were:

VEC 45-dimensional vectors of image color features compared by the quadratic distance measure reflecting correlations between individual colors.

URL Sets of URL addresses visited by users during work sessions with the Masaryk University information system. The distance measure applied is based on the similarity of sets, specifically using Jaccard's coefficient.

STR Sentences of a Czech language corpus compared using an edit distance measure that counts the minimum number of insertions, deletions or substitutions to transform one string (sentence) into another.

For illustration see Figure 3.22, showing the distance densities for all our datasets. Notice that VEC is practically normally distributed, whereas the distribution of URL is discrete and that of STR is highly skewed.

In all our experiments, the query objects are not necessarily chosen from the indexed datasets, but follow the same distance distribution. Search costs were measured in terms of distance computations and block reads (number of disk accesses), which is sufficient to correctly estimate CPU and I/O costs. The L_∞ distance measures used in the pivot-based filtering of the D-index are deliberately ignored, because according to our tests, the costs of computing such distances are several orders of magnitude smaller than the costs needed to compute any of the distance functions applied in the experiments. Since the query execution costs very much depend on the specific instance of the

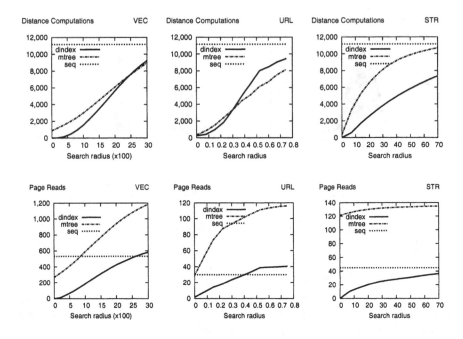

Figure 3.23. Comparison of the range search efficiency in the number of distance computations (above) and block accesses (below) for VEC, URL, and STR.

query object, the reported cost values are the mean values obtained from fifty executions of queries with different query objects and search selectivity held constant, i.e., with queries using the same search radius or the same number of nearest neighbors.

3.2 Performance Comparison

In the first group of experiments, we focus on three different approaches, namely the M-tree, D-index, and the sequential scan (SEQ) which serves us as a baseline – the sequential scan forms the basic cost model both in terms of disk accesses and the number of distance function evaluations. Obviously, the sequential file stands for the most economical organization with respect to the disk space, but needs the maximum number of distance comparisons to evaluate a query. The M-tree and D-index are, respectively, appropriate representatives for tree-based and hash-based categories of similarity search indexes. The results of experiments for range queries are reported in Figure 3.23. All datasets consist of about 11,000 objects. The maximal query radii were selected to keep the response set size at about 20% of the database.

For all queries tested, the M-tree and D-index required fewer distance computations than the sequential scan, which is desirable and is in fact a prerequisite for any index organization. We can also observe that the D-index outperforms the other structures in many situations, especially when queries with small selectivity are posed – the effectiveness of the pivot-based filtering inside the D-index strongly depends on the data distribution and the query size. Because of the normal data distribution of the vector dataset, the pivot-based filtering in the D-index becomes less efficient for query radii greater than 2,500. Where many pairs of objects are at such a distance, the pruning effect is diminishing. Observe that, with the URL dataset, the D-index is competitive for just a few small query radii. In general, we observe that the highly skewed and discrete distribution together with the fixed hashing schema of the D-index hands an advantage to the fully-adaptive M-tree, especially for queries with higher radii. The authors of the D-index also observe that the problem of selecting a good pivot is more difficult for discrete distributions, where an object different from any other object can easily be promoted without actually being a good pivot.

The global increasing trends in the number of disk page accesses are merely the same as those for distance computations. Observe that the sequential scan is often more efficient than the sophisticated M-tree, because the M-tree typically needs twice the disk space to store the same data as the SEQ. As a result, it is usually worse than the linear scan, since the ratio of wasted disk space markedly influences I/O search costs. This drawback is addressed in some extensions of the M-tree, but the improvements are only marginal. In contrast, the D-index is very economical of space and needs slightly more disk memory than the SEQ. Only for some queries from the VEC dataset does the M-tree require fewer disk reads than the SEQ, but the D-index almost always remains beneath the linear scan threshold for this data. However, elevated disk costs can be tolerated when an index structure saves many distance evaluations by a distance function very demanding of CPU time. Of course, I/O costs become crucial when the distance function is very easy to compute. In this respect, the hashing schema of the D-index is more promising than that of the M-tree.

Figure 3.23 reveals another interesting observation. To run an exact-match query, i.e., a range search with $r = 0$, the D-index needs to access only one disk page. Compare, in the same figure, the number of block reads for the M-tree. They are one half that of the SEQ for vectors, practically equal to the SEQ for the URL sets, and actually three times higher for the sentences. Note that an exact-match search is important when a specific object must be eliminated – the location of the deleted object forms the main cost. In this respect, the D-index is able to manage deletions far more efficiently than the M-tree. The outcome of the same test with $r = 0$ in terms of distance computations can be summarized as follows: The D-index needed just twelve and five distance evaluations for the VEC and STR datasets, respectively. Even for the URL collection, the D-index performed better than the M-tree. In summary, the D-index is very efficient in insertions or deletions of objects compared to the other techniques explored. It is also the preferable type of organization for range queries with narrow radii.

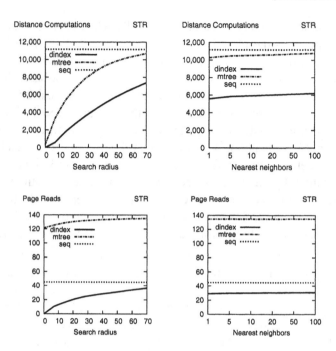

Figure 3.24. Comparison of the range search efficiency in the number of distance computations (above) and block accesses (below) for the kNN search on STR.

3.3   Different Query Types

The objective of the second group of tests is to show that costs also depend on various query types. Figure 3.24 shows results of experiments for range and nearest neighbor queries. We use the STR collection, because the performance contrast is most marked here. For the kNN queries, both indexes tested exhibit more or less the same behavior and the greatest advantage of the D-index, the fast processing of small queries, decreases. This reveals the fact that a kNN query execution, even for small k, is very expensive and many unqualified data objects must be inspected to get the result. The experiments also show that the difference in search costs for $k = 1$ and $k = 100$ is insignificant. However, the D-index is still twice as fast as the M-tree as far as distance computations go, and four times faster in terms of disk accesses.

We also evaluated similarity joins, probably the most demanding operation even for small thresholds of μ. Figure 3.25 shows results for the VEC and STR datasets, again containing about 11,000 objects. In the figure, three algorithms are compared. NL (nested loops) represents the naive approach, which incrementally compares all object pairs against the join constraint μ. The RJ (range join) algorithm is based on the D-index, and the OJ (overloading join) algorithm uses the eD-index. For details of these algorithms, please refer to

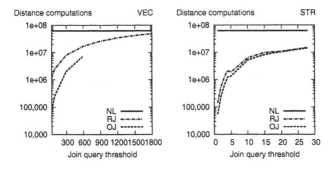

Figure 3.25. Join queries on the VEC and STR datasets.

Section 2.2. To illustrate the complexity of this search execution, take as an example the STR collection and the similarity self-join $SJ(1)$. In this case, the execution requires 54,908 distance computations even for the most efficient OJ algorithm. The kNN query, by contrast, with $k = 1$, needs only 5,567, and the range query with $r = 1$ just several tens of distance evaluations.

In both graphs, query selectivity increases up to $\mu = 28$ and $\mu = 1800$ for the STR and VEC datasets, respectively, retrieving about 1,000,000 pairs. As expected, the number of distance evaluations performed by the RJ and OJ algorithms increases rapidly with growing μ. However, the OJ outperforms the RJ by more than twice for smaller joins on the STR dataset. The limitation of the OJ algorithm can be observed in the figure for the VEC data. It is due to the fact that the exclusion overloading principle requires $2\mu \leq \rho$, i.e., $\mu \leq 600$ for VEC. Here, the OJ is even more efficient and achieves seven times better performance than the RJ. This is mainly caused by the distance distribution of the VEC dataset, where the average distance between each pair of objects is high, so the small query selectivity can benefit from the higher pruning effectiveness of the pivot-based filtering. On the other hand, the same distance distribution incurs poor performance for $\mu = 1800$. The reason is analogous, that is, objects are not contrasted enough for the pivot-base filtering to remain effective.

3.4 Scalability

We have shown that some access structures are able to outperform others, and that search costs depend not only on the structure but also on query type and the distance distribution of datasets. However, considering the amount of available data on the web, scalability of search structures is probably the most important issue to investigate. In the elementary case, it is necessary to study what happens to performance as the amount of data grows. An investigation of this phenomenon formed the objective of our final group of experiments.

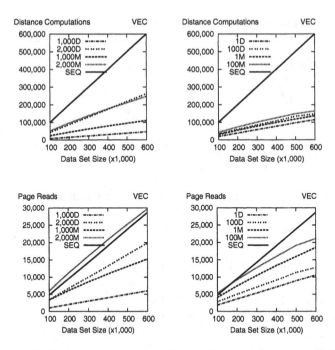

Figure 3.26. Scalability of range (left) and nearest neighbor queries (right) for the VEC dataset.

Figure 3.26 presents scalability of range and nearest neighbor queries in terms of distance computations and block accesses. In these experiments, the VEC dataset is used and the amount of data grows from 100,000 up to 600,000 objects. Apart from the SEQ organization, individual curves are labeled by a number indicating either the count of nearest neighbors or the search radius, and a letter, where 'D' stands for the D-index and 'M' for the M-tree. Query size is not provided for the results of SEQ because sequential organization has the same costs no matter the query. The results indicate that on the level of distance computations, the D-index is usually slightly better than the M-tree, but the differences are not significant – the D-index and M-tree can each save a considerable number of distance computations over the SEQ. To solve a query, the M-tree needs significantly more block reads than the D-index and for some queries (see the 2,000M curve) this number is even higher than for the SEQ. The reason for such behavior has been given earlier.

In general, the D-index can be said to behave strictly linearly when the size of the dataset grows, i.e., search costs depend linearly upon the amount of data. In this regard, the M-tree came out slightly better, because execution costs for querying a file twice as large were not twice as high. This sublinear behavior should be attributed to the fact that the M-tree incrementally reorganizes its structure by splitting blocks and, in this way, improves data clustering. On the

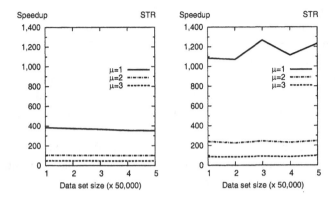

Figure 3.27. Scalability measured in speedup for RJ (left) and OJ (right) algorithms on the STR dataset.

other hand, the D-index used a constant bucket structure, where only the number of blocks changed. However, the static hashing schema allows the D-index to have constant costs for exact-match queries. The D-index required one block access and eighteen distance comparisons, independent of dataset size. This was in sharp contrast to the M-tree, which needed about 6,000 block reads and 20,000 distance computations to find the exact match in a set of 600,000 vectors. Moreover, the D-index has constant costs to insert one object, while the M-tree exhibits logarithmic behavior.

For similarity self-join queries, the situation is comparable. In [Dohnal et al., 2003b], the STR database was used and the data size varied from 50,000 to 250,000 sentences – the decreased maximum data size was applied due to the join complexity. Figure 3.27 reports the results in terms of speedup, i.e., how many times faster the algorithm is than the NL (nested loops) approach. The experiments were conducted for queries of small selectivity typically used in applications like data cleaning or copy detection. The results indicate that both RJ and OJ have practically constant speedup, which corresponds to costs growing quadratically with data size. An exception can be observed for $\mu = 1$, where the RJ slightly deteriorates, while the OJ improves its performance. This is very simple to understand because costs for the smallest queries are highly influenced by the distance distribution, which may change as the dataset grows. All in all, the OJ performs at least twice faster than the RJ algorithm.

The basic lessons learned from these experiments are twofold:

- similarity search is expensive;
- the scalability of centralized indexes is linear.

Of course, there are differences in search costs among individual techniques, but the global outcome is that search costs grow linearly with dataset size. This property prohibits their applicability for huge data archives, because, after a certain point, centralized indexes become inefficient for users' needs.

Suitable solutions arise from two possibilities. First, increased performance may be obtained by sacrificing some precision in search results. This technique is called approximate similarity search and we discuss it in Chapter 4. Second, more storage and computational resources may be used to speed up executions of queries. The main idea here is to modify centralized solutions by considering parallel environments and developing distributed structures. An advantage of distributed processing is that we can spread the problem over a network and computations can consequently be parallelized. Parallel and distributed access structures are the subject of Chapter 5.

Chapter 4

APPROXIMATE SIMILARITY SEARCH

The general algorithms for executing approximate range and nearest neighbor queries in metric spaces discussed in Section 9.2 of Chapter 1 are able to implement different strategies by means of a properly defined pruning condition and stop condition. In this chapter, we present some relevant approximate similarity search strategies based on either one or both these conditions. The choice between methods is constrained by each method's ability to support structures that organize data on disk memories. Finally, the pros and cons of approximate similarity search are treated, and evidence provided by tests conducted on real datasets is discussed.

1.   Relative Error Approximation

An approximation strategy proposal for range and nearest neighbor queries which guarantees the relative error on distances remains smaller than a user-specified value, was presented in [Zezula et al., 1998a, Amato, 2002].

Let $\mathcal{R}_q = (q, r_q)$ be a query region and $\mathcal{R}_i = (p_i, r_i)$ be a data region. Precise similarity search algorithms discard the region $\mathcal{R}_i$ when there is no overlap between $\mathcal{R}_q$ and $\mathcal{R}_i$, because it is guaranteed that no qualifying objects are contained in $\mathcal{R}_i$. Formally, the region $\mathcal{R}_i$ is not accessed when:

$$d(q, p_i) - r_i > r_q \qquad (4.1)$$

As Section 1.1 of Chapter 3 explains, the power of this test can be further enhanced by methods which exploit hierarchical space decomposition like the M-tree. Let $\mathcal{R}_p = (p_p, r_p)$ be the parent region of $\mathcal{R}_i$, which implies that $\mathcal{R}_i$ is completely contained inside $\mathcal{R}_p$. An additional pruning condition can be applied in order to avoid the region completely. So, the overlap test given by

Equation 4.1 is not needed, and the entire sub-tree rooted in $\mathcal{R}_i$ can be safely pruned if the following inequality holds:

$$|d(q, p_p) - d(p_i, p_p)| - r_i > r_q \qquad (4.2)$$

These two "exact" pruning tests can be conveniently relaxed to obtain an approximate similarity search algorithm in which the quality of the result-set is constrained by a user-defined relative error on distances.

Let o^N be the actual nearest neighbor of q, and o^A some other object in the searched collection. The object o^A is called the *(1+ε)-approximate-nearest-neighbor* [Arya et al., 1998] of object q if its distance from q is within a factor $(1 + \epsilon)$ of that of the nearest neighbor o^N, that is when

$$\frac{d(o^A, q)}{d(o^N, q)} \leq 1 + \epsilon.$$

In other words, when the previous formula holds, the distance of object o^A from q is at most $1 + \epsilon$ times bigger than the distance to the actual nearest neighbor o^N.

This idea can be generalized for the k-th nearest neighbor of q, for $1 \leq k \leq n$, where n is the size of the database. Using o_k^A and o_k^N to designate the k-th approximate and the k-th actual nearest neighbors respectively, we state that

$$\frac{d(o_k^A, q)}{d(o_k^N, q)} \leq 1 + \epsilon.$$

Again, o_k^A is called the *(1+ε)-k-th-approximate-nearest-neighbor* of q. In both cases, ϵ represents the relative error on distances to o^A or o_k^A.

The pruning tests in Equations 4.1 and 4.2 can be relaxed to discard regions even if they overlap the query region, while still guaranteeing a relative error on distance not exceeding a user-specified value of ϵ. To this aim, let us consider the following alternate expressions for Equations 4.1 and 4.2:

$$\begin{cases} \frac{r_q}{d(p_i,q)-r_i} < 1 & \text{if } d(p_i, q) - r_i > 0 \\ \\ false & \text{otherwise} \end{cases} \qquad (4.3)$$

and

$$\begin{cases} \frac{r_q}{|d(p_p,q)-d(p_i,p_p)|-r_i} < 1 & \text{if } |d(p_p, q) - d(p_i, p_p)| - r_i > 0 \\ \\ false & \text{otherwise} \end{cases} \qquad (4.4)$$

The numerators in the fractions above represent the distance to the k-th nearest neighbor of q (as discovered to that point in the nearest neighbor search), or

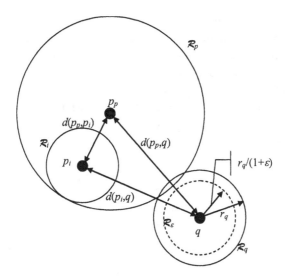

Figure 4.1. The region $\mathcal{R}_i = (p_i, r_i)$, its parent region $\mathcal{R}_p = (p_p, r_p)$, the query region $\mathcal{R}_q(q, r_q)$, and the reduced query region $\mathcal{R}_\epsilon = (q, r_q/(1 + \epsilon))$

the maximum accepted distance from q, in case of range search. Provided the nearest neighbor search has not been completed, this distance can also be interpreted as the distance from q to the current approximate neighbor. The denominators, on the other hand, stand for lower bounds on distances between q and objects within the region $\mathcal{R}_i$. To put it differently, the denominators represent the minimum distance an object in the given region might have with respect to q. Naturally, if the lower bounds (i.e., denominators) are greater than the current radius of q, the region $\mathcal{R}_i$ cannot contain any qualifying object and can therefore be ignored in the search process.

In order to modify these tests for approximate searching, the relative factor ϵ can be used to relax the lower bounds in the following way:

$$\begin{cases} \frac{r_q}{d(p_i,q)-r_i} < 1 + \epsilon & \text{if } d(p_i, q) - r_i > 0 \\ false & \text{otherwise} \end{cases} \tag{4.5}$$

and

$$\begin{cases} \frac{r_q}{|d(p_p,q)-d(p_i,p_p)|-r_i} < 1 + \epsilon & \text{if } |d(p_p, q) - d(p_i, p_p)| - r_i > 0 \\ false & \text{otherwise} \end{cases} \tag{4.6}$$

Naturally, this can never increase similarity search costs, because the number of distance computations and the number of node reads can both only be reduced.

In fact, the relaxation has the effect of using a smaller query region $\mathcal{R}_\epsilon = (q, r_q/(1+\epsilon))$ than the original, as Figure 4.1 illustrates. The precise similarity search algorithm would use the radius r_q and thus access the region $\mathcal{R}_p$. But in the approximate approach, the reduced region $\mathcal{R}_\epsilon$ no longer intersects $\mathcal{R}_p$.

Let us label the approximate pruning test $\epsilon Prune(\mathcal{R}_q, \mathcal{R}_i, \epsilon)$ defined by Equation 4.5, and that defined by Equation 4.6 $\epsilon PrePrune(\mathcal{R}_q, \mathcal{R}_i, \epsilon)$. The pruning condition dictated by the approximate similarity search algorithms presented in Section 9.2 of Chapter 1 is as follows:

$$
Prune(\mathcal{R}_q, \mathcal{R}_i, \epsilon) = \quad \textbf{if } \epsilon PrePrune(\mathcal{R}_q, \mathcal{R}_i, \epsilon)
$$
$$
\textbf{return } true
$$
$$
\textbf{else}
$$
$$
\textbf{return } \epsilon Prune(\mathcal{R}_q, \mathcal{R}_i, \epsilon).
$$

As far as the stop condition is concerned, we have that

$$
Stop(\texttt{response}, x_s) = false,
$$

because the Relative Error Approximation technique is based only on the relaxed branching strategy and the stop condition is not defined. In this respect, the stop condition is always false.

2.   Good Fraction Approximation

The nearest neighbor search algorithm presented in Section 6.1 of Chapter 1, gradually improves upon the result-set in a series of iteration steps. With each iteration, whenever a new object o is found with distance from the query object q less than some object in the current result-set, the k-th nearest o_k of the result set is removed and o is inserted in its place.

In [Zezula et al., 1998a, Amato, 2002], an approximate nearest neighbors search algorithm is proposed. It prematurely stops search execution as soon as all objects of the result-set belong to a user-specified fraction of objects closest to the query object q. To explain the idea, suppose that the dataset X contains 10,000 objects $o_1, o_2, \ldots, o_{10,000}$ ordered with respect to their distances from the query object q. If the fraction chosen is $1/200$ (that is 0.5%), the approximation algorithm will halt when the result-set is a subset of $\{o_1, o_2, ..., o_{50}\}$, since $10,000/200 = 50$. If the fraction determines subset smaller than or equal to k, approximation is not possible and the precise result-set is retrieved.

An efficient implementation of this idea uses a probabilistic approach which exploits the concept of the distance distribution. The properties of the distribution of distances in metric space are discussed in Section 10.1.2 of Chapter 1.

Suppose we have a metric space $\mathcal{M} = (\mathcal{D}, d)$. The distance distribution relative to p_i, $F_{p_i}(x) = \Pr\{d(p_i, o) \leq x\}$, gives the probability that an object o chosen at random from $\mathcal{D}$ will have a distance from p_i which is less than x. Suppose the dataset $X \subseteq \mathcal{D}$ forms a representative sample of the domain $\mathcal{D}$,

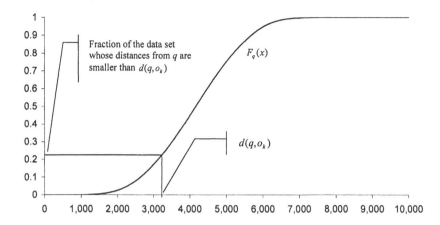

Figure 4.2. An estimation of the fraction of the objects closest to q, whose distances from q are less than $d(q, o_k)$, can be obtained by using $F_q(x)$.

i.e., the distribution of distances in X is statistically similar to that of $\mathcal{D}$. This can generally be assumed to be true given a large enough number of objects in X. In this case, $F_{p_i}(x), p_i \in X$, represents that fraction of objects in X for which the distance from p_i is less than or equal to x. If the number of objects in X is n, the expected number of objects in X with distance from p_i less than x is $n \cdot F_{p_i}(x)$.

Let response represent the temporary result-set obtained at a certain intermediate iteration of the nearest neighbor search execution. Let o_k be the current k-th object in the response and $d(q, o_k)$ its distance from q. We have that $F_q(d(q, o_k))$ corresponds to the fraction of objects in X whose distances from q are less than or equal to $d(q, o_k)$, as also shown in Figure 4.2. Since all other objects in the response have a distance from q less than or equal to $d(q, o_k)$, all objects in the response are included in that fraction. For instance, when $F_q(d(q, o_k)) = 1/200$, the response is expected to be included in the set corresponding to the 0.5% of objects which lie closest to q.

So far, we have assumed that the distribution function F_q is known. However, computing and maintaining this information for any possible query object is unrealistic in practice, because query objects $q \in \mathcal{D}$ are not known a priori. A solution is to use the overall distance distribution, defined as $F(x) = \Pr\{d(o_1, o_2) \leq x\}$, instead of F_q. Since, as discussed in Section 10.1.2, the homogeneity of viewpoints is typically high, F can reliably be used as a substitute for any F_q.

The approximate nearest neighbor search algorithm prematurely stops execution when $F(d(q, o_k))$ is less than a user-specified threshold $frac$, corre-

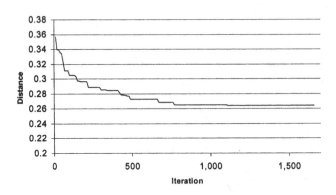

Figure 4.3. Trend of $d_{it}(iter)$ as the search algorithm progresses.

sponding to the desired fraction of the entire dataset. The stop condition is defined as:

$$Stop(\texttt{response}, frac) = F_q(d(q, o_k)) \le frac,$$

where o_k is the k-th object in the response.

This approximation method only applies the stop condition. The pruning condition therefore performs nothing special aside from the usual exact overlap test:

$$Prune(\mathcal{R}_q, \mathcal{R}_i, x_p) = d(q, p_i) > r_q + r_i,$$

where $\mathcal{R}_q = (q, r_q)$ is the query region, $\mathcal{R}_i = (p_i, r_i)$ is a data region, and the parameter x_p is obviously left unused.

3.   Small Chance Improvement Approximation

As precise nearest neighbor search algorithms iterate, the distance $d(o_k, q)$ of the k-th current object o_k from the query object q becomes smaller and smaller. The improvement due to radius reduction is initially rapid but progressively slows down. The approximate strategy for nearest neighbor search first proposed in [Zezula et al., 1998a] and later refined in [Amato, 2002] halts execution as soon as improvement in the result-set slows down below a user-specified threshold. This strategy is presented more formally in what follows.

Let $d_{it}(iter)$ be the distance of the query object q from the k-th object in the response set at iteration $iter$. The function is defined as

$$d_{it}(iter) = d(o_k(iter), q),$$

where $o_k(iter)$ is the k-th nearest object in the response set at iteration $iter$. Figure 4.3 shows the characteristic trend of $d_{it}(iter)$ as a function of the number

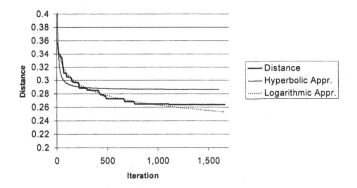

Figure 4.4. Trend of $d_{it}(iter)$ and two possible approximation curves.

of iterations. It can be seen that refinements of the distance are considerable during the initial iteration steps but then become less significant, with little or no improvement after a certain number of iterations. Observe that $d_{it}(iter)$ often assumes several consecutive constant values. This happens when accessed regions do not contain better objects, and the length of such (no improvement) sequences is growing with an increasing number of iteration steps.

The problem here is how to determine the moment, i.e., the iteration, when the chances for distance improvements are conveniently low. In fact, $d_{it}(iter)$ is a function that is not known a priori since its values become available as the search algorithm proceeds. In addition, it is a piecewise constant function, i.e., there are intervals where it assumes constant values, but it may decline again later. To cope with these problems, $d_{it}(iter)$ is approximated by a continuous function, designated $\varphi(iter)$, which is used to decide if search algorithms should be stopped or not.

The approximation of $d_{it}(iter)$ is obtained by using the method of *discrete least-squares* approximation (see, e.g., [Burden et al., 1978]). Specifically, the curve $\varphi(iter)$ approximating $d_{it}(iter)$ has the following form:

$$\varphi(iter) = c_1 \cdot \varphi_1(iter) + c_2.$$

The least-squares approximation technique finds values of c_1 and c_2 for which $\varphi(iter)$ optimally approximates $d_{it}(iter)$, once a specific curve φ_1 is chosen. Successful results were obtained using the hyperbolic function $\varphi_1(i) = 1/i$ and the logarithmic function $\varphi_1(i) = log(i)$. For illustration, Figure 4.4 shows a specific function $d_{it}(iter)$ and its two approximations.

The fact that $\varphi(iter)$ is a continuous decreasing function leads to the following definition of a stop condition: Informally, we want to stop the algorithm when $\varphi(iter)$ ceases to decline dramatically and the change between consecutive iterations drops below a threshold value. From the mathematical point of view, we use the derivative $\varphi'(iter)$ to characterize the shape of the curve $\varphi(iter)$. Because $\varphi(iter)$ is decreasing, its derivative will always be negative. The more rapidly the function decreases, the higher the negative number the derivative returns. Thus a parameter der can be chosen so that the algorithm halts when $\varphi'(iter) \geq der$, since this indicates that $\varphi(iter)$ is now decreasing only very slowly. The parameter der is fixed in such a way as to control the tradeoff between approximation quality and performance improvement. Of course, der approaching zero results in poor performance but high approximation quality, because the algorithm may stop very close to its natural end. Higher negative values of der, on the other hand, result in higher performance but poorer quality, because the algorithm may stop prematurely, when the current result-set is still quite different from the precise result-set. Obviously, with the threshold der set to zero, the algorithm behaves like a precise nearest neighbors search.

This method is based only on the stop condition, so the pruning condition performs the usual (exact) overlap test and only discards a node when its bounding region fails to overlap the query region, i.e.:

$$Prune(\mathcal{R}_q, \mathcal{R}_i, x_p) = d(q, p_i) > r_q + r_i,$$

where $\mathcal{R}_q = (q, r_q)$ is the query region and $\mathcal{R}_i = (p_i, r_i)$ is a data region, and the parameter x_p is again left unused.

On the other hand, the stop condition refines $\varphi(iter)$ iteration by iteration and checks if the derivative $\varphi'(iter)$ is above the approximation threshold:

$$Stop(\texttt{response}, der) = \quad \begin{aligned} &\text{let } iter \text{ denotes the iteration number;} \\ &\text{let } o_k \text{ be the } k\text{-th element of } \texttt{response;} \\ &\text{compute } \varphi(iter) \text{using the new} \\ &\quad \text{point } (iter, d(o_k, q)) \text{in addition} \\ &\quad \text{to the points previously used;} \\ &\textbf{if } iter{==}1 \\ &\quad \textbf{return } false; \\ &\textbf{else} \\ &\quad \textbf{return}(\varphi'(iter) \geq der); \end{aligned}$$

4.   Proximity-Based Approximation

As we have already explained, there is no guarantee that qualifying objects will be found in the intersection of data and query regions. Depending on specific distribution of data, it may happen that the overlap covers a portion of the space containing very few or no objects. Therefore, some regions are more likely to contain the query response than others.

An approach proposed in [Amato et al., 2003, Amato, 2002] attempts to detect these situations and is based on the relaxed branching strategy. It relies for its underlying concept upon the proximity of ball regions discussed in Section 10.2 of Chapter 1. In fact, the proximity $prox(\mathcal{R}_q, \mathcal{R}_i)$ of two ball regions $\mathcal{R}_q, \mathcal{R}_i$ is defined as the probability that a randomly chosen object o over the same metric space $\mathcal{M}$ appears in both the regions.

The basic idea here is to use the proximity measure to decide if a region should be accessed or not, so that only data regions with proximity to the query region greater than a specified threshold px are accessed. Of course, some regions containing qualifying objects may be falsely discarded by the algorithm, so the results obtained are only approximate. When the threshold is set to zero, search results are precise – the higher the proximity threshold, the less accurate the results, but the faster the query execution.

Let $\mathcal{R}_q$ be a query region and $\mathcal{R}_i$ a data region. The pruning condition of the approximate range and nearest neighbors search is defined as follows:

$$Prune(\mathcal{R}_q, \mathcal{R}_i, px) = prox(\mathcal{R}_q, \mathcal{R}_i) < px.$$

This technique is among those that omit a stop condition, so the stop condition always evaluates to false:

$$Stop(\texttt{response}, x_s) = false.$$

5. PAC Nearest Neighbor Searching

In [Ciaccia and Patella, 2000b], an approach called the *Probably Approximately Correct* (PAC) nearest neighbor search in metric spaces is proposed. The idea is to bound the error on distance of the approximate nearest neighbor so that a $(1+\epsilon)$-approximate-nearest-neighbor is found. In addition, the proposed algorithm may halt prematurely when the probability of the current $(1+\epsilon)$-approximate-nearest-neighbor satisfies the threshold δ. In fact, the approximation is controlled by two parameters. The ϵ parameter is used to specify the upper bound on the desired relative error on distance of the approximate nearest neighbor, while the δ parameter specifies the degree of confidence that the upper bound ϵ has not been exceeded. If δ is set to zero, the algorithm stops when the resulting object is guaranteed to be the $(1+\epsilon)$-approximate-nearest-neighbor. Values of δ greater than zero may return an object that is not a $(1+\epsilon)$-approximate-nearest-neighbor. On the other hand, when ϵ is set to zero, δ controls the probability that the retrieved object is not the actual nearest neighbor. Of course, when both ϵ and δ are set to zero, a precise nearest neighbor search is performed.

More formally, let q be the query object, o^N the actual nearest neighbor, and o^A the approximate nearest neighbor found. Let ϵ_{act} be the actual error on distances of o^A and o^N, that is

$$\epsilon_{act} = \frac{d(q, o^A)}{d(q, o^N)} - 1.$$

The PAC nearest neighbor algorithm retrieves a $(1+\epsilon)$-approximate-nearest-neighbor with confidence δ. That is, the algorithm stops when o^A is such that

$$\Pr\{\epsilon_{act} \geq \epsilon\} \leq \delta.$$

The pruning condition for this strategy is defined in the same way as that of the Relative Error Approximation technique given in Section 1. Besides the usual exact overlap test, it incorporates the extended pruning test which exploits a tree-like hierarchical structure and is specified in Equation 4.2 (pg. 146). For convenience, we give the pruning condition in the pseudocode below:

$$Prune(\mathcal{R}_q, \mathcal{R}_i, \epsilon) = \quad \textbf{if } \epsilon PrePrune(\mathcal{R}_q, \mathcal{R}_i, \epsilon)$$
$$\textbf{return } true$$
$$\textbf{else}$$
$$\textbf{return } \epsilon Prune(\mathcal{R}_q, \mathcal{R}_i, \epsilon).$$

The stop condition is based on the distribution of nearest neighbors in X (of cardinality n) with respect to q, designated as $G_q(x)$ and defined as follows:

$$G_q(x) = \Pr\{\exists o \in X : d(q, o) \leq x\} = 1 - (1 - F_q(x))^n.$$

As previously stated, the algorithm stops when $\Pr\{\epsilon_{act} \geq \epsilon\} \leq \delta$, where ϵ_{act} is the actual relative error on distances. That is when

$$\Pr\{\exists o \in X : d(q, o^A)/d(q, o) - 1 \geq \epsilon\} =$$
$$= \Pr\{\exists o \in X : d(q, o) \leq d(q, o^A)/(1 + \epsilon)\} \leq \delta.$$

This leads to the definition of the stop condition as:

$$Stop(\textbf{response}, \epsilon, \delta) = G_q(d(q, o^A)/(1 + \epsilon)) \leq \delta.$$

The limitation of this approach is due to its only being defined for $1NN$ similarity queries.

6.   Performance Trials

In this section, we provide the reader with a comparison of the techniques introduced within this chapter. We have used implementations provided by respective authors. These prototypes are all based on the publicly available implementation of the M-tree [Ciaccia et al., 1997a]. To assess performance objectively, we performed various experiments using the collection of 11,000

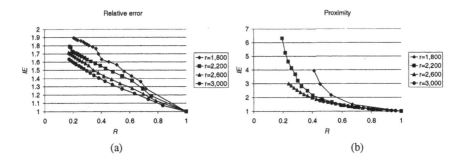

Figure 4.5. Approximate range query results: (a) Relative Error Approximation and (b) Proximity-based Approximation techniques.

objects of the VEC dataset described in Section 3.1 of Chapter 3. Data partitioning on this dataset results in highly overlapping regions and precise similarity search typically has high costs. In this respect, this dataset is a good candidate for demonstrating the advantages of the approximate similarity search. Note that when precise similarity search is already efficiently executed, there is obviously not much space for further improvements.

We experimentally varied approximation parameters, query radii, and the number of objects retrieved. For each test configuration, approximate search algorithms were executed using fifty different query objects (not occurring in the dataset), the costs presented being averaged values. Results of the trials are shown in Figure 4.5 for range queries and in Figure 4.6 for the nearest neighbor queries. In the following, we discuss these results in greater depth.

6.1 Range Queries

The approximate range search can only be implemented using the Relative Error Approximation technique or the Proximity-based Approximation technique. We executed range queries with radii varying from 1,800 to 3,000, so the response size varied between 1% and 20% of objects in the dataset. The approximation parameters of the two methods were varied, and for each test configuration the improvement in efficiency IE and recall R, as defined in Section 9.3 of Chapter 1, were computed. Results are shown in Figure 4.5, where the curves illustrate the dependence of improvement in efficiency IE on recall R for different query radii.

As would be expected, both methods obtained high values for IE in correspondence to small values of R – the improvement in efficiency is paid for by lower recall. Performance is generally better when small query radii are used.

Observe that the improvement in efficiency for approximate range search algorithms is not very high. In fact, it is always below one order of magnitude. For example, the Relative Error Approximation method executes a range query

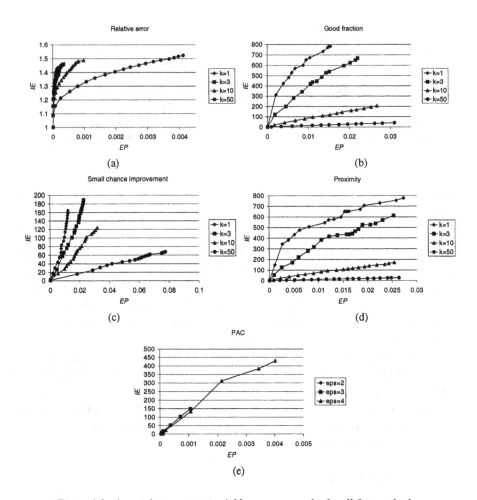

Figure 4.6. Approximate nearest neighbors query results for all five methods.

with radius 2,200 1.8 times faster with recall $R = 0.2$, that is 20% of objects retrieved by the precise search occur in the approximate result. On the other hand, the Proximity-based Approximation method with the same recall is able to execute the same query six times faster than the precise execution. The difference in performance of these two methods is mainly due to the superiority of the Proximity-based Approximation method in detecting regions which can be discarded.

6.2 Nearest Neighbors Queries

All the methods presented in this chapter can be used for approximate nearest neighbor searches. In general, the improvements in efficiency obtained are high even for good quality results. Nearest neighbor queries in our experiments were executed varying k between 1 and 50 with the exception of the PAC method, which is limited to using $k = 1$ only. We varied the approximation parameters of the methods and for each configuration computed improvement in efficiency IE and error on position EP, as defined in Section 9.3 of Chapter 1. Since the PAC method depends upon two approximation parameters, δ and ϵ, we used δ varying over several values of EP for three fixed values of the relative distance error ϵ. Results are depicted in Figure 4.6, where we plot IE versus EP. Large improvements in efficiency can be observed for all methods, but the specific values depend upon accuracy as measured in terms of error on position EP. Performance is systematically higher for small values of k.

The Relative Error Approximation method proved to be the least efficient. The method seems to saturate for high values of the approximation parameters, with no additional improvements in efficiency obtained. Result-sets are consequently quite precise and the difference in efficiency from precise execution is negligible. When $k = 1$, approximate execution is about 1.5 times faster than precise execution for $EP = 0.0002$. All other methods offer substantially greater improvements, roughly speaking several orders of magnitude. Let us focus on a value for EP of 0.0005, with $k = 1$. This value of EP implies that the approximate nearest neighbor is on average the fifth actual nearest neighbor. The Good Fraction Approximation method offers an improvement in efficiency of about sixty, i.e., the approximate search is executed sixty times faster than a precise search. In other words, if the precise execution takes one minute, then the approximate execution needs just one second. The same can be observed for the Proximity-based Approximation method. For the Small Chance Improvement Approximation method, we see an improvement in efficiency of about ten times, and for the PAC method with $\epsilon = 4$, $IE = 50$.

The approximate algorithms, however, perform much faster for lower values of accuracy. For example, with $EP = 0.003$, i.e., the approximate nearest neighbor is the thirtieth actual nearest neighbor, the Small Chance Improvement Approximation is thirty times faster. For the same configuration, the Good Fraction Approximation, Proximity-based Approximation, and PAC methods are about 300 times faster – if precise execution takes five minutes, the approximate execution still takes just one second.

We observe that the chief reason for the markedly poor performance of the Relative Error Approximation method (with respect to the others) is that precise nearest neighbors algorithms find good candidates for the result-sets soon on, and then spend the remainder of their time mostly in refining the current results. Very efficient methods have the property of stopping the search execution early, i.e., as soon as the current result-set is good enough. In fact, the Good Fraction Approximation, Small Chance Improvement Approximation, and PAC methods are based on early termination strategies, which aim at identifying this situation. The Proximity-based Approximation method, even if it is defined as a relaxed branching strategy, implicitly behaves like an early termination strategy, as explained in the following.

Our experiments have shown that after a certain number of iterations of the approximate nearest neighbors algorithm with the Proximity-based Approximation strategy, all entries contained in the priority queue PR (see Section 9 of Chapter 1 for a description of the approximate nearest neighbors search algorithm) are suddenly discarded and the algorithm terminates. This is the main reason for the big improvement in query execution speed. We call the iteration in which the remaining entries are discarded the *cut-off iteration*. We have also observed that small values of k anticipate the occurrence of the cut-off iteration, which can be explained as follows:

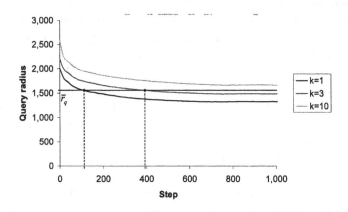

Figure 4.7. Trend of the query radius during the precise nearest neighbors search execution.

1 The proximity of two ball regions is less than or equal to the probability that a randomly chosen point belongs to the smaller of the two regions. This probability can be approximated by $F(r)$, where F (see Section 10.1.2 of Chapter 1) is the overall distance distribution and r is the radius of the smaller region.

2 At each iteration of the nearest neighbors search algorithm, the query radius is changed and set to the distance between the query and the current k-th nearest neighbor. Let x be the approximation threshold. When the dynamic radius r_q of the query region is reduced so that $x > F(r_q)$, then all regions in the queue PR are pruned (due to Property 1 above), so the cut-off iteration occurs and the search algorithm terminates.

3 At any specific iteration of the nearest neighbors search algorithm, higher values of k result in a larger query radius. To illustrate this, consider Figure 4.7 which relates the current query radius and the number of iteration

steps of the precise nearest neighbors search algorithm, individually for $k = 1, 3$, and 10. Observe that query radii for $k = 1$ are systematically below those for $k = 3$, and these are systematically below those for $k = 10$. This means lower k methodically results in smaller query regions, which is quite obvious. Given a specific approximation threshold $\bar{x}$, let $\bar{r}_q$ be the maximum radius such that $\bar{x} > F(\bar{r}_q)$. Figure 4.7 shows that $\bar{r}_q$ is reached faster with small values of k and may never be reached when $\bar{x}$ is too small or when k is too big. Since the cost for a precise similarity search is almost independent of k, IE is higher for lower values of k.

The previous arguments can also be used to explain the performance improvements observed for approximate nearest neighbors queries vis à vis range queries. In fact, given that the query radius is fixed during execution of the range search algorithm, the cut-off iteration either never occurs or is the very first iteration. In the latter case, however, even though execution costs are very low, the result-set is empty because all regions are discarded. As a consequence, range queries with larger radii are often posed but their evaluation is not accelerated that significantly.

6.3   Global Considerations

In summary, the approximation methods described afford moderate improvement in efficiency for range queries and substantial improvement for nearest neighbors queries. The Good Fraction Approximation method achieves the highest performance, but it can only be used for nearest neighbors queries. On the other hand, the Proximity-based Approximation method offers nearly the same results, with the advantage of also being applicable to range queries. Improvement in efficiency of the Small Chance Improvement Approximation method may also reach two orders of magnitude, but the technique is always less efficient than the two previous competitors. The Relative Error Approximation method can hardly be recommended, because its performance improvements are only marginal. The (minor) drawback of the Good Fraction Approximation and the Proximity-based Approximation methods is that they require precomputing, storing, and manipulating the distribution and density functions of the searched data. However, as discussed in Section 10.1.2 of Chapter 1, this overhead is realistic. The Relative Error Approximation and the Small Chance Improvement Approximation methods do not need any pre-analysis of datasets and do not require any other storage overhead but their performance is worse than that of the other two methods. Finally, the PAC method also achieves very good performance. However, it is limited to nearest neighbor searches ($k = 1$) only.

Chapter 5

PARALLEL AND DISTRIBUTED INDEXES

Centralized metric indexes achieve a significant speedup (both in terms of distance computations and disk-page reads) when compared to a baseline approach, the sequential scan. However, experience with centralized methods (see, e.g., Section 3 of Chapter 3) reveals a strong correlation between the dataset size and search costs. More specifically, costs increase linearly with the growth of the dataset, i.e., it is practically twice as expensive to compute a similarity query in a dataset of a given size as it would be with a dataset of half that size. Thus, the ability of centralized indexes to maintain a reasonable query response time when the dataset multiplies in size, its *scalability*, is limited.

In this chapter, we present methods which solve this problem by exploiting parallel computing power. The idea behind it is easy in principle: As the dataset grows in size, more independent computation and storage resources are added (CPUs, disks, etc.), keeping the query response time low.

The basis of parallel and distributed index structures as well as differences between the two approaches can be found in Section 1. In Section 2, we present a modification of the M-tree structure for a parallel environment, where multiple processors and disks are used to accelerate the evaluation of similarity queries. A dynamic index structure which exploits a distributed environment to enhance similarity search is explained in Section 3. As the experiments in Section 4 demonstrate, this structure attains practically constant response times even as the dataset grows, provided sufficient computational resources are available.

1. Preliminaries

The field of architectures and paradigms for parallel and distributed computing environments is quite large due to the numerous research challenges it offers for different objectives. In this book, we concentrate on the database perspective. We start by describing some basic requirements for parallel and distributed index structures, and also briefly discuss some of the advantages and drawbacks of the parallel and distributed paradigms.

1.1   Parallel Computing

We use a definition of parallel systems similar to [Leopold, 2001]: A parallel system is a device composed of multiple independent processing units and/or multiple independent storage places. All the units share dedicated communication media and data. Accordingly, a parallel computing environment can be a multi-processor computer with several disk units. The processors (CPUs) share operating memory (RAM) and use a shared internal bus for communicating with the disks.

In order to fully exploit the parallel environment, an index structure should have the following properties:

- *shared data* – any object from a stored dataset is available to any processor at any time. Of course, there are situations, when, for consistency reasons, some objects will be locked by a processor and not immediately accessible to another. But such a condition should occur only intermittently;

- *multiple operations at the same time* – the system can evaluate several independent operations on different processors. The number of tasks processed in parallel is limited by the number of processing units (CPUs);

- *parallel storage* – data can be stored on multiple disks and each disk is available to all processors. There is the possibility of moving data from one disk to another.

The first two requirements allow a parallel index structure to process objects from a stored dataset using multiple processors at the same time. The third property allows data to be efficiently distributed across disks, thus enabling parallel access to stored objects while processing queries.

In order to measure the effectiveness of parallel search implementations, [DeWitt and Gray, 1992] define two factors: *speedup* and *scaleup*. Specifically, given a fixed job run on a small system and a run on a large (big) system, the speedup afforded by the larger system is measured as:

$$speedup = \frac{ST}{BT},$$

where ST is the Small system elapsed Time, and BT is the Big system elapsed Time. Speedup is linear if an n-times bigger (more powerful) system yields a speedup of n. Speedup keeps the problem size constant and expands the system.

Scaleup measures the ability to expand both the system and the problem size. It is defined as the ability of an n-times larger system to perform an n-

times larger job in the same elapsed time as the original system for the original problem size. The scaleup metric is:

$$scaleup = \frac{STSP}{BTBP},$$

where $STSP$ is the Small system elapsed Time on Small Problem, and $BTBP$ is the Big system elapsed Time on Big Problem. If this scaleup equation evaluates to one, scaleup is said to be linear.

In spite of the fact that parallel processing can accelerate query execution, only a fixed amount of resources are available. Thus, processing can only be enhanced by a factor that is strictly bounded by the number of added resources. The paradigm of distributed processing further extends these possibilities.

1.2 Distributed Computing

In distributed environments, computers (network nodes) are connected via a high-speed network (such as a corporate local network, the Internet, etc.). They share the processing power of their CPUs as well as the storage resources of their disks. Objects of distributed organizations are allocated and processed over such an infrastructure. In order to solve queries, store new data, or remove unneeded objects, network nodes pass requests to other nodes by means of a specific *navigation* or *routing* mechanism. In the following, we concentrate on the two most important paradigms for distributed indexes, those of *Scalable and Distributed Data Structures* (SDDS) and *Peer-to-Peer* (P2P) data networks.

1.2.1 Scalable and Distributed Data Structures

The paradigm of Scalable and Distributed Data Structures was originally proposed by [Litwin et al., 1996] for simple search keys like numbers and strings. Data objects are stored in a distributed file on specialized network nodes called *servers*. More servers are employed as the file grows and additional storage capacity is required. The file is modified and queried by network nodes called *clients* through insert, delete, and search operations. The number of clients is unlimited and any client can request an operation at any time. To ensure high effectiveness, the following three properties should be built into the system:

- *scalability* – data migrate to new network nodes gracefully, and only when the network nodes already used are sufficiently loaded;

- *no hotspot* – there is no master site that must be accessed for resolving addresses of searched objects, e.g., there is no centralized directory;

- *independence* – the file access and maintenance primitives, such as the search, insertion, or node split, never require atomic updates on multiple nodes.

There are several practical reasons why the second property should be satisfied. In particular, if hotspots such as centralized directories exist, they would sooner or later turn into bottlenecks as the files grow. Structures without hotspots are also potentially more efficient in terms of the number and the distribution of messages sent over the network during the execution of an operation.

The third property is vital in a distributed environment, because informing other nodes may be either inefficient or even impossible in large-scale networks. Since they do not support techniques like multicast or broadcast, update operations cannot efficiently contact multiple servers with only one message. As an alternative, they would flood the network with multiple independent messages to all the respective nodes, which is certainly undesirable. Moreover, when several updates occur simultaneously on different servers, it may be difficult to maintain data consistency on individual nodes.

1.2.2   Peer-to-Peer Data Networks

Another distributed paradigm has led to the definition of the Peer-to-Peer (P2P) data network. In this environment, network nodes are called peers, equal in functionality and typically operating as part of a large-scale, potentially unreliable, network. Basically, a peer offers some computational resources, but can also use resources of the others [Aberer and Hauswirth, 2002]. In principle, the P2P network inherits the basic principles of SDDSs with added new requirements to overcome the problems of unreliability in the underlying network. These can be summarized as follows:

- *peer* – every node participating in the structure behaves as both client and server, i.e., the node can perform queries and at the same time store a part of the processed data file.

- *fault tolerance* – the failure of a network node participating in the structure is not fatal. All defined operations can still be performed, but the affected part of the dataset is inaccessible.

- *redundancy* – data components are replicated on multiple nodes to increase availability. Search algorithms must respect the possibility of multiple paths leading to specific instances.

Not every P2P structure proposed so far satisfies all these properties. However, these are the rules that any P2P system should be aware of and which ensure maximal scalability and effectiveness of the system.

2.   Processing M-trees with Parallel Resources

In this section, we describe a parallel version of the M-tree algorithms (see Chapter 3 for description of the M-tree) as proposed in [Zezula et al., 1998b].

The main objective of this parallel implementation is to decrease both CPU and I/O costs of executing similarity queries. In principle, there are two specific problems (restrictions) to be considered. First, we must respect the hierarchical dependencies between a parent node and its respective child nodes. Specifically, the search starts at the root node of the M-tree and continues recursively by traversing the relevant child nodes until leaf nodes with possibly qualifying objects are found, or search on a given path is terminated. In any case, a node on a given level cannot be accessed unless all its ancestors have already been processed. Thus, only nodes on the same level can be processed in parallel. Second, the use of priority queues for searching represents another serial component in the algorithms. For example, in a nearest neighbors search, the validity and significance of nodes in different branches of the M-tree can change, because paths that seem to qualify at a certain stage of the search may be eliminated when more relevant objects are found, possibly in some other parts of the M-tree.

In the following, we outline the principles of CPU and I/O parallel strategies for similarity-query execution in M-trees. Then we discuss qualitatively the results of known experimental evaluations.

2.1 CPU Parallelism

The order in which the M-tree nodes are accessed is determined by the (priority) queue, which is dynamically built and maintained in course of query execution (refer to Chapter 3). For coordination reasons, the queue is exclusively maintained by a dedicated CPU. Thus, the additional processors can only be used to accelerate performance while computing distances of objects within individual accessed nodes. Specifically, at each step, a node containing m keys is selected from the queue and up to m CPUs are used to compute distances between the query object and the particular keys. Similarly, multiple CPUs are applied to parallel computations of distances in leaf nodes, where data objects actually reside.

2.2 I/O Parallelism

As we have already anticipated, the order of accessing nodes is determined by their position in the priority queue. Thus, the processing strategy is to fetch in parallel as many nodes from the queue as possible, and bring them into main memory. To this aim, the key approach to achieve good performance resides in using an adequate *declustering* method to distribute nodes among available disks.

The problem of declustering can be seen in choosing a particular disk upon which to place a new node, resulting from splitting an overflowing M-tree node. The disk should be chosen in such a way that it does not contain many similar objects or object regions. In other words, the nodes are distributed among disks, so that the probability of accessing n disks during a search for n nodes is high. [Zezula et al., 1998b] have considered two different types of data placement strategies which can be briefly characterized as follows.

Global Allocation Declustering Method

With the global allocation strategy, the content of nodes is not taken into account, but the number of nodes on a disk is practically constant, thus no *data skew* occurs. The global allocation strategy does not consider similarity between node objects, but typically depends upon the order in which new nodes are created. In particular, the *round robin* strategy stores the j-th node on the (j mod n)-th disk of an n-disk system, while the *random strategy* decides which disk should store the j-th node using a random number generator.

Proximity-Based Allocation Declustering Method

This approach, by contrast, does not consider the data load on individual disks, but makes use of the proximity of node regions to locally avoid putting similar objects on the same disk. Proximity-based strategies allocate nodes respecting the proximity of their covering ball regions as described in Section 10.2 of Chapter 1. When choosing a destination disk, the sum of proximities between the new region and the regions of nodes already stored on the disk is minimized.

Efficiency Testing

Experiments by [Zezula et al., 1998b] demonstrate relatively high I/O speedup and scaleup, and the effects of the sequential components of the M-tree algorithms seem not to be very restrictive. The approach also seems not to be dependent on query type, number of objects retrieved, or type of object used.

During the experimental evaluation, the authors observed a practically linear speedup of M-tree CPU costs. The scaleup as investigated by the authors remained constant near a value of one when the initial 10,000-object file supported by five processors was expanded to a file size four times larger (40,000 objects) executed by four times as many processors, i.e., twenty processors.

Although the results show significant improvements, they are still limited considering the scalability, because the parallelized M-tree cannot dynamically increase the number of processors to preserve query response time as the file grows in size. The number of processors that can be actively used is also bounded by the maximum number of keys in a node. Moreover, the serial nature of the priority queue used during the search also implies a possible bottleneck.

2.3 Object Declustering in M-trees

A slightly different version of the parallel M-tree is proposed in [Alpkocak et al., 2002]. The algorithm does not try to decluster the nodes of the M-tree but instead distributes the nodes' objects across multiple disks. The M-tree leaf nodes are modified – they contain only addresses of particular objects stored on respective disks. The search algorithm proceeds exactly in the same way as for the standard M-tree until the leaf node is reached. After that, the object-declustered storage allows parallel acceleration of retrieval. In particular, the technique tries to distribute the objects according to their distance – specifically, similar objects are stored on different disks. Thus objects accessed by a similarity query are maximally distributed, allowing maximal parallelization during retrieval.

The specific declustering algorithm works as follows: After inserting a new object o_N into the M-tree, but before actually storing the object on a disk, we issue a range query $R(o_N, d(o_N, p))$, where p is the pivot of the M-tree leaf node where the object is to be logically stored. The evaluation of the query gives us objects similar to o_N, and, more importantly, the identifications of disks on which these objects are stored. The disk with the minimum number of retrieved objects is then selected for storing the object o_N.

On the basis of the criterion defined by the authors, i.e., the best utilization of parallel disks during similarity queries, the proposed declustering technique is nearly optimal. The declustering algorithm considers both object proximity and data load on disks as the experimental results provided have shown.

3. Scalable Distributed Similarity Search Structure

The parallel paradigm has shown that a certain speedup of a centralized index is possible. However it has still limited scalability due to the nature of parallel computing. Moreover, computers with a large number of processors (tens or hundreds) as well as disk arrays with huge storage are far more expensive than a network of several common workstations.

The first distributed index to support similarity search in generic metric spaces is based on the idea of the Generalized Hyperplane Tree, designated GHT* [Batko et al., 2004]. The structure allows storing datasets from any metric space and has many essential properties of the SDDS and P2P approaches. It is scalable, because every peer can perform an autonomous split and distribute the data over several peers at any time. It has no hotspot, and all peers use an addressing schema as precise as possible, while learning from misaddressing. Updates are performed locally and splitting never requires sending multiple messages to many peers. Finally, every peer can store data and perform similarity queries simultaneously. In what follows, we present the main characteristics of the GHT* index.

3.1   Architecture

In general, the GHT* exploits the P2P paradigm, i.e., it consists of network nodes (peers) that can insert, update and delete objects in the structure, and retrieve them using similarity queries.

In the GHT*, the dataset is distributed among peers participating in the network. Every peer holds sets of objects in its storage areas called *buckets*. A bucket is a limited space dedicated to storing objects. It may, for example, be a memory segment or a block on a disk. The number of buckets managed by a peer depends on its own potentialities – a peer can have multiple buckets, only one bucket, or no bucket at all. In the latter case, the peer is unable to hold objects, but can still issue similarity queries and insert or update objects.

Since the GHT* structure is dynamic and new objects can be inserted at any time, a bucket on a peer may reach its capacity limit. In this situation, a new bucket is created and some objects from the full bucket are moved to it. This new bucket may be located on a different peer than the original one. Thus, the GHT* structure grows as new data come in. The opposite operation – merging two buckets into one – is also possible, and may be used when objects are deleted from the GHT*.

The core of the algorithm lays down a mechanism for locating appropriate peers which hold requested objects. The part of the GHT* responsible for this navigation is called the *Address Search Tree* (AST). In order to avoid hotspots which may be caused by the existence of a centralized node accessed by every request, an instance of the AST structure is present in every peer. Whenever a peer wants to access or modify the data in the GHT* structure, it must first consult its own AST to get locations, i.e., peers, where the data resides. Then, it contacts the peers via network communication to actually process the operation.

Since we are in a distributed environment, it is practically impossible to maintain a precise address for every object in every peer. Thus, the ASTs in the peers contain only limited navigation information which may be imprecise. The locating step is then repeated on contacted peers until the desired peers are reached. It is guaranteed by the algorithm that the destination peers are always found. The GHT* also provides a mechanism called *image adjustment* for updating the imprecise parts of the AST automatically.

In the following, we summarize the foregoing information and provide some necessary identifiers which will be employed in the remainder of this chapter:

- Each peer maintains data objects in a set of *buckets*. Within a peer, the *Bucket IDentifier* (BID) is used to address a bucket.

- Every object is stored in exactly one bucket.

- Each peer participating in the network has a unique *Network Node IDentifier* (NNID).

- A structure called an *Address Search Tree* (AST) is present in every peer.

- Subtrees of the AST are automatically updated during the evaluation of queries using an algorithm called *image adjustment*.

- Peers communicate through the *message passing* paradigm. For consistency reasons, each *request message* expects a confirmation by a proper *acknowledgment message*.

3.2   Address Search Tree

The AST is a binary search tree based on the Generalized Hyperplane Tree (GHT) [Uhlmann, 1991], one of the centralized metric space indexing structures explained in Section 2.2 of Chapter 2. Its inner nodes hold the routing information of the GHT, a pair of pivots each. Each leaf node represents a pointer to either a bucket (using BID) or a peer (using NNID) holding the data. Whenever the data is in a bucket on the local peer, a leaf node is a BID pointer. An NNID pointer is used if the data is on a remote peer. An example of the AST is depicted in Figure 5.1. The NNID and BID pointers in leaf nodes are denoted by BID_i and $NNID_i$ symbols, while pivots of inner nodes are designated as p_i. Observe that every inner node has exactly two pivots. In order to recognize inconsistencies between ASTs on different peers, every inner node has a serial number. It is initially set to one and incremented whenever a particular part of the AST is modified. The serial numbers of inner nodes are shown above the inner nodes in Figure 5.1.

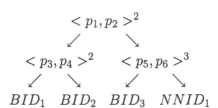

Figure 5.1. An example of an Address Search Tree.

Figure 5.2 illustrates the instances of AST structure in a network of three peers. The dashed arrows indicate the NNID pointers while the solid arrows represent the BID pointers. Observe that Peer 1 has no buckets, while the other two peers contain objects located only under specific leaves.

3.3   Storage Management

As we have already explained, the atomic storage unit of the GHT* is a bucket. The number of buckets and their capacity on a peer always have upper

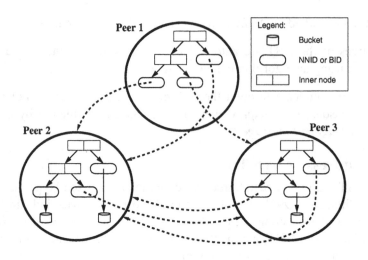

Figure 5.2. The GHT* network of three peers.

bounds, but these can be different for different peers. Since the bucket identifiers are only unique within a peer, a bucket in the global context is addressed by a pair (NNID, BID). To achieve scalability, the GHT* must be able to split buckets and allocate new storage and network resources. As is intuitively clear, splitting one bucket into two implies changes in the AST, i.e., the tree must grow. The complementary operation, merging two buckets into one, forces the AST to shrink.

3.3.1   Bucket Splitting

The bucket splitting operation is triggered by the insertion of an object into an already-full bucket. The procedure consists of the following three steps:

- A new bucket is allocated. If the capacity exists on the local peer, the bucket is created there. Otherwise, the bucket is allocated either to another peer with free capacity, or a new peer is used.

- A pair of pivots is chosen from objects of the overflowing bucket as detailed in Section 3.3.2.

- Objects from the overflowing bucket closer to the second pivot than to the first one are moved to the new bucket.

Figure 5.3 illustrates splitting one bucket into two. First, two objects are selected from the original bucket as pivots p_1 and p_2. Then, the distances between the pivots and every object in the original bucket are computed. All objects closer to the pivot p_2 are moved into a new bucket BID_2. A new inner node with the two pivots is added into the AST.

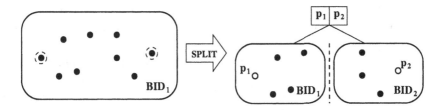

Figure 5.3. Splitting of a bucket in GHT.

3.3.2 Choosing Pivots

A specific choice of pivot mechanism directly impacts the performance of the GHT* structure. However, the selection can be a time-consuming operation, typically requiring many distance computations. To smooth this process, the authors use an incremental pivot selection algorithm which is based on the hypothesis that the GHT structure performs better if the distance between pivots is great.

First, the first two objects inserted into an empty bucket become pivot candidates. Then, distances to the candidates are computed for every other object inserted. If at least one of these distances is greater than the distance between the current candidates, the new object replaces one of the candidates, so the distance between the new pair of candidates is greater. After a sufficient number of insertions, the distance between the candidates is large with respect to the bucket dataset. However, the technique need not choose the most distant pair of objects. When the bucket overflows, the candidates become pivots and the split is executed.

3.4 Insertion of Objects

Inserting an object o_N starts in a peer by traversing its local AST from the root. For every inner node $< p_1, p_2 >$, the left branch is followed if $d(p_1, o_N) \leq d(p_2, o_N)$, otherwise the right branch is followed. Once a leaf node has been reached, a BID or NNID pointer is obtained. If it is the BID pointer, the inserted object is stored in the local bucket that the BID points to. Otherwise, the NNID pointer found is applied to forward the request to the peer, where the insertion continues recursively until an AST leaf with the BID pointer is reached.

For an example refer to Figure 5.1 again, where the AST is shown. To insert object o_N, the peer starts traversing the AST from the root. Assume that $d(p_1, o_N) > d(p_2, o_N)$, so the right branch is taken where distances $d_1 = d(p_5, o_N)$ and $d_2 = d(p_6, o_N)$ are evaluated. If $d_1 \leq d_2$ the left branch is taken which is a leaf node with BID_3. Therefore, the object o_N is stored locally in a bucket denoted by BID_3. In the opposite situation, i.e., $d_1 > d_2$, the right branch leading to a leaf with $NNID_1$ is traversed. Reaching the leaf with NNID, the insertion must be forwarded to the peer denoted by $NNID_1$ and the insert operation continues there.

In order to avoid redundant distance computations when searching the AST on the other peer, a path, once-determined, in the original AST is forwarded as well. The path is encoded as a bit-string called BPATH, where each node is represented by one bit – "0" represents the left branch, "1" represents the right branch. Every bit in this path is also accompanied by the respective serial number of the inner node. This is used to recognize possible out-of-date entries and if such entries are found, to update the AST with a more recent version. (The mechanism is explained in Section 3.8).

When a BPATH is received by a peer, it helps to quickly traverse the AST, because the distance computations to pivots are not repeated. During this quick traversal, the only check is to see if the serial number of the respective inner node equals the serial number stored in the BPATH. If not, the search resumes with standard AST traversal, and the pivot distances are evaluated until the traversal is finished.

To clarify the concept, see Figure 5.1. A BPATH representing the traversal to the leaf node BID_3 can be expressed as "1[2], 0[3]". First, the right branch from the root (the first bit thus being one) is taken and the serial number of the root node is two (denoted by the number in brackets). Then, the left branch with serial number three (thus "0[3]" is the next item) is taken. Finally, reaching a leaf node, the traversal is finished.

3.5   Range Search

Range search for query $R(q, r)$ is processed as follows. By analogy to insertion, the evaluation of a range search operation in GHT* also starts by traversing the local AST of the peer which issued the query. However, a different traversal condition is used in every inner node $< p_1, p_2 >$, specifically:

$$d(p_1, q) - r \leq d(p_2, q) + r, \tag{5.1}$$

$$d(p_1, q) + r > d(p_2, q) - r. \tag{5.2}$$

The right subtree of the inner node is traversed if Condition 5.1 qualifies and the left subtree is traversed whenever Condition 5.2 holds. From the equations derived from Lemma 1.4 of Chapter 1, it is clear that both conditions may qualify for a particular range search. Therefore, multiple paths may qualify and finally, multiple leaf nodes may be reached.

For all qualifying paths having an NNID pointer in their leaves, the query request is recursively forwarded (including known BPATH) to identified peers until a BID pointer is found in every leaf. If multiple paths point to the same peer, only one request with multiple BPATH attachments is sent. The range search condition is evaluated by the peers in every bucket determined by the BID pointers, together forming the response as a set of qualifying objects.

3.6 Nearest Neighbor Search

In principle, there are two strategies for evaluating kNN queries. The first starts with a very large query radius, covering all the data in a given dataset, to identify the degree to which specific regions might contain searched neighbors. The information is stored in a priority stack (queue) so that the most promising regions are accessed first. As suitable objects are found, the search radius is reduced and the stack adjusted accordingly. Though this strategy never accesses regions which do not intersect the query region bounded by the distance from the query object to its k-th nearest neighbor, processing of regions is strictly serial. On a single computer, the approach is optimal [Hjaltason and Samet, 1995], but it is not convenient for distributed environments aiming at exploiting parallelism. The second strategy starts with a zero radius to locate the first region to explore and then extends the radius to locate other candidate regions, if the result-set is still not complete. The nearest neighbors search in the GHT* structure adopts the second approach.

The algorithm first searches for a bucket which has a high probability of containing nearest neighbors. In particular, it seeks a bucket in which the query object would be stored using an insert operation. The accessed bucket's objects are sorted according to their distances with respect to the query object q. Assume there are at least k objects in the bucket, so that the first k objects, the objects with the shortest distances to q, are candidates for the result-set. However, there may be other objects in different buckets that are closer to the query object than some of the candidates. In order to check this, a range search is issued with the radius equal to the distance of the k-th candidate. In this way, a set of objects is obtained which always has cardinality greater than or equal to k. If all the retrieved objects are sorted and only the first k possessing the shortest distances are retained, the exact answer to the query is obtained.

If less than k objects are found during the search in the first bucket, another strategy must be applied because the upper bound on the distance to the k-th nearest neighbor is unknown. The range search operation is once again executed, but the radius must be estimated. If enough objects are returned from the range query (at least k), the search is complete – the result is again the first k objects from the sorted result of the range search. Otherwise, the radius must be expanded and the search done again until enough objects are obtained. There are two possible strategies for estimating the radius: (1) the optimistic strategy, in which the number of distance computations is kept low but multiple incremental range searches might be performed in order to retrieve all necessary objects, and (2) the pessimistic strategy, which prefers bigger range radii at the expense of additional distance computations.

Optimistic strategy. The objective is to minimize the costs, i.e., the number of buckets accessed and distance computations carried out, using a smallish radius, at the risk of more iterations being necessary if not enough objects are found. In the first iteration, the bounding radius of the candidates is used, i.e., the distance to the last candidate, even though there are fewer than k candidates. The optimistic strategy hopes that there will be enough objects in the other buckets within this radius. Let x be the number of objects returned from the last range query. If $x \geq k$, the search is finished, because the result is guaranteed, otherwise, the radius is expanded by factor $1 + \frac{k-x}{k}$ and the algorithm iterates again. The higher the number of missing objects, the more the radius is enlarged.

Pessimistic strategy. The estimated radius is chosen rather large so that the probability of a next iteration is minimized, while risking excessive (though parallel) bucket accesses and distance computations. To estimate the radius, the distance between pivots of inner nodes is used, because the algorithm presumes pivots are very distant. More specifically, the pessimistic strategy traverses the AST from the leaf up to the tree root, using the distance between pivots of the current node as the range radius. Every iteration climbs up one level in the AST until the search terminates or the root is encountered. If there are still not enough objects retrieved, the maximum distance of the metric is used and all objects in the structure are examined.

3.7   Deletions and Updates of Objects

For simplicity reasons, the updates are not handled specifically. Instead, if the algorithm needs to update an object, it first deletes the previous instance of this object and inserts the new one.

The deletion of an object o takes place in two phases. First, a search is made for a particular peer and a bucket containing the object being deleted. The insert traversal algorithm is used for this. More specifically, the algorithm searches for the leaf node in the AST containing the BID pointer b, where object o would be inserted.

The bucket b is sought to determine whether the object is really there. If not, the algorithm finishes, because the object is not present in the structure. Otherwise, the object is removed from the bucket b.

At this point, an object has been removed from the structure. However, if many objects are removed from buckets, the overall load of the GHT* structure would degrade. Many nearly-empty buckets would also worsen efficiency at the whole-system level. Therefore, an algorithm is provided to merge two buckets into one in order to increase the load factor of the bucket.

First, the algorithm must detect (after a deletion) that the bucket has become underfilled and needs to be merged. This can be easily implemented by, e.g., a minimal-load threshold for a bucket. Let N_b be the leaf node representing

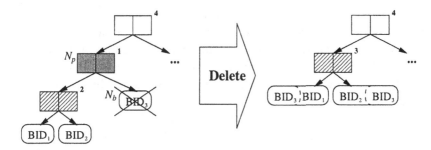

Figure 5.4. Removing a bucket pointer from the AST.

the pointer to the underfilled bucket b. A bucket to merge with the underfilled bucket must be found. The algorithm, as a rule, always merges the right bucket with the left one, because after a split the original bucket stays in the left and the new one goes to the right.

Let N_p be the parent inner node of the node N_b. If the node N_b is a right sub-node of the node N_p, then the algorithm reinserts all the objects from the underfilled bucket to the left subtree of node N_p and removes node N_p from the AST, shrinking the path from the root. Similarly, if N_b is a left sub-node, all the objects from the right branch are taken and reinserted into the left branch, and N_p is removed from the AST. Possible bucket overflows are handled as usual. To allow other peers to detect changes in the AST, the serial numbers of all inner nodes in the subtree with root N_p are incremented by one.

Figure 5.4 outlines the concept. We are removing the bucket BID_3, so first we reinsert the data to the left subtree of its parent (the shaded node). For every object in BID_3 we decide according to pivots in the left subtree (specifically, the hatch-marked node) whether to go to bucket BID_1 or bucket BID_2. Then we remove the leaf node with BID_3 and, preserving the binary tree, we also remove the parent node. One can also see that the serial numbers of the affected nodes are incremented.

3.8   Image Adjustment

An important advantage of the GHT* structure is update independence. During object insertion, a peer can split an overflowing bucket without informing other nodes in the network. Similarly, deletions may merge buckets. Consequently, peers need not have their ASTs up-to-date with respect to the data, but the advantage is that the network is not flooded with many "adjustment" messages for every update. AST updates are thus postponed and actually done when the respective insertion, deletion, or search operations are executed.

The inconsistency in the ASTs is recognized on a peer that receives an operation request with corresponding BPATH from another peer. In fact, if the

BPATH derived from the AST of the current peer is longer than the received BPATH, this indicates that the sending peer has an out-of-date version of the AST and must be updated. The other possibility is inconsistency between serial numbers in the BPATH and the inner nodes of the AST. The current peer easily determines a subtree that is missing or outdated on the sending peer because the root of this subtree is the last correct element of the received BPATH. Such a subtree is sent back to the peer through an *Image Adjustment Message*, IAM.

If multiple BPATHs are received by the current peer (which can occur in case of range queries) several subtrees can be sent back through one IAM (including all found inconsistencies). Naturally, the IAM process can also involve multiple peers. Whenever a peer finds an NNID in its AST leaf during the path expansion, the request must be forwarded to the located peer. This peer can also detect an inconsistency and respond with an IAM. This image adjustment message updates the ASTs of all previous peers, including the first peer starting the operation. This is a recursive procedure which guarantees that, for an insertion, deletion or a search operation, every involved peer is correctly updated.

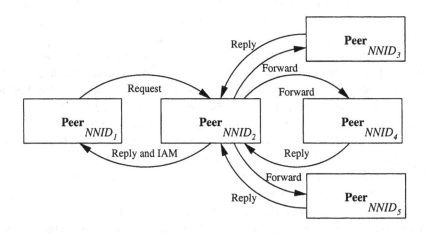

Figure 5.5. Message passing during a query and image adjustments.

An example of a communication during a query execution is given by Figure 5.5. At the beginning, the peer with $NNID_1$ starts to evaluate a query. According to its local AST the query must be forwarded to peer $NNID_2$. However, this peer detects that the BPATHs from the forwarded request are not complete – i.e., using local AST of peer $NNID_2$ the BPATHs are extended and new leaf nodes with $NNID_3$, $NNID_4$, and $NNID_5$ are reached. Therefore, the request is forwarded to those peers and processed there. The peers were contacted by $NNID_2$, so they respond with the query results back to peer $NNID_2$. Finally, peer $NNID_2$ passes the responses to peer $NNID_1$ as the final result-set along with image adjustment, which is represented by the respective subtrees of the local AST of the peer $NNID_2$.

3.9   Logarithmic Replication Strategy

As explained previously, every inner node of the AST contains two pivots and the AST structure is present in a more or less accurate form on every peer. Therefore, the number of replicated pivots increases linearly with the number of peers used. In order to reduce replication, the authors propose a more economical strategy which achieves logarithmic replication among peers at the cost of a moderately increased number of forwarded requests.

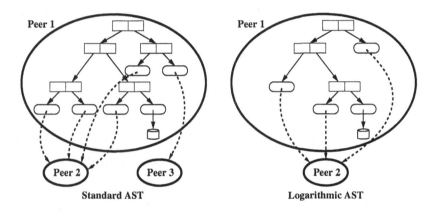

Figure 5.6. Example of the logarithmic AST.

Inspired by the *lazy updates* strategy by [Johnson and Krishna, 1993], the logarithmic replication scheme uses a slightly modified AST containing only the necessary number of inner nodes. More precisely, the AST on a specific peer stores only those nodes containing pointers to local buckets (i.e., leaf nodes with BID pointers) and all their ancestors. However, the resulting AST is still a binary tree which substitutes all subtrees leading exclusively to leaf nodes with NNID pointers by the leftmost leaf node of the subtree. The rationale for choosing the leftmost leaf node derives from the split strategy, which always retains the left node and adds the right one. Figure 5.6 illustrates this principle. In a way, the logarithmic AST can be seen as the minimum subtree of the fully updated AST. The search operation with the logarithmic replication scheme may require more forwarding (compared to the full replication scheme), but replication is significantly reduced.

3.10   Joining the Peer-to-Peer Network

The GHT* scales-up to process a large volume of data by utilizing more and more peers. In principle, such an extension can be solved in several ways. In the GRID infrastructure, for example, new peers are added by standard commands. In the prototype implementation, authors use a pool of available peers known to every active peer. They do not use a centralized registering service. Instead, they exploit *broadcast messaging* to notify active peers about a new peer that has become available. When a new network node becomes available, the following actions occur:

- The new node with its NNID sends a broadcast message saying "I am here". This message is received by each active peer in the network.

- The receiving peers add the announced NNID to their local pool of available peers.

Additional storage and computational resources required by an active peer are extended as follows:

- The active peer picks up one item from the pool of available peers. An activation message is sent to the chosen peer.

- With another broadcast message, the chosen peer announces: "I am being used now" so that other active peers can remove its NNID from their pools of available peers.

- The chosen peer initializes its own pool of available peers, creates a copy of the AST, and sends the caller the "Ready to serve" reply message.

The algorithm is illustrated in Figure 5.7, where the numbers represent the messages sent in the order they appear. The white computer is a new peer that has just joined the network. It announces its presence by an "I am here" message (1) delivered to all other active peers. Then an active overloaded peer (at top left) needs a new peer. It contacts the white peer in order to activate it (2). The white peer broadcasts "I am being used now" to all others (3) and responds with "Ready to serve" to the first peer (4).

If a peer does not want to be activated, it might respond to the first message immediately saying that it is not available any more. The requesting peer then removes it from its pool and continues with the next one.

3.11   Leaving the Peer-to-Peer Network

As stated in Section 1.2.2, peers may want to leave the network. The proposed technique does not deal with the unexpected exit of peers which may occur due to the unreliability in the network, operating system crashes among peers, etc. To recover from such situations, replication and fault tolerance mechanisms are

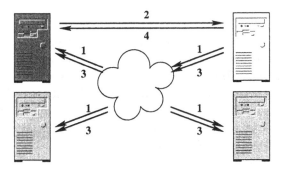

Figure 5.7. New peer allocation using broadcast messages.

required to preserve data even if part of the system goes down unexpectedly. However, this is stated by the authors of the GHT* to be a future research challenge and has not yet been addressed. Therefore, if a peer wants to leave the network, it must perform a clean-up first.

There are two kinds of peers – peers which store some data in their local buckets and peers which do not. Those which do not provide use of their storage may leave the system safely without causing problems and need not inform the others. However, peers which hold data must first ensure that data is not lost. In general, such a peer uses the deletion mechanism and reinserts the data again, but without offering its storage capacity to the network any longer. The peer thus gets rid of all its objects and does not receive new ones.

4.   Performance Trials

In this section, we report on our experience with the distributed index GHT* using the prototype implementation provided by its authors. This section further expands upon Section 3 of Chapter 3, where we have provided some experimental results for centralized disk-based structures. To obtain experimental results comparable to those of centralized structures, we have used the same datasets and provide total costs incurred by similarity queries in GHT* in Section 4.2.1. In Section 4.2.2, we show the enhancement of distributed computing, i.e., the parallel costs, which represent the actual response time of the search system. In both sections, we show results of range and nearest neighbors queries, which are then compared with each other in Section 4.2.3.

The final group of experiments concentrates on the scalability aspects of the GHT*. The point we would most like to emphasize in this section is that, even with a huge and permanently growing dataset, the index distributed on sufficient number of peers is able to maintain practically constant response times to similarity queries.

4.1   Datasets and Computing Infrastructure

We conducted our experiments using two real-life datasets. The first was a dataset of 45-dimensional vectors of color image features (labeled VEC) compared via the quadratic form distance function. The second dataset consisted of sentences from the Czech language corpus (labeled STR), with the edit distance function used to quantify sentence proximity. Both datasets contained 100,000 objects, vectors or sentences, respectively. Further details about these datasets can be found in Section 3 of Chapter 3.

We used a local network of 100 workstations, which are publicly available for students. The computers are connected by a high-speed 100Mbit switched network with access times approximately 5ms. Since the computers have enough memory, we used the simplest setting of the GHT* implementation, in which the buckets are implemented as unordered lists of objects stored in RAM. However, more advanced settings are possible, such as organizing the buckets by a centralized index, for example the M-tree or D-index, storing data on disks. Such schemas would additionally extend the efficiency of the distributed index, but would also further complicate the evaluation of results and the comparison with centralized indexes.

To achieve deterministic and reliable experimental results, we used the logarithmic replication schema for all participating peers. We also used a constant number of buckets per peer and the same capacity for all buckets. Specifically, every peer was capable of holding up to five buckets with a maximum 1,000 objects per bucket.

The computers were not exclusively dedicated to our performance trials. In such an environment, it is practically impossible to maintain identical behavior for each participating computer, and the speed and actual response times of the computers may vary depending on their actual computational load. Therefore we do not report absolute response times but rather the number of distance computations to characterize CPU costs, the number of buckets accessed for I/O costs, and the number of messages sent to indicate network communication costs.

4.2   Performance of Similarity Queries

In order to study the performance of the GHT* for changing queries, we have measured the costs of range and nearest neighbors queries for different sizes of query radii and different numbers of neighbors, respectively. All inputs for graphs in this section were obtained by averaging the results of fifty queries with a different set of (randomly chosen) query objects and constant search radius or number of neighbors, respectively.

4.2.1 Global Costs

A distributed structure uses the power of networked computers to speed up query evaluation by parallel execution. However, every participating peer must employ its resources and that naturally incurs some costs. In this section, we provide the total costs needed to evaluate a query, i.e., the sum of costs for each peer employed during the query execution.

In general, total costs are directly comparable to those of centralized indexes, because these represent the costs the distributed structure would need if run on a single computer. Of course, there are some additional costs due to the distributed nature of the algorithms. In particular, a centralized structure incurs no network communication costs.

Buckets Accessed (I/O costs). The first experiment focused on relationships between query size and total number of buckets and peers accessed. For different radii of range queries, Figure 5.8 reports these results separately for the VEC and STR datasets together with the number of retrieved objects (divided by 100 for easier exposition). If the radius increases, the number of peers accessed grows practically linearly, the number of accessed buckets a bit faster. However, the number of retrieved objects satisfying the query, i.e., the result-set size, may grow exponentially. In general, this is in accordance with the I/O behavior of centralized metric indexes such as the M-tree or the D-index on the global (not distributed) scale.

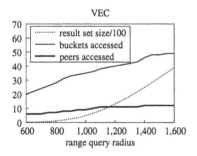
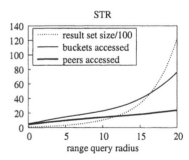

Figure 5.8. Average number of buckets, peers, and objects retrieved as a function of radius.

We have also measured these characteristics for kNN queries, and the results are shown in Figure 5.9. We again report the number of buckets and peers accessed with respect to the increasing value of k. As should be clear, the value k also represents the number of objects retrieved. These trials once again reveal a behavior similar to centralized indexes – total costs are low for small values of k, but grow very rapidly as the number of neighbors increases.

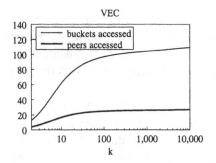
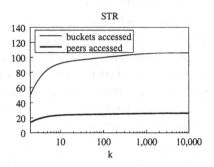

Figure 5.9. Average number of buckets, peers, and objects retrieved as a function of k.

Distance Computations (CPU costs). In the following experiments, we have concentrated on the total cost of the similarity queries measured by the number of distance computations. Specifically, Figure 5.10 shows the results for increasing radii of range queries. The total cost is the sum of all distance computations performed by every accessed peer in accessed buckets plus "navigation" costs. The navigation cost is measured in terms of distance computations in the AST (shown as a separate line). Since these costs are well below 1%, they can be neglected for practical purposes. Observe that total costs have once again been divided by 100.

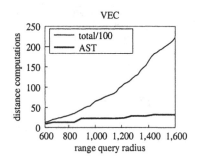
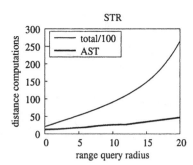

Figure 5.10. Total and AST distance computations as a function of radius.

In Figure 5.11, we show total distance computation costs of kNN queries for different values of k. The results were obtained similarly as for range queries, and for convenience we provide the AST computations as well. It can be seen that, even for the computationally more expensive nearest neighbors queries, AST navigation costs are only marginal and can be neglected.

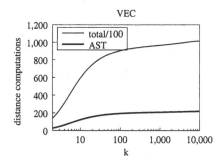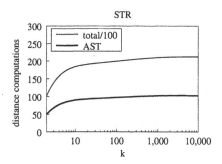

Figure 5.11. Total and AST distance computations as a function of k.

Compared to centralized indexes, the GHT* performs better than the sequential scan, but the M-tree and D-index achieve better results. However, the GHT* can perform distance computations in parallel, which is the main advantage of the distributed index. We elaborate on this issue in the next section.

Messages Sent (communication cost). Algorithms for the evaluation of similarity queries in GHT* send messages whenever they need to access other peers. More specifically, if an NNID pointer for the peer is encountered in a leaf node during evaluation, a message is sent to that peer. These are termed request messages. Messages destined for the same peer are sent together within one message. Figures 5.12 and 5.13 depict the total number of request messages sent by peers involved in a range and kNN search, respectively. We have also measured the number of messages that had to be forwarded because of improper addressing. This situation occurs when a request message arrives at a peer that does not evaluate the query in its local buckets and only passes (forwards) the message to a more appropriate peer. This cost is a little higher for the kNN algorithm because its first phase needs to navigate to the proper bucket first.

Intuitively, the total number of (request) messages is strictly related to the number of peers accessed. This fact is confirmed by trials using both range and nearest neighbors queries. We have also observed that, even with the logarithmic replication strategy, the average number of messages forwarded is below 15% of the total number of messages sent during query execution. The process of sending messages is specific to a distributed environment and therefore has no adequate counterpart in centralized structures.

4.2.2 Parallel Costs

The objective of this section is to report results using the distributed structure GHT*, with an emphasis on parallel costs. As opposed to the total costs, these

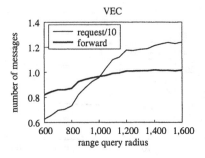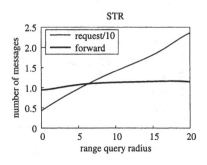

Figure 5.12. Average number of request and forward messages as a function of the radius.

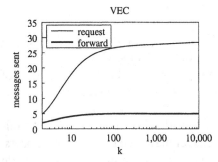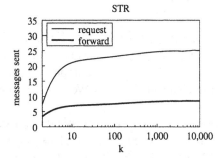

Figure 5.13. Average number of request and forward messages as a function of the k.

correspond to the actual response time of the GHT* index structure to execute similarity queries.

For our purposes, we define the parallel cost as the maximum of the serial costs from all accessed peers. For example, to measure a parallel distance computations cost during a range query, we gather the number of distance computations on each peer accessed during the query. The maximum of those values is the query's parallel cost, since the range query evaluation has practically no serial component (except for the search in the AST on the first peer, which is very low-cost and so can be neglected).

A different situation occurs during the execution of kNN queries, because the kNN search algorithm consists of two phases, which cannot be performed simultaneously. The parallel cost is therefore the sum of the parallel costs of the respective phases. As explained in Section 3.6, the first phase navigates to a single bucket seeking candidates for neighbors. The second phase consists of a range query, for which we have already defined the parallel cost. However, the second phase can be repeated when the number of objects retrieved is still smaller than k. Finally, the parallel cost of a nearest neighbors query is the sum of the cost of the first phase plus the parallel costs of every needed second phase.

Buckets Accessed (I/O costs). The parallel costs for range queries, measured as the maximal number of accessed buckets per peer, are summarized in Figure 5.14. Since the number of buckets per peer is bounded – our trials employed maximally five buckets per peer – the parallel cost remains stable at around 4.3 buckets per peer. For this reason, the parallel range query cost scales well with increasing query radius.

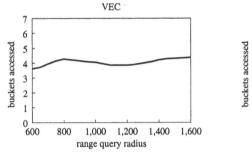 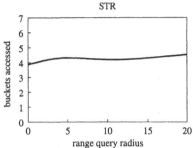

Figure 5.14. Parallel cost in accessed buckets as a function of radius.

A nearest neighbors query always requires one bucket access for the first phase. Then multiple second phases may be required and their costs are added to the resulting parallel cost. Figure 5.15 shows these results, with the number of iterations in the second phase of the algorithm represented by the lower curve. It can be seen that, for smaller values of k, only one iteration is needed and the cost is somewhere around the value 5.4, consisting of 1.0 for the initial bucket and 4.4 for the range query. As the value of k grows above the number of objects in one bucket, more iterations are needed. Obviously, each additional iteration represents a serial step of query execution, so the cost slightly increases, but the increase is not doubled, because the algorithm never accesses buckets which have already been processed. In any case, the number of iterations is not high and in our experiments maximally two iterations were always sufficient.

Distance Computations (CPU costs). Parallel distance computations represented the major query execution cost in our trials, and can be considered an accurate approximation to actual query response time. This is mainly thanks to the fact that the time to access buckets and send messages is practically negligible compared to the evaluation of used distance metric functions. Recall

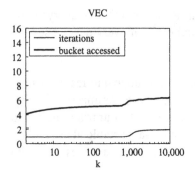
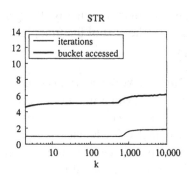

Figure 5.15. Parallel cost in accessed buckets with the number of iterations as a function of k.

that the computations of edit distance and quadratic form metric functions are very time demanding – accessing a bucket in local memory costs microseconds, while network communications can be achieved in tens of milliseconds.

We have applied a standard methodology: We have measured the number of distance computations evaluated by each peer, and taken as the reported cost the maximum of these values. Figure 5.16 shows results averaged for the same set of fifty randomly chosen query objects and a specific radius. Since the number of objects stored per peer is bounded (maximum five buckets per peer and 1,000 objects per bucket), the cost would never exceed this value. Recall that we do not consider AST costs, which are of no practical significance. Thus the structure retains an essentially constant response time for any size of query radius.

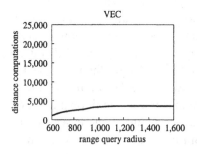
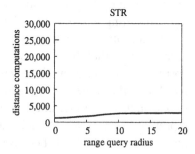

Figure 5.16. Parallel cost in distance computations as a function of radius.

The situation is similar for kNN queries but the sequential components of the search algorithm must be properly considered. The results are shown in Figure 5.17 and represent the parallel costs for different numbers of neighbors k, measured in terms of distance computations. It can be seen that costs grow very quickly to a value of around 5,000 distance computations. This value represents the parallel cost of the range query plus the initial search for the first bucket. Some increase in distance computations with k around 800 can also be seen. This is caused by the added sequential phase of the algorithm, i.e., the next iteration. The increase is not dramatic, since only some additional buckets are searched to amend the result-set to k objects. This is in accordance with the buckets accessed in parallel shown in Figure 5.14. It can be seen there that only one additional "parallel" bucket was searched during the second iteration, thus the increase in parallel distance computations may be maximally 1,000 (the capacity of a bucket).

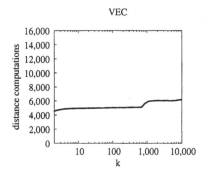
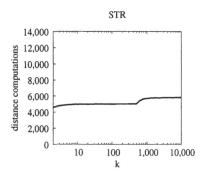

Figure 5.17. Parallel cost in distance computations as a function of k.

Messages Sent (communication cost). Parallel communication cost is a bit different from previous cases, since we cannot compute it "per peer". During the evaluation of a query, every peer can send messages to several other peers, but we can consider the cost of sending several messages to different peers equal to the cost of sending only one message to a specific peer, since a peer sends them all at once. Thus, the parallel communication cost consists of a chain of forwarded messages, the sequential passing of the request to other peers. The number of peers sequentially contacted during a search, is usually called the *hop count*. In the GHT* algorithm, there can be several different "hop" paths. For our purposes, we have taken the longest hop path, i.e., the path with maximal hop count, as the parallel communication cost.

Figures 5.18 and 5.19 present the number of hops during a range and kNN search, respectively. Our experimental trials show parallel communication is essentially logarithmically proportional to the number of peers accessed (see Figure 5.8), a desirable property in any distributed structure. The time spent communicating can also be deduced from these graphs. However, it is hard to see the contribution of this cost to the overall response time of a query, since each peer first traverses its AST and forwards messages to the respective peers (if needed), and only then it begins to compute distances inside its buckets. So the communication time is only added to the time spent computing the distances in peers contacted subsequently, but these can have only a few objects in their buckets. In this case, the overall response time is practically unaffected by communication costs.

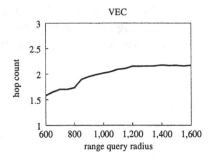
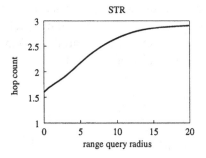

Figure 5.18. Number of parallel messages as a function of radius.

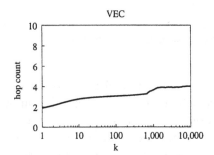
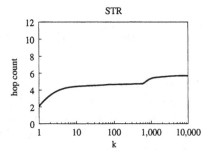

Figure 5.19. Number of parallel messages as a function of k.

4.2.3   Comparison of Search Algorithms

In principle, the nearest neighbors search can be solved by a range query, provided a specific radius is known. After a kNN query has been solved, it becomes trivial to execute the corresponding range query with a precisely measured radius, i.e., using the distance from the query object to the k-th retrieved object. However, such radius is generally unknown, so kNN queries are typically more expensive. We have compared the costs in terms of distance computations of the original nearest neighbors query execution with the costs of the respective range query with exact radius. In what follows, we provide both the parallel and total costs measured according to the methodology used throughout this section.

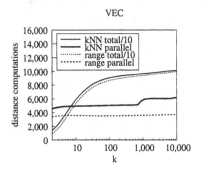
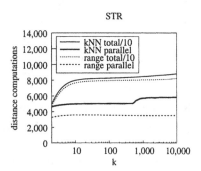

Figure 5.20. Comparison of a kNN and range query returning k objects as a function of k.

The trials show kNN query execution costs are always slightly higher than those of a comparable range query execution. In particular, total costs are practically equal to those of the range query, mainly because the kNN algorithm never accesses the same bucket twice. The difference is caused by the fact that the estimated radius need not be optimal. A different situation can be observed for parallel costs, since the kNN search needs some sequential execution steps, thus diminishing the possibility for parallel execution. In Figure 5.20, the effects of accessing the first bucket during the first phase of the kNN algorithm can be clearly seen in the difference between the range and kNN parallel cost lines in the graphs. The costs of the second iteration become visible after $k > 800$, which further worsens the parallel response time of the nearest neighbors query. However, the parallel response time is still comparable to that of the range query. It is practically stable and does not grow markedly.

4.3   Data Volume Scalability

In this section, we detail our tests of scalability of the GHT*, i.e., the ability to adapt to expanding datasets. To measure this experimentally, we have fixed the query parameters by choosing two distinct query radii and three different values for nearest neighbors k. The same set of fifty randomly chosen query objects was employed during the experiment, with the graphs depicting average values. Moreover, we have gradually expanded the original dataset to 1,000,000 objects. The following results were obtained as measures at particular stages of incremental insertion. More specifically, we have measured *intraquery* and *interquery* parallelism costs after every block of 2,000 inserted objects.

We quantify the intraquery parallelism cost as the parallel response of a query measured in terms of distance computations. This is defined to be the maximum

of costs incurred on peers involved in the query, including navigation costs in
the AST. Specifically, each accessed peer computes its internal cost as the sum
of the computations in its local AST, and the computations in its buckets visited
during the evaluation. The intraquery cost is then determined as the maximum
of the internal costs of all peers accessed during the evaluation.

Interquery parallelism is more difficult to quantify. To simplify it, we characterize the interquery parallelism as the ratio of the number of peers involved
in a query to the total number of peers. In this way, we assume that the lower
the ratio, the higher the chances for other queries to be executed in parallel.
Naturally, such an assumption is valid only if each peer is used with equal
probability. In summary, the intraquery parallelism is proportional to the response time of a query, while the interquery parallelism represents the relative
utilization of available computing resources.

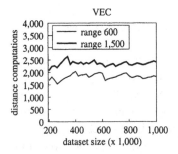 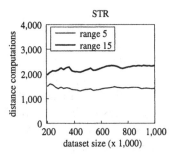

Figure 5.21. Parallel cost as a function of dataset size for two different radii.

The results summarized in Figure 5.21 show intraquery parallelism remains
very stable, independently of dataset size. Thus the parallel search time, which
is proportional to this cost, remains practically constant, which is to be expected
from the fact that storage and computing resources are added gradually as the
size of the dataset grows. Of course, the number of distance computations
needed for traversing the AST grows with the size of the dataset. However, this
contribution is not visible. The reason is that AST growth is logarithmic, while
peer expansion is linear.

The nearest neighbors results shown in Figure 5.22 exhibit similar behavior,
only the absolute cost is a bit higher. This is incurred by the sequential steps of
the nearest neighbors search algorithm, consisting of locating the first bucket,
followed by possibly multiple sequential iterations. However, the cost is still
nearly constant, thus the query response remains unchanged even if the file
grows in size.

By contrast, the ratio shown in Figure 5.23 characterizing interquery parallelism actually decreases as the dataset grows in size. This means the number
of peers involved during the query grows much more slowly than the number of

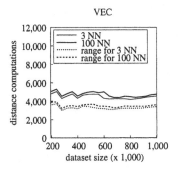

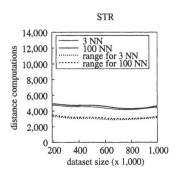

Figure 5.22. Parallel cost as a function of dataset size for three different k.

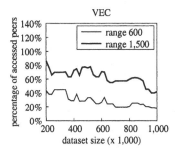

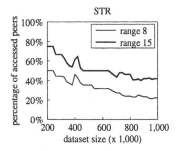

Figure 5.23. Percentage of peers used as a function of dataset size for two different radii.

active peers, and thus the percentage of peers used to evaluate the query drops. For example, with 1,000,000 objects inserted in the structure, only 21% of all active peers were accessed in order to satisfy the query with the smaller radius. This also means that, assuming an equal distribution of accessed peers, there can be almost five totally independent queries solved on peers at the same time. In other words, compared to the centralized solution, nearly five independent queries are solved simultaneously with a response time identical to one such query. Of course, this situation represents the ideal. But assuming a heavily loaded system (one with a huge amount of queries executed), the response of a particular query will not degrade as much as for a centralized structure, which executes queries in a strictly serial way.

Concluding Summary

There is no doubt that the proliferation of new data types will lead to dramatic change or the significant extension of a fundamental data processing paradigm, that of search. It seems certain that the binary "YES" or "NO" classification for retrieved versus undesired data will be replaced by an approximate assessment of relevance. This naturally implies a sort of ranking with respect to a user-defined reference, model, or other idealized specification of the data desired. Though other possibilities are expected in the future, such a search paradigm is typically fulfilled by similarity search.

Traditionally, search has been applied to structured (attribute-type) data yielding records that exactly match the query. A more modern type of search, similarity search, is used in content-based retrieval for queries involving complex data types such as images, videos, time series, text documents and DNA sequences. Similarity search is based on approximate rather than exact relevance using a distance metric that, together with the database, forms a mathematical metric space. The obvious advantage of similarity search is that the results can be ranked according to their estimated relevance. But currently prevalent centralized similarity search mechanisms are time-consuming and not scalable, thus only suitable for relatively small data collections.

Google-like Web search engines are based on specialized search mechanisms for text documents and for HTML pages. Since less than 1% of Web data is in text form, the rest being of a multimedia/streaming nature, the next-generation of search needs to be expanded to accommodate these heterogeneous data types, also taking into account datastreams produced by data sensors, the mobility of data resources, as well as the variety of formats in which data may appear. It is believed that the diversity and uncertainty of terminologies and schema-like annotations will make precise querying on a Web scale elusive if not hopeless, and that the same argument holds for large-scale networks of intra- and inter-organizational data sources. As a consequence, traditional query processing and search technology need to be supported by a powerful distributed computing platform that will empower the next-generation relevance-ranked similarity search methods.

It is estimated that 93% of data produced today is in digital format, and the amount of data added each year is more than an exabyte (i.e. 10^{18} bytes). This is due in part to people and organizations collecting more data, e.g., digital photographs, and making the data more accessible. It is also caused by new technologies like peer-to-peer networks offering and exchanging huge volumes of (mostly) multimedia data which already make up the majority of network traffic on the Internet. The problem is visible not only on the World Wide Web, but also in large data-producing organizations. The trend is toward a small and shrinking subset of corporate information managed in database management systems (10 to 15% today), with more and more relevant information existing outside corporate databases. This trend is inevitable, due to the decentralization and personalization of control and data. Examples include: office documents, legal papers, technical references, regulations, marketing material, customer relationship information, scientific and statistical data collections, biological data, streams of volatile data from sensor networks, news tickers, video tapes, telephone recordings, e-mail etc. An effective search solution to cope with this exponential growth and diversity of data sources must consider two related issues:

effectiveness - formulating (dis)similarity or proximity paradigms, and

efficiency - achieving the required performance over huge volumes of data.

The effectiveness of next-generation search requires new query techniques that deal with inexact matching and heterogeneous data forms. The efficiency of search requires innovative ideas about how to arrange and adjust computation power, storage, and network resources to meet the requirements set by the queries in a given context.

In this book, we have summarized the latest efforts in similarity searching using metric space as a suitable theoretical abstraction. We have demonstrated the extensibility of this approach by examples of various distance measures, which can be defined for virtually any application. We have specified theoretical constraints that can be applied for partitioning metric data into subsets, with the aim of achieving efficient pruning during similarity query execution. Partitioning principles lead to the formation of hierarchical (e.g. tree-like) index structures. Building on such a hypothetical structure, we have explained related theoretical research achievements to support efficient query processing, performance prediction, and similarity search application through the transformation of metric measures. Many similarity search index structures have been reported in an extensive survey including corresponding search algorithms. Whenever possible, specific ideas have been contrasted with theoretical essentials. In greater detail, we have described disk-oriented search structures, demonstrated how the notion of approximation can significantly speed up retrieval, and reported on the latest parallel and distributed efforts to cope with the problem of scalability.

In the future, finding a scalable solution to the search problem for large-scale distributed heterogeneous data will constitute an important scientific and technological breakthrough, overcoming the scalability limitations of present solutions and today's research perspectives. It will have a big economic impact, since it can generate technology for the next generation of integrated and multipurpose search and query processing engines on the scale of the Web as well as for intranet-scale information management infrastructures.

Searching for the most relevant data is essential, not only for personal use, but also for applications like e-science, e-business, e-health, catastrophe management, and many others. These new application domains require the relevance of specific searches to be determined autonomously to avoid information overload with false results. Furthermore, these application domains require new search strategies for automatically searching multimedia data. Traditional centralized search structures, as employed by today's search machines, will require radical redesign and re-engineering to address these issues.

The biggest challenge for the search paradigm is to find self-organizing solutions that evolve over time and still scale into the expected data volume quantities. Such an initiative must be based on solid theoretical grounds to avoid a quick but ad hoc solutions; these will sooner or later fail because their definitions lack rigor, and because their behavior is unpredictable. The research should certainly go beyond the capabilities of the traditional computer science. It should try to find inspiration in other areas, such as the social sciences, biology, or mathematical theories of epidemic diseases.

Future pervasive computing and communication systems represent a big challenge for the new kinds of searching. But at the same time, they offer a great opportunity to find a successful solution. With the massive deployment of computational resources, we need solutions which will fully exploit available computational power, which very often lies idle or partly utilized. Such an environment nevertheless not only provides a framework for scalability, it also offers a possibility for performance tuning and customization for communities of users.

In order to successfully replace or enhance still-predominant exact-match search mechanisms, future solutions should be general-purpose and highly extensible. Only in this way will they be able to serve the vast collective of potential users from different applications. Though a strong emphasis should be placed upon theories and formal definitions, all hypotheses must be diligently verified by extensive trials on the road to becoming candidates for successful products.

References

[Aberer and Hauswirth, 2002] Aberer, K. and Hauswirth, M. (2002). An overview of Peer-to-Peer information systems. In Litwin, W. and Lévy, G., editors, *Distributed Data & Structures 4, Records of the 4th International Meeting (WDAS 2002), Paris, France, March 20-23, 2002,* volume 14 of *Proceedings in Informatics,* pages 171–188. Carleton Scientific.

[Alpkocak et al., 2002] Alpkocak, A., Danisman, T., and Ulker, T. (2002). A parallel similarity search in high dimensional metric space using M-Tree. In Grigoras, D., Nicolau, A., Toursel, B., and Folliot, B., editors, *Proceedings of the NATO Advanced Research Workshop on Advanced Environments, Tools, and Applications for Cluster Computing-Revised Papers (IWCC 2001), Mangalia, Romania, September 1-6, 2001,* volume 2326 of *Lecture Notes in Computer Science,* pages 166–171. Springer.

[Alt et al., 1991] Alt, H., Behrends, B., and Blömer, J. (1991). Approximate matching of polygonal shapes (extended abstract). In *Proceedings of the 7th Annual Symposium on Computational Geometry (SCG 1991),* pages 186–193. ACM Press.

[Amato, 2002] Amato, G. (2002). *Approximate similarity search in metric spaces.* PhD thesis, Computer Science Department - University of Dortmund, August-Schmidt-Str. 12, 44221, Dortmund, Germany. http://pc-erato2.iei.pi.cnr.it/amato/thesis/.

[Amato et al., 2003] Amato, G., Rabitti, F., Savino, P., and Zezula, P. (2003). Region proximity in metric spaces and its use for approximate similarity search. *ACM Transactions on Information Systems (TOIS 2003),* 21(2):192–227. ACM Press.

[Apostolico and Galil, 1997] Apostolico, A. and Galil, Z. (1997). *Pattern Matching Algorithms.* Oxford University Press.

[Arya et al., 1998] Arya, S., Mount, D. M., Netanyahu, N. S., Silverman, R., and Wu, A. Y. (1998). An optimal algorithm for approximate nearest neighbor searching in fixed dimensions. *Journal of ACM (JACM 1998),* 45(6):891–923. ACM Press.

[Aurenhammer, 1991] Aurenhammer, F. (1991). Voronoi diagrams - a survey of a fundamental geometric data structure. *ACM Computing Surveys (CSUR 1991),* 23(3):345–405. ACM Press.

[Baeza-Yates, 1997] Baeza-Yates, R. A. (1997). Searching: an algorithmic tour. In Kent, A. and Williams, J. G., editors, *Encyclopedia of Computer Science and Technology*, volume 37, pages 331–359. Marcel Dekker, Inc.

[Baeza-Yates et al., 1994] Baeza-Yates, R. A., Cunto, W., Manber, U., and Wu, S. (1994). Proximity matching using fixed-queries trees. In Crochemore, M. and Gusfield, D., editors, *Proceedings of the 5th Annual Symposium on Combinatorial Pattern Matching (CPM 1994), Asilomar, California, USA, June 5-8, 1994*, volume 807 of *Lecture Notes in Computer Science*, pages 198–212. Springer, Berlin.

[Baeza-Yates and Navarro, 1998] Baeza-Yates, R. A. and Navarro, G. (1998). Fast approximate string matching in a dictionary. In *Proceedings of the 5th International Symposium on String Processing and Information Retrieval (SPIRE 1998), Santa Cruz, Bolivia, September 9-11, 1998*, pages 14–22. IEEE Computer Society.

[Barbará et al., 1997] Barbará, D., DuMouchel, W., Faloutsos, C., Haas, P. J., Hellerstein, J. M., Ioannidis, Y. E., Jagadish, H. V., Johnson, T., Ng, R. T., Poosala, V., Ross, K. A., and Sevcik, K. C. (1997). The new jersey data reduction report. *IEEE Data Engineering Bulletin*, 20(4):3–45. IEEE Computer Society.

[Batko et al., 2004] Batko, M., Gennaro, C., Savino, P., and Zezula, P. (2004). Scalable similarity search in metric spaces. In *Proceedings of the 6th Thematic Workshop of the EU Network of Excellence DELOS on Digital Library Architectures, Cagliari, Italy, 24-25 June, 2004*, pages 213–224. Edizioni Libreria Progetto, Padova.

[Beckmann et al., 1990] Beckmann, N., Kriegel, H.-P., Schneider, R., and Seeger, B. (1990). The R*-Tree: An efficient and robust access method for points and rectangles. In Garcia-Molina, H. and Jagadish, H. V., editors, *Proceedings of the ACM International Conference on Management of Data (SIGMOD 1990), Atlantic City, NJ, May 23-25, 1990*, pages 322–331. ACM Press.

[Berchtold et al., 1997] Berchtold, S., Keim, D. A., and Kriegel, H.-P. (1997). A cost model for nearest neighbor search in high-dimensional data space. In *Proceedings of the 16th ACM Symposium on Principles of Database Systems (PODS 1997), Tucson, Arizona, USA, May 12-14, 1997*, pages 78–96. ACM Press.

[Bern et al., 1993] Bern, M. W., Eppstein, D., and Teng, S.-H. (1993). Parallel construction of quadtrees and quality triangulations. In Dehne, F. K. H. A., Sack, J.-R., Santoro, N., and Whitesides, S., editors, *Proceedings of the 3rd Algorithms and Data Structures (WADS 1993), Montréal, Canada, August 11-13, 1997*, volume 709 of *Lecture Notes in Computer Science*, pages 188–199. Springer.

[Bespamyatnikh, 1995] Bespamyatnikh, S. (1995). An optimal algorithm for closest pair maintenance (extended abstract). In Peckham, J., editor, *Proceedings of the 11th ACM Symposium on Computational Geometry (SCG 1995), Vancouver, B.C., Canada, June 5-12, 1995*, pages 152–161. ACM Press.

[Böhm et al., 2001] Böhm, C., Berchtold, S., and Keim, D. A. (2001). Searching in high-dimensional spaces: Index structures for improving the performance of multimedia databases. *ACM Computing Surveys (CSUR 2001)*, 33(3):322–373. ACM Press.

[Bozkaya and Özsoyoglu, 1997] Bozkaya, T. and Özsoyoglu, Z. M. (1997). Distance-based indexing for high-dimensional metric spaces. In Peckham, J., editor, *Proceedings of the*

ACM International Conference on Management of Data (SIGMOD 1997), Tucson, Arizona, USA, May 13-15, 1997, pages 357–368. ACM Press.

[Bozkaya and Özsoyoglu, 1999] Bozkaya, T. and Özsoyoglu, Z. M. (1999). Indexing large metric spaces for similarity search queries. *ACM Transactions on Database Systems (TODS 1999)*, 24(3):361–404. ACM Press.

[Brin, 1995] Brin, S. (1995). Near neighbor search in large metric spaces. In Dayal, U., Gray, P. M. D., and Nishio, S., editors, *Proceedings of the 21th International Conference on Very Large Data Bases (VLDB 1995), Zurich, Switzerland, September 11-15, 1995*, pages 574–584. Morgan Kaufmann.

[Bugnion et al., 1993] Bugnion, E., Fhei, S., Roos, T., Widmayer, P., and Widmer, F. (1993). A spatial index for approximate multiple string matching. In Baeza-Yates, R. A. and Ziviani, N., editors, *Proceedings of the 1st South American Workshop on String Processing (WSP 1993), Belo Horizonte, Brazil, September 13-15, 1993*, pages 43–53.

[Burden et al., 1978] Burden, R., Faires, J. D., and Reynolds, A. (1978). *Numerical Analysis*. Prindle, Weber & Schmidt.

[Burkhard and Keller, 1973] Burkhard, W. A. and Keller, R. M. (1973). Some approaches to best-match file searching. *Communications of the ACM (CACM 1973)*, 16(4):230–236. ACM Press.

[Bustos et al., 2001] Bustos, B., Navarro, G., and Chávez, E. (2001). Pivot selection techniques for proximity searching in metric spaces. In *Proceedings of the 21st Conference of the Chilean Computer Science Society (SCCC 2001), Punta Arenas, Chile, November 6-8, 2001*, pages 33–40. IEEE Computer Society.

[Callahan and Kosaraju, 1995] Callahan, P. B. and Kosaraju, S. R. (1995). Algorithms for dynamic closest pair and n-body potential fields. In *Proceedings of the 6th ACM-SIAM Symposium on Discrete Algorithms (SODA 1995), San Francisco, California, January 22-24, 1995*, pages 263–272. ACM Press.

[Carreira-Perpinan, 1997] Carreira-Perpinan, M. A. (1997). A review of dimension reduction techniques. Technical Report CS–96–09, Department of Computer Science, University of Sheffield, UK.

[Castelman, 1996] Castelman, K. R. (1996). *Digital Image Processing*. Prentice-Hall, Inc.

[Cetintemel et al., 2000] Cetintemel, U., Franklin, M. J., and Giles, C. L. (2000). Self-adaptive user profiles for large-scale data delivery. In *Proceedings of the 16th International Conference on Data Engineering (ICDE 2000), San Diego, California, USA, February 28 - March 3, 2000*, pages 622–633. IEEE Computer Society.

[Chávez et al., 1999a] Chávez, E., Marroquín, J. L., and Baeza-Yates, R. A. (1999a). Spaghettis: An array based algorithm for similarity queries in metric spaces. In *Proceedings of the 6th International Symposium on String Processing and Information Retrieval & International Workshop on Groupware (SPIRE/CRIWG 1999), Cancun, Mexico, September 21-24, 1999*, pages 38–46. IEEE Computer Society.

[Chávez et al., 1999b] Chávez, E., Marroquín, J. L., and Navarro, G. (1999b). Overcoming the curse of dimensionality. In *Procedings of the European Workshop on Content-Based Multimedia Indexing (CBMI 1999), Toulouse, France, October 25-27, 1999*, pages 57–64.

[Chávez et al., 2001a] Chávez, E., Marroquín, J. L., and Navarro, G. (2001a). Fixed Queries Array: A fast and economical data structure for proximity searching. *Multimedia Tools and Applications*, 14(2):113–135. Kluwer Academic Publishers.

[Chávez et al., 2001b] Chávez, E., Navarro, G., Baeza-Yates, R. A., and Marroquín, J. L. (2001b). Searching in metric spaces. *ACM Computing Surveys (CSUR 2001)*, 33(3):273–321. ACM Press.

[Chiueh, 1994] Chiueh, T. (1994). Content-based image indexing. In Bocca, J. B., Jarke, M., and Zaniolo, C., editors, *Proceedings of the 20th International Conference on Very Large Data Bases (VLDB 1994), Santiago de Chile, Chile, September 12-15, 1994*, pages 582–593. Morgan Kaufmann.

[Chomicki, 2002] Chomicki, J. (2002). Querying with intrinsic preferences. In Jensen, C. S., Jeffery, K. G., Pokorný, J., Saltenis, S., Bertino, E., Böhm, K., and Jarke, M., editors, *Proceedings of the 8th International Conference on Extending Database Technology (EDBT 2002), Prague, Czech Republic, March 25-27, 2002*, volume 2287 of *Lecture Notes in Computer Science*, pages 34–51. Springer.

[Ciaccia et al., 2000] Ciaccia, P., Montesi, D., Penzo, W., and Trombetta, A. (2000). Imprecision and user preferences in multimedia queries: A generic algebraic approach. In *Proceedings of the 1st International Symposium on Foundations of Information and Knowledge Systems (FoIKS 2000), Burg, Germany, February 14-17, 2000*, volume 1762 of *Lecture Notes in Computer Science*, pages 50–71. Springer.

[Ciaccia et al., 1999] Ciaccia, P., Nanni, A., and Patella, M. (1999). A query-sensitive cost model for similarity queries with M-tree. In *Proceedings of the 10th Australasian Database Conference (ADC 1999), Auckland, New Zealand, January 18-21, 1999*, volume 21(2) of *Australian Computer Science Communications*, pages 65–76. Springer.

[Ciaccia and Patella, 1998] Ciaccia, P. and Patella, M. (1998). Bulk loading the M-tree. In *Proceedings of the 9th Australasian Database Conference (ADC 1998), Perth, Australia, February 2-3, 1998*, volume 20(2) of *Australian Computer Science Communications*, pages 15–26. Springer.

[Ciaccia and Patella, 2000a] Ciaccia, P. and Patella, M. (2000a). The M^2-tree: Processing complex multi-feature queries with just one index. In *Proceedings of the First DELOS Network of Excellence Workshop on Information Seeking, Searching and Querying in Digital Libraries, Zurich, Switzerland, December 11-12, 2000*.

[Ciaccia and Patella, 2000b] Ciaccia, P. and Patella, M. (2000b). PAC nearest neighbor queries: Approximate and controlled search in high-dimensional and metric spaces. In *Proceedings of the 16th International Conference on Data Engineering (ICDE 2000), San Diego, California, USA, February 28 - March 3, 2000*, pages 244–255. IEEE Computer Society.

[Ciaccia and Patella, 2002] Ciaccia, P. and Patella, M. (2002). Searching in metric spaces with user-defined and approximate distances. *ACM Transactions on Database Systems (TODS 2002)*, 27(4):398–437. ACM Press.

[Ciaccia et al., 1997a] Ciaccia, P., Patella, M., Rabitti, F., and Zezula, P. (1997a). *The M-tree Project*. Available at http://www-db.deis.unibo.it/Mtree/.

[Ciaccia et al., 1997b] Ciaccia, P., Patella, M., and Zezula, P. (1997b). M-tree: An efficient access method for similarity search in metric spaces. In Jarke, M., Carey, M. J., Dittrich,

K. R., Lochovsky, F. H., Loucopoulos, P., and Jeusfeld, M. A., editors, *Proceedings of the 23rd International Conference on Very Large Data Bases (VLDB 1997), Athens, Greece, August 25-29, 1997*, pages 426–435. Morgan Kaufmann.

[Ciaccia et al., 1998a] Ciaccia, P., Patella, M., and Zezula, P. (1998a). A cost model for similarity queries in metric spaces. In *Proceedings of the 17th ACM Symposium on Principles of Database Systems (PODS 1998), Seattle, Washington, USA, June 1-3, 1998*, pages 59–68. ACM Press.

[Ciaccia et al., 1998b] Ciaccia, P., Patella, M., and Zezula, P. (1998b). Processing complex similarity queries with distance-based access methods. In Schek, H.-J., Saltor, F., Ramos, I., and Alonso, G., editors, *Proceedings of the 6th International Conference on Extending Database Technology (EDBT 1998), Valencia, Spain, March 23-27, 1998*, volume 1377 of *Lecture Notes in Computer Science*, pages 9–23. Springer.

[Clarkson, 1997] Clarkson, K. L. (1997). Nearest neighbor queries in metric spaces. In *Proceedings of the 29th Annual ACM Symposium on Theory of Computing (STOC 1997), El Paso, Texas, USA, May 4-6, 1997*, pages 609–617. ACM Press.

[Cobena et al., 2002] Cobena, G., Abiteboul, S., and Marian, A. (2002). Detecting changes in XML documents. In *IEEE International Conference on Data Engineering (ICDE 2002), San Jose, California, USA, February 26 - March 1, 2002*, pages 41–52. IEEE Computer Society.

[Comer, 1979] Comer, D. (1979). Ubiquitous B-Tree. *ACM Computing Surveys (CSUR 1979)*, 11(2):121–137. ACM Press.

[Critchlow, 1985] Critchlow, D. E. (1985). *Metric Methods for Analyzing Partially Ranked Data*, volume 34 of *Lecture Notes in Statistics*. Springer.

[Dehne and Noltemeier, 1987] Dehne, F. K. H. A. and Noltemeier, H. (1987). Voronoi trees and clustering problems. *Information Systems (IS 1987)*, 12(2):171–175. Elsevier.

[DeWitt and Gray, 1992] DeWitt, D. J. and Gray, J. (1992). Parallel database systems: The future of high performance database systems. *Communications of the ACM (CACM 1992)*, 35(6):85–98. ACM Press.

[Diaconis, 1988] Diaconis, P. (1988). *Group Representations in Probability and Statistics*, volume 11 of *IMS Lecture Notes - Monograph Series*. Institute of Mathematical Statistics, Hawyard California.

[Dohnal, 2004] Dohnal, V. (2004). *Indexing Structures fro Searching in Metric Spaces*. PhD thesis, Faculty of Informatics, Masaryk University in Brno, Czech Republic. http://www.fi.muni.cz/~xdohnal/phd-thesis.pdf.

[Dohnal et al., 2001] Dohnal, V., Gennaro, C., Savino, P., and Zezula, P. (2001). Separable splits in metric data sets. In Celentano, A., Tanca, L., and Tiberio, P., editors, *Proceedings of the 9th Italian Symposium on Advanced Database Systems (SEBD 2001), Venezia, Italy, June 27-29, 2001*, pages 45–62. LCM Selecta Group - Milano.

[Dohnal et al., 2003a] Dohnal, V., Gennaro, C., Savino, P., and Zezula, P. (2003a). D-Index: Distance searching index for metric data sets. *Multimedia Tools and Applications*, 21(1):9–33. Kluwer Academic Publishers.

[Dohnal et al., 2002] Dohnal, V., Gennaro, C., and Zezula, P. (2002). A metric index for approx-
imate text management. In *Proceedings of the IASTED International Conference Information
Systems and Databaseso (ISDB 2002), Tokyo, Japan, September 25-27, 2002*, pages 37–42.
ACTA Press.

[Dohnal et al., 2003b] Dohnal, V., Gennaro, C., and Zezula, P. (2003b). Similarity join in metric
spaces using eD-Index. In Mařík, V., Retschitzegger, W., and Štěpánková, O., editors, *Proceedings of the 14th International Conference on Database and Expert Systems Applications
(DEXA 2003), Prague, Czech Republic, September 1-5, 2003*, volume 2736 of *Lecture Notes
in Computer Science*, pages 484–493. Springer.

[Duda and Hart, 1973] Duda, R. O. and Hart, P. E. (1973). *Pattern Classification and Scene
Analysis*. Wiley, New York.

[Dunteman, 1989] Dunteman, G. H. (1989). *Principal Component Analysis (Quantitative Applications in the Social Sciences)*. SAGE Publications.

[Dwork et al., 2001] Dwork, C., Kumar, R., Naor, M., and Sivakumar, D. (2001). Rank ag-
gregation methods for the web. In *Proceedings of the 10th International World Wide Web
Conference (WWW 2001), Hong Kong, China, May 1-5, 2001*, pages 613–622. ACM Press.

[Egecioglu and Ferhatosmanoglu, 2000] Egecioglu, Ö. and Ferhatosmanoglu, H. (2000). Dimensionality reduction and similarity computation by inner product approximations. In
*Proceedings of the ACM International Conference on Information and Knowledge Manage-
ment (CIKM 2000), McLean, Virginia, USA, November 6-11, 2000*, pages 219–226. ACM
Press.

[Fagin, 1996] Fagin, R. (1996). Combining fuzzy information from multiple systems. In *Proceedings of the 15th ACM Symposium on Principles of Database Systems (PODS 1996),
Montreal, Canada, June 3-5, 1996*, pages 216–226. ACM Press.

[Fagin, 1998] Fagin, R. (1998). Fuzzy queries in multimedia database systems. In *Proceedings
of the 17th ACM Symposium on Principles of Database Systems (PODS 1998), Seattle,
Washington, June 1-3, 1998*, pages 1–10. ACM Press.

[Faloutsos et al., 1994] Faloutsos, C., Barber, R., Flickner, M., Hafner, J., Niblack, W., Petkovic,
D., and Equitz, W. (1994). Efficient and effective querying by image content. *Journal of
Intelligent Information Systems (JIIS 1994)*, 3(3/4):231–262. Kluwer Academic Publishers.

[Faloutsos and Kamel, 1994] Faloutsos, C. and Kamel, I. (1994). Beyond uniformity and independence: Analysis of R-trees using the concept of fractal dimension. In *Proceedings of
the 13th ACM Symposium on Principles of Database Systems (PODS 1994), Minneapolis,
Minnesota, USA, May 24-26, 1994*, pages 4–13. ACM Press.

[Faloutsos and Lin, 1995] Faloutsos, C. and Lin, K.-I. (1995). FastMap: A fast algorithm for
indexing, data-mining and visualization of traditional and multimedia datasets. In Carey,
M. J. and Schneider, D. A., editors, *Proceedings of the 18th ACM International Conference
on Management of Data (SIGMOD 1995), San Jose, California, USA, May 22-25, 1995*,
pages 163–174. ACM Press.

[Ferhatosmanoglu et al., 2000] Ferhatosmanoglu, H., Tuncel, E., Agrawal, D., and Abbadi,
A. E. (2000). Vector approximation based indexing for non-uniform high dimensional data
sets. In *Proceedings of the ACM International Conference on Information and Knowledge*

Management (CIKM 2000), McLean, Virginia, USA, November 6-11, 2000, pages 202–209. ACM Press.

[Ferhatosmanoglu et al., 2001] Ferhatosmanoglu, H., Tuncel, E., Agrawal, D., and Abbadi, A. E. (2001). Approximate nearest neighbor searching in multimedia databases. In *Proceedings of the 17th International Conference on Data Engineering (ICDE 2001), Heidelberg, Germany, April 2-6, 2001*, pages 503–511. IEEE Computer Society.

[Frakes and Baeza-Yates, 1992] Frakes, W. and Baeza-Yates, R. A. (1992). *Information Retrieval: Data Structures and Algorithms*, chapter 10, pages 219–240. Prentice-Hall, Inc.

[Fukunaga, 1990] Fukunaga, K. (1990). *Introduction to Statistical Pattern Recognition*. Academic Press, second edition.

[Gaede and Günther, 1998] Gaede, V. and Günther, O. (1998). Multidimensional access methods. *ACM Computing Surveys (CSUR 1998)*, 30(2):170–231. ACM Press.

[García et al., 1998] García, Y. J., Lopez, M. A., and Leutenegger, S. T. (1998). On optimal node splitting for R-trees. In Gupta, A., Shmueli, O., and Widom, J., editors, *Proceedings of the 24th International Conference on Very Large Data Bases (VLDB 1998), New York City, New York, USA, August 24-27, 1998*, pages 334–344. Morgan Kaufmann.

[Gennaro et al., 2001] Gennaro, C., Savino, P., and Zezula, P. (2001). Similarity search in metric databases through hashing. In *Proceedings of the 3rd ACM Multimedia 2001 Workshop on Multimedia Information Retrieval (MIR 2001), Ottawa, Ontario, Canada, October 5, 2001*, pages 1–5. ACM Press.

[Gravano et al., 2001] Gravano, L., Ipeirotis, P. G., Jagadish, H. V., Koudas, N., Muthukrishnan, S. M., and Srivastava, D. (2001). Approximate string joins in a database (almost) for free. In Apers, P. M. G., Atzeni, P., Ceri, S., Paraboschi, S., Ramamohanarao, K., and Snodgrass, R. T., editors, *Proceedings of the 27th International Conference on Very Large Data Bases (VLDB 2001), Roma, Italy, September 11-14, 2001*, pages 491–500. Morgan Kaufmann.

[Gresho and Gray, 1992] Gresho, A. and Gray, R. M. (1992). *Vector Quantization and Signal Compression*, volume 159. Kluwer Academic Publishers, Boston, MA.

[Guha et al., 2002] Guha, S., Jagadish, H. V., Koudas, N., Srivastava, D., and Yu, T. (2002). Approximate XML joins. In Franklin, M. J., Moon, B., and Ailamaki, A., editors, *Proceedings of the ACM International Conference on Management of Data (SIGMOD 2002), Madison, Wisconsin, USA, June 3-6, 2002*, pages 287–298. ACM Press.

[Guttman, 1984] Guttman, A. (1984). R-Trees: A dynamic index structure for spatial searching. In Yormark, B., editor, *Proceedings of the ACM International Conference on Management of Data (SIGMOD 1984), Boston, Massachusetts, USA, June 18-21, 1984*, pages 47–57. ACM Press.

[Hafner et al., 1995] Hafner, J. L., Sawhney, H. S., Equitz, W., Flickner, M., and Niblack, W. (1995). Efficient color histogram indexing for quadratic form distance functions. *IEEE Transactions on Pattern Analysis and Machine Intelligence (TPAMI 1995)*, 17(7):729–736. IEEE Computer Society.

[Hjaltason and Samet, 1995] Hjaltason, G. R. and Samet, H. (1995). Ranking in spatial databases. In Egenhofer, M. J. and Herring, J. R., editors, *Proceedings of the 4th International Symposium on Advances in Spatial Databases (SSD 1995), Portland, Maine, USA, August 6-9, 1995*, volume 951 of *Lecture Notes in Computer Science*, pages 83–95. Springer.

[Hjaltason and Samet, 1999] Hjaltason, G. R. and Samet, H. (1999). Distance browsing in spatial databases. *ACM Transactions on Database Systems (TODS 1999)*, 24(2):265–318. ACM Press.

[Hjaltason and Samet, 2000] Hjaltason, G. R. and Samet, H. (2000). Incremental similarity search in multimedia databases. Technical Report CS-TR-4199, Computer Science Department, University of Maryland, College Park.

[Hjaltason and Samet, 2003a] Hjaltason, G. R. and Samet, H. (2003a). Index-driven similarity search in metric spaces. *ACM Transactions on Database Systems (TODS 2003)*, 28(4):517–580. ACM Press.

[Hjaltason and Samet, 2003b] Hjaltason, G. R. and Samet, H. (2003b). Properties of embedding methods for similarity searching in metric spaces. *IEEE Transactions on Pattern Analysis and Machine Intelligence (TPAMI 2003)*, 25(5):530–549. IEEE Computer Society.

[Hoel et al., 1971] Hoel, P. G., Port, S. C., and Stone, C. J. (1971). *Introduction to Probability Theory*. Houghton Mifflin Company.

[Huttenlocher et al., 1993] Huttenlocher, D. P., Klanderman, G. A., and Rucklidge, W. J. (1993). Comparing images using the Hausdorff distance. *IEEE Transactions on Pattern Analysis and Machine Intelligence (TPAMI 1993)*, 15(9):850–863. IEEE Computer Society.

[Johnson and Krishna, 1993] Johnson, T. and Krishna, P. (1993). Lazy updates for distributed search structure. In *Proceedings of the ACM International Conference on Management of Data (SIGMOD 1993), Washington, D.C., May 26-28, 1993*, volume 22(2), pages 337–346. ACM Press.

[Kailath, 1985] Kailath, T. (1985). *Modern Signal Processing*. Springer.

[Kalantari and McDonald, 1983] Kalantari, I. and McDonald, G. (1983). A data structure and an algorithm for the nearest point problem. *IEEE Transactions on Software Engineering (TSE 1983)*, 9(5):631–634. IEEE Computer Society.

[Kamel and Faloutsos, 1993] Kamel, I. and Faloutsos, C. (1993). On packing R-Trees. In Bhargava, B. K., Finin, T. W., and Yesha, Y., editors, *Proceedings of the 2nd International conference on Information and Knowledge Management (CIKM 1993), Washington, D.C., USA, November 1-5, 1993*, pages 490–499. ACM Press.

[Kaufman and Rousseeuw, 1990] Kaufman, L. and Rousseeuw, P. J. (1990). *Finding Groups in Data: An Introduction to Cluster Analysis*. Wiley-Interscience.

[Kelly, 1955] Kelly, J. L. (1955). *General Topology*. D. Van Nostrand, New York.

[Kohonen, 1984] Kohonen, T. (1984). *Self-Organization and Associative Memory*. Springer.

[Kollios et al., 1999] Kollios, G., Gunopulos, D., and Tsotras, V. J. (1999). Nearest neighbor queries in a mobile environment. In *Proceedings of the Internation Workshop on Spatio-Temporal Database Management (STDBM 1999), Edinburgh, Scotland, September 10-11, 1999*, volume 1678 of *Lecture Notes in Computer Science*, pages 119–134. Springer.

[Korn and Muthukrishnan, 2000] Korn, F. and Muthukrishnan, S. M. (2000). Influence sets based on reverse nearest neighbor queries. In *Proceedings of the ACM International Conference on Management of Data (SIGMOD 2000), Dallas, Texas, USA, May 16-18, 2000*, pages 201–212. ACM Press.

[Kruskal, 1956] Kruskal, J. B. (1956). On the shortest spanning subtree of a graph and the traveling salesman problem. In *Proceedings of the American Mathematical Society*, volume 7, pages 48–50. American Mathematical Society.

[Lee, 2002] Lee, D. (2002). *Query Relaxation for XML Model*. PhD thesis, University of California, Los Angeles, California, USA.

[Leopold, 2001] Leopold, C. (2001). *Parallel and Distributed Computing: A Survey of Models, Paradigms and Approaches*. John Wiley & Sons, Inc.

[Levenshtein, 1965] Levenshtein, V. I. (1965). Binary codes capable of correcting spurious insertions and deletions of ones. *Problems of Information Transmission*, 1:8–17. Kluwer Academic Publishers.

[Li et al., 2002] Li, C., Chang, E., Garcia-Molina, H., and Wiederhold, G. (2002). Clustering for approximate similarity search in high-dimensional spaces. *IEEE Transactions on Knowledge and Data Engineering (TKDE 2002)*, 14(4):792–808. IEEE Computer Society.

[Litwin et al., 1996] Litwin, W., Neimat, M.-A., and Schneider, D. A. (1996). LH* - a scalable, distributed data structure. *ACM Transactions on Database Systems (TODS 1996)*, 21(4):480–525. ACM Press.

[MacQueen, 1967] MacQueen, J. B. (1967). Some methods for classification and analysis of multivariate observations. In *Proceedings of the 5th Berkeley Symposium on Mathematical Statistics and Probability*, pages 281–297. University of California Press.

[Micó et al., 1996] Micó, M. L., Oncina, J., and Carrasco, R. C. (1996). A fast branch & bound nearest neighbour classifier in metric spaces. *Pattern Recognition Letters*, 17(7):731–739. Elsevier.

[Micó et al., 1992] Micó, M. L., Oncina, J., and Vidal, E. (1992). An algorithm for finding nearest neighbors in constant average time with a linear space complexity. In *Proceedings of the 11th International Conference on Pattern Recognition (ICPR 1992), The Hague, The Netherlands*, volume II, pages 557–560.

[Micó et al., 1994] Micó, M. L., Oncina, J., and Vidal, E. (1994). A new version of the nearest-neighbour approximating and eliminating search algorithm (AESA) with linear preprocessing time and memory requirements. *Pattern Recognition Letters*, 15(1):9–17. Elsevier.

[Moreno-Seco et al., 2003] Moreno-Seco, F., Micó, M. L., and Oncina, J. (2003). A modification of the LAESA algorithm for approximated k-NN classification. *Pattern Recognition Letters*, 24(1-3):47–53. Elsevier.

[Narasimhalu et al., 1997] Narasimhalu, A. D., Kankanhalli, M. S., and Wu, J.-K. (1997). Benchmarking multimedia databases. *Multimedia Tools and Applications*, 4(3):333–356. Kluwer Academic Publishers.

[Navarro, 1999] Navarro, G. (1999). Searching in metric spaces by spatial approximation. In *Proceedings of the 6th International Symposium on String Processing and Information Retrieval (SPIRE 1999), Cancun, Mexico, September 21-24, 1999*, pages 141–148. IEEE Computer Society.

[Navarro, 2001] Navarro, G. (2001). A guided tour to approximate string matching. *ACM Computing Surveys (CSUR 2001)*, 33(1):31–88. ACM Press.

[Navarro, 2002] Navarro, G. (2002). Searching in metric spaces by spatial approximation. *The VLDB Journal*, 11(1):28–46. Springer.

[Navarro and Reyes, 2002] Navarro, G. and Reyes, N. (2002). Fully dynamic spatial approximation trees. In Laender, A. H. F. and Oliveira, A. L., editors, *Proceedings of the 9th International Symposium on String Processing and Information Retrieval (SPIRE 2002), Lisbon, Portugal, September 11-13, 2002*, volume 2476 of *Lecture Notes in Computer Science*, pages 254–270. Springer.

[Noltemeier, 1989] Noltemeier, H. (1989). Voronoi trees and applications. In *International Workshop on Discrete Algorithms and Complexity, Fukuoka, Japan, November, 1989*, pages 69–74.

[Noltemeier et al., 1992a] Noltemeier, H., Verbarg, K., and Zirkelbach, C. (1992a). A data structure for representing and efficient querying large scenes of geometric objects: MB* Trees. In *Geometric Modelling*, volume 8 of *Computing Supplement*, pages 211–226. Springer.

[Noltemeier et al., 1992b] Noltemeier, H., Verbarg, K., and Zirkelbach, C. (1992b). Monotonous Bisector* Trees - a tool for efficient partitioning of complex scenes of geometric objects. In *Data Structures and Efficient Algorithms*, volume 594 of *Lecture Notes in Computer Science*, pages 186–203. Springer.

[Ogras and Ferhatosmanoglu, 2003] Ogras, Ü. Y. and Ferhatosmanoglu, H. (2003). Dimensionality reduction using magnitude and shape approximations. In *Proceedings of the ACM International Conference on Information and Knowledge Management (CIKM 2003), New Orleans, Louisiana, USA, November 3-8, 2003*, pages 99–107. ACM Press.

[Oppenheim et al., 1999] Oppenheim, A. V., Schafer, R. W., and Buck, J. R. (1999). *Discrete-Time Signal Processing (2nd edition)*. Prentice-Hall, Inc.

[Ortega-Binderberger et al., 2002] Ortega-Binderberger, M., Chakrabarti, K., and Mehrotra, S. (2002). An approach to integrating query refinement in sql. In Jensen, C. S., Jeffery, K. G., Pokorný, J., Saltenis, S., Bertino, E., Böhm, K., and Jarke, M., editors, *Proceedings of the 8th International Conference on Extending Database Technology (EDBT 2002), Prague, Czech Republic, March 25-27, 2002*, volume 2287 of *Lecture Notes in Computer Science*, pages 15–33. Springer.

[Papadopulos and Manolopoulos, 1997] Papadopulos, A. and Manolopoulos, Y. (1997). Performances of nearest-neighbor queries in R-Trees. In *Proceedings of the 6th International Conference on Database Theory (ICDT 1997), Delphi, Greece, January 8-10, 1997*, volume 1186 of *Lecture Notes in Computer Science*, pages 394–408. Springer.

[Parnas and Ron, 2001] Parnas, M. and Ron, D. (2001). Testing metric properties. In *Proceedings of the 33rd Annual ACM Symposium on Theory of Computing (STOC 2001), Heraklion, Crete, Greece, July 6-8, 2001*, pages 276–285. ACM Press.

[Pramanik et al., 1999a] Pramanik, S., Alexander, S., and Li, J. (1999a). An efficient searching algorithm for approximate nearest neighbor queries in high dimensions. In *Proceedings of the IEEE International Conference on Multimedia Computing and Systems (ICMCS 1999), Florence, Italy, June 7-11, 1999*, volume 1. IEEE Computer Society.

[Pramanik et al., 1999b] Pramanik, S., Li, J., Ruan, J., and Bhattacharjee, S. K. (1999b). Efficient search scheme for very large image databases. In Beretta, G. B. and Schettini, R., editors, *Proceedings of the International Society for Optical Engineering (SPIE) on Internet Imaging, San Jose, California, USA, January 26, 2000,* volume 3964, pages 79–90. The International Society for Optical Engineering.

[Rammal et al., 1986] Rammal, R., Toulouse, G., and Virasoro, M. A. (1986). Ultrametricity for physicists. *Reviews of Modern Physics,* 58(3):765–788. The American Physical Society.

[Rico-Juan and Micó, 2003] Rico-Juan, J. R. and Micó, M. L. (2003). Comparison of AESA and LAESA search algorithms using string and tree-edit-distances. *Pattern Recognition Letters,* 24(9-10):1417–1426. Elsevier.

[Samet, 1984] Samet, H. (1984). The quadtree and related hierarchical data structures. *ACM Computing Surveys (CSUR 1984),* 16(2):187–260. ACM Press.

[Sankoff and Kruskal, 1983] Sankoff, D. and Kruskal, J. B. (1983). *Time Warps, String Edits, and Macromolecules.* Addison-Wesley, Reading, Mass.

[Seidl and Kriegel, 1997] Seidl, T. and Kriegel, H.-P. (1997). Efficient user-adaptable similarity search in large multimedia databases. In Jarke, M., Carey, M. J., Dittrich, K. R., Lochovsky, F. H., Loucopoulos, P., and Jeusfeld, M. A., editors, *Proceedings of the 23rd International Conference on Very Large Data Bases (VLDB 1997), Athens, Greece, August 25-29, 1997,* pages 506–515. Morgan Kaufmann.

[Shapiro, 1977] Shapiro, M. (1977). The choice of reference points in best-match file searching. *Communications of the ACM (CACM 1977),* 20(5):339–343. ACM Press.

[Shasha and Wang, 1990] Shasha, D. and Wang, J. T.-L. (1990). New techniques for best-match retrieval. *ACM Transactions on Information Systems (TOIS 1990),* 8(2):140–158. ACM Press.

[Skopal, 2004] Skopal, T. (2004). Pivoting M-tree: A metric access method for efficient similarity search. In Snášel, V., Pokorný, J., and Richta, K., editors, *Proceedings of the Annual International Workshop on DAtabases, TExts, Specifications and Objects (DATESO 2004), Desna, Czech Republic, April 14-16, 2004,* volume 98 of *CEUR Workshop Proceedings.* Technical University of Aachen (RWTH).

[Skopal et al., 2003] Skopal, T., Pokorný, J., Krátký, M., and Snášel, V. (2003). Revisiting M-Tree building principles. In Kalinichenko, L. A., Manthey, R., Thalheim, B., and Wloka, U., editors, *Proceedings of the 7th East European Conference on Advances in Databases and Information Systems (ADBIS 2003), Dresden, Germany, September 3-6, 2003,* volume 2798 of *Lecture Notes in Computer Science.* Springer.

[Skopal et al., 2005] Skopal, T., Pokorný, J., and Snášel, V. (2005). Nearest neighbours search using the PM-Tree. In *Proceedings of the 10th International Conference on Database Systems for Advanced Applications (DASFAA 2005), Beijing, China, April 17-20, 2005,* volume 3453 of *Lecture Notes in Computer Science,* pages 803–815. Springer.

[Stanoi et al., 2000] Stanoi, I., Agrawal, D., and Abbadi, A. E. (2000). Reverse nearest neighbor queries for dynamic databases. In *Proceedings of the ACM SIGMOD Workshop on Research Issues in Data Mining and Knowledge Discovery, Dallas, Texas, USA, May 14, 2000,* pages 44–53. ACM Press.

[Stanoi et al., 2001] Stanoi, I., Riedewald, M., Agrawal, D., and Abbadi, A. E. (2001). Discovery of influence sets in frequently updated databases. In *Proceedings of the 27th International*

Conference on Very Large Data Bases (VLDB 2001), Roma, Italy, September 11-14, 2001, pages 99–108. Morgan Kaufmann.

[Theodoridis and Sellis, 1996] Theodoridis, Y. and Sellis, T. K. (1996). A model for the prediction of R-tree performance. In *Proceedings of the 15th ACM Symposium on Principles of Database Systems (PODS 1996), Montreal, Canada, June 3-5, 1996*, pages 161–171. ACM Press.

[Traina, Jr. et al., 1999] Traina, Jr., C., Traina, A. J. M., and Faloutsos, C. (1999). Distance exponent: A new concept for selectivity estimation in metric trees. Technical Report CMU-CS-99-110, Computer Science Department, School of Computer Science, Carnegie Mellon University.

[Traina, Jr. et al., 2000a] Traina, Jr., C., Traina, A. J. M., and Faloutsos, C. (2000a). Distance exponent: A new concept for selectivity estimation in metric trees. In *Proceedings of the 16th International Conference on Data Engineering (ICDE 2000), San Diego, California, USA, February 28 - March 3, 2000*, page 195. IEEE Computer Society.

[Traina, Jr. et al., 2002] Traina, Jr., C., Traina, A. J. M., Faloutsos, C., and Seeger, B. (2002). Fast indexing and visualization of metric data sets using Slim-Trees. *IEEE Transactions on Knowledge and Data Engineering (TKDE 2002)*, 14(2):244–260. IEEE Computer Society.

[Traina, Jr. et al., 2000b] Traina, Jr., C., Traina, A. J. M., Seeger, B., and Faloutsos, C. (2000b). Slim-Trees: High performance metric trees minimizing overlap between nodes. In Zaniolo, C., Lockemann, P. C., Scholl, M. H., and Grust, T., editors, *Proceedings of the 7th International Conference on Extending Database Technology (EDBT 2000), Konstanz, Germany, March 27-31, 2000*, volume 1777 of *Lecture Notes in Computer Science*, pages 51–65. Springer.

[Tuncel et al., 2002] Tuncel, E., Ferhatosmanoglu, H., and Rose, K. (2002). VQ-index: an index structure for similarity searching in multimedia databases. In *Proceedings of the 10th ACM International Conference on Multimedia 2002, Juan les Pins, France, December 1-6, 2002*, pages 543–552. ACM Press.

[Uhlmann, 1991] Uhlmann, J. K. (1991). Satisfying general proximity/similarity queries with metric trees. *Information Processing Letters*, 40(4):175–179. Elsevier.

[Vidal, 1986] Vidal, E. (1986). An algorithm for finding nearest neighbors in (approximately) constant average time. *Pattern Recognition Letters*, 4(3):145–157. Elsevier.

[Vidal, 1994] Vidal, E. (1994). New formulation and improvements of the nearest-neighbour approximating and eliminating search algorithm (AESA). *Pattern Recognition Letters*, 15(1):1–7. Elsevier.

[Vilar, 1995] Vilar, J. M. (1995). Reducing the overhead of the AESA metric-space nearest neighbour searching algorithm. *Information Processing Letters*, 56(5):265–271. Elsevier.

[Volmer, 2002] Volmer, S. (2002). Fast approximate nearest-neighbor queries in metric feature spaces by buoy indexing. In *Proceedings of the 5th International Conference on Visual Information Systems (VISUAL 2002), Hsin Chu, Taiwan, March 11-13, 2002*, volume 2314 of *Lecture Notes in Computer Science*, pages 36–49. Springer.

[Wall et al., 2003] Wall, M. E., Rechtsteiner, A., and Rocha, L. M. (2003). Singular value decomposition and principal component analysis. In Berrar, D., Dubitzky, W., and Granzow,

M., editors, *A Practical Approach to Microarray Data Analysis*, pages 91–109. Kluwer Academic Publishers, Norwell, MA.

[Wang et al., 2000] Wang, X., Wang, J. T.-L., Lin, K.-I., Shasha, D., Shapiro, B. A., and Zhang, K. (2000). An index structure for data mining and clustering. In *Knowledge and Information Systems*, volume 2, pages 161–184. Springer.

[Weber and Böhm, 2000] Weber, R. and Böhm, K. (2000). Trading quality for time with nearest neighbor search. In Zaniolo, C., Lockemann, P. C., Scholl, M. H., and Grust, T., editors, *Proceedings of the 7th International Conference on Extending Database Technology (EDBT 2000), Konstanz, Germany, March 27-31, 2000*, volume 1777 of *Lecture Notes in Computer Science*. Springer.

[Weber et al., 1998] Weber, R., Schek, H.-J., and Blott, S. (1998). A quantitative analysis and performance study for similarity-search methods in high-dimensional spaces. In Gupta, A., Shmueli, O., and Widom, J., editors, *Proceedings of the 24th International Conference on Very Large Data Bases (VLDB 1998), New York City, New York, USA, August 24-27, 1998*, pages 194–205. Morgan Kaufmann.

[White and Jain, 1996] White, D. A. and Jain, R. (1996). Similarity indexing with the SS-tree. In Su, S. Y. W., editor, *Proceedings of the 12th International Conference on Data Engineering (ICDE 1996), New Orleans, Louisiana, USA, February 26 - March 1, 1996*, pages 516–523. IEEE Computer Society.

[Yang and Lin, 2001] Yang, C. and Lin, K.-I. (2001). An index structure for efficient reverse nearest neighbor queries. In *Proceedings of the 17th International Conference on Data Engineering (ICDE 2001), Heidelberg, Germany, April 2-6, 2001*, pages 485–492. IEEE Computer Society.

[Yianilos, 1993] Yianilos, P. N. (1993). Data structures and algorithms for nearest neighbor search in general metric spaces. In *Proceedings of the 4th Annual ACM Symposium on Discrete Algorithms (SODA 1993), Austin, Texas, USA, January 25-27, 1993*, pages 311–321. ACM Press.

[Yianilos, 1999] Yianilos, P. N. (1999). Excluded middle vantage point forests for nearest neighbor search. In *Proceedings of the 6th DIMACS Implementation Challenge: Near Neighbor Searches (ALENEX 1999), Baltimore, Maryland, USA, January 15-16, 1999*.

[Zezula et al., 1998a] Zezula, P., Savino, P., Amato, G., and Rabitti, F. (1998a). Approximate similarity retrieval with M-Trees. *The VLDB Journal*, 7(4):275–293. Springer.

[Zezula et al., 1998b] Zezula, P., Savino, P., Rabitti, F., Amato, G., and Ciaccia, P. (1998b). Processing M-trees with parallel resources. In *Procedings of the 8th International Workshop on Research Issues in Data Engineering (RIDE 1998), Orlando, Florida, USA, February 23-24, 1998*, pages 147–154. IEEE Computer Society.

[Zhou et al., 2003] Zhou, X., Wang, G., Yu, J. X., and Yu, G. (2003). M^+-tree: A new dynamical multidimensional index for metric spaces. In Schewe, K.-D. and Zhou, X., editors, *Proceedings of the 14th Australasian Database Conference on Database Technologies (ADC 2003), Adelaide, South Australia, February 4-7, 2003*, volume 17 of *CRPIT*, pages 161–168. Australian Computer Society.

[Zhou et al., 2005] Zhou, X., Wang, G., Zhou, X., and Yu, G. (2005). BM$^+$-Tree: A hyperplane-based index method for high-dimensional metric spaces. In *Proceedings of the 10th International Conference on Database Systems for Advanced Applications (DASFAA 2005), Beijing, China, April 17-20, 2005*, volume 3453 of *Lecture Notes in Computer Science*, pages 398–409. Springer.

Author Index

Abbadi, A. E. 17, 42, 90
Aberer, K. 164
Abiteboul, S. 13
Agrawal, D. 17, 42, 90
Alexander, S. 92, 93
Alpkocak, A. 167
Alt, H. 15
Amato, G. 55, 57, 60, 98, 99, 145, 148, 150, 153, 164, 166
Apostolico, A. 13
Arya, S. 48, 90, 146
Aurenhammer, F. 83

Baeza-Yates, R. A. 67–69, 71, 72, 80
Barbará, D. 3
Barber, R. 11
Batko, M. 167
Beckmann, N. 40
Behrends, B. 15
Berchtold, S. 6, 52
Bern, M. W. 91
Bespamyatnikh, S. 91
Bhattacharjee, S. K. 92–94
Blömer, J. 15
Blott, S. 90
Böhm, C. 6
Böhm, K. 90
Bozkaya, T. 63–65, 74, 81, 82
Brin, S. 65, 82, 84, 106
Buck, J. R. 40
Bugnion, E. 78
Burden, R. 151
Burkhard, W. A. 68
Bustos, B. 65

Callahan, P. B. 91
Carrasco, R. C. 80
Carreira-Perpinan, M. A. 41
Castelman, K. R. 40
Cetintemel, U. 38

Chakrabarti, K. 38
Chang, E. 94
Chávez, E. 65, 67, 68, 70–72, 80
Chiueh, T. 74
Chomicki, J. 38
Ciaccia, P. 19, 36, 39, 52, 54, 55, 58–60, 87, 88, 99, 105, 107–111, 124, 136, 153, 154, 164, 166
Clarkson, K. L. 7
Cobena, G. 13
Comer, D. 77, 106
Critchlow, D. E. 49
Cunto, W. 69

Danisman, T. 167
Dehne, F. K. H. A. 77
DeWitt, D. J. 162
Diaconis, P. 49
Dohnal, V. 34, 88, 89, 126, 130, 131, 137, 143
Duda, R. O. 96
DuMouchel, W. 3
Dunteman, G. H. 40
Dwork, C. 49

Egecioglu, Ö. 89
Eppstein, D. 91
Equitz, W. 11, 37

Fagin, R. 18, 19
Faires, J. D. 151
Faloutsos, C. 3, 11, 40, 52, 60–62, 88, 90, 113–116, 118
Ferhatosmanoglu, H. 42, 89, 90, 95, 96
Fhei, S. 78
Flickner, M. 11, 37
Frakes, W. 71
Franklin, M. J. 38
Fukunaga, K. 39, 40

Gaede, V. 6

Galil, Z. 13
Garcia-Molina, H. 94
García, Y. J. 116
Gennaro, C. 88, 89, 126, 130, 131, 143, 167
Giles, C. L. 38
Gravano, L. 131
Gray, J. 162
Gray, R. M. 96
Gresho, A. 96
Guha, S. 13
Gunopulos, D. 17
Günther, O. 6
Guttman, A. 106

Haas, P. J. 3
Hafner, J. 11
Hafner, J. L. 11, 37
Hart, P. E. 96
Hauswirth, M. 164
Hellerstein, J. M. 3
Hjaltason, G. R. 25, 27, 39, 40, 67, 79, 85, 87,
    173
Hoel, P. G. 51
Huttenlocher, D. P. 14

Ioannidis, Y. E. 3
Ipeirotis, P. G. 131

Jagadish, H. V. 3, 13, 131
Jain, R. 40, 92
Johnson, T. 3, 177

Kailath, T. 40
Kalantari, I. 76
Kamel, I. 52, 60
Kankanhalli, M. S. 49
Kaufman, L. 96
Keim, D. A. 6, 52
Keller, R. M. 68
Kelly, J. L. 6
Klanderman, G. A. 14
Kohonen, T. 14
Kollios, G. 17
Korn, F. 17
Kosaraju, S. R. 91
Koudas, N. 13, 131
Krátký, M. 112, 116
Kriegel, H.-P. 11, 37, 40, 52
Krishna, P. 177
Kruskal, J. B. 13, 113
Kumar, R. 49

Lee, D. 13, 15
Leopold, C. 162
Leutenegger, S. T. 116
Levenshtein, V. I. 12
Li, C. 94
Li, J. 92–94

Lin, K.-I. 17, 40, 90
Litwin, W. 163
Lopez, M. A. 116

MacQueen, J. B. 96
Manber, U. 69
Manolopoulos, Y. 52
Marian, A. 13
Marroquín, J. L. 67, 68, 70–72, 80
McDonald, G. 76
Mehrotra, S. 38
Micó, M. L. 79, 80
Montesi, D. 19
Moreno-Seco, F. 80
Mount, D. M. 48, 90, 146
Muthukrishnan, S. M. 17, 131

Nanni, A. 60
Naor, M. 49
Narasimhalu, A. D. 49
Navarro, G. 13, 65, 67, 68, 70–72, 85–87
Neimat, M.-A. 163
Netanyahu, N. S. 48, 90, 146
Ng, R. T. 3
Niblack, W. 11, 37
Noltemeier, H. 76, 77

Ogras, Ü. Y. 90
Oncina, J. 79, 80
Oppenheim, A. V. 40
Ortega-Binderberger, M. 38
Özsoyoglu, Z. M. 63–65, 74, 81, 82

Papadopulos, A. 52
Parnas, M. 9
Patella, M. 19, 36, 39, 52, 54, 55, 58–60, 87, 88,
    99, 105, 107–111, 124, 136, 153, 154
Penzo, W. 19
Petkovic, D. 11
Pokorný, J. 112, 116, 121
Poosala, V. 3
Port, S. C. 51
Pramanik, S. 92–94

Rabitti, F. 55, 57, 60, 98, 99, 136, 145, 148,
    150, 153, 154, 164, 166
Rammal, R. 9
Rechtsteiner, A. 41
Reyes, N. 87
Reynolds, A. 151
Rico-Juan, J. R. 80
Riedewald, M. 17
Rocha, L. M. 41
Ron, D. 9
Roos, T. 78
Rose, K. 95, 96
Ross, K. A. 3

Rousseeuw, P. J. 96
Ruan, J. 92–94
Rucklidge, W. J. 14

Samet, H. 25, 27, 39, 40, 67, 79, 85, 87, 91, 173
Sankoff, D. 13
Savino, P. 55, 57, 60, 88, 89, 98, 99, 126, 130,
    131, 145, 148, 150, 153, 164, 166, 167
Sawhney, H. S. 11, 37
Schafer, R. W. 40
Schek, H.-J. 90
Schneider, D. A. 163
Schneider, R. 40
Seeger, B. 40, 61, 62, 88, 113–116, 118
Seidl, T. 11, 37
Sellis, T. K. 52
Sevcik, K. C. 3
Shapiro, B. A. 40, 90
Shapiro, M. 63, 80
Shasha, D. 40, 78, 90
Silverman, R. 48, 90, 146
Sivakumar, D. 49
Skopal, T. 112, 116, 118, 121
Snášel, V. 112, 116, 121
Srivastava, D. 13, 131
Stanoi, I. 17
Stone, C. J. 51

Teng, S.-H. 91
Theodoridis, Y. 52
Toulouse, G. 9
Traina, A. J. M. 60–62, 88, 113–116, 118
Traina, Jr., C. 60–62, 88, 113–116, 118
Trombetta, A. 19
Tsotras, V. J. 17
Tuncel, E. 42, 90, 95, 96

Uhlmann, J. K. 20, 77, 78, 169
Ulker, T. 167

Verbarg, K. 76
Vidal, E. 78, 79
Vilar, J. M. 80
Virasoro, M. A. 9
Volmer, S. 97

Wall, M. E. 41
Wang, G. 121, 123, 124
Wang, J. T.-L. 40, 78, 90
Wang, X. 40, 90
Weber, R. 90
White, D. A. 40, 92
Widmayer, P. 78
Widmer, F. 78
Wiederhold, G. 94
Wu, A. Y. 48, 90, 146
Wu, J.-K. 49
Wu, S. 69

Yang, C. 17
Yianilos, P. N. 20, 21, 63, 72–75
Yu, G. 121, 123, 124
Yu, J. X. 121, 123
Yu, T. 13

Zezula, P. 19, 52, 54, 55, 57–60, 87–89, 98, 99,
    105, 108, 109, 124, 126, 130, 131, 136,
    143, 145, 148, 150, 153, 154, 164, 166,
    167
Zhang, K. 40, 90
Zhou, X. 121, 123, 124
Zirkelbach, C. 76

Index

$\mathcal{A}_0$ algorithm, *19*, 125
Address Search Tree (AST), 168, *169*, 170–172, 175
   logarithmic, 177
Angle property technique, 92
Approximate similarity search, 41, 44, 89, 144, 145, 155, 159
Approximating and Eliminating Search Algorithm (AESA), *78*, 80, 125
   linear (LAESA), *79*, 80, 118
   reduced overhead (ROAESA), 80
   tree linear (TLAESA), 80

Balanced Box Decomposition tree (BBD), 91
Bisector Tree (BST), *76*, 78
BM$^+$-tree, 124
Bounding constraints, 23, 27
   double-pivot, *33*, 78, 86, 172
   object-pivot, *28*, 32, 34, 74, 79, 80, 108, 111
   pivot filtering, *34*, 63, 70, 81, 121, 126, 134, 137, 139
   pivot-pivot, 31
   range-pivot, *30*, 32, 68, 72, 76, 84, 87, 108
Bounding region, *see* Region
Bulk loading, 88, *109*
Buoy index, 97
Burkhard-Keller Tree (BKT), 68, 71

Chessboard distance, *see* Minkowski distance
City-block distance, *see* Minkowski distance
Clustering for Index (Clindex), 94
Contractive mapping, *35*, 42, 65
Coordinate space, 6, 35, 39, 40, 52
Covering radius, 60, *76*, 86, 106, 112, 113, 116, 119, 124
Cross talk, 7, 11
Cut-off iteration, 158

Declustering, 165–167

Density
   data, 52
   distance, 52, *53*, 57, 59, 63, 64, 137
   function, *51*, 52, 59, 159
Dimensionality curse, 7, 40
Dimensionality reduction, *40*, 42, 89
Discrete least-squares approximation, 151
Distance function, *see* Metric
   continuous, *10*, 71, 72
   discrete, *9*, 68, 71, 72
   time complexity, 14
Distance index (D-index), 88, *126*, 131, 138, 179
Distance space, *see* Metric space
Distribution
   data, 52, 58, 63
   distance, 48, 52, 54–56, 60, 137, 148, 158
   function, *51*, 149, 159

Early termination, 42, 44, 157
Edit distance, *12*, 15, 18, 37, 137
Error on position, 50, 157
Euclidean distance, *see* Minkowski distance
   weighted, 11
Exact match, 6, *15*, 114, 139, 143
Excluded Middle Vantage Point Forest (VPF), *75*, 88
Exclusion bucket, *128*
Exclusion set, 21, *75*, *127*
   overloading, *131*
Extended D-index (eD-index), 131
Extensibility, 5, 7

False dismissal, 41, 47
False hit, 35, 41, 42, 47, 89
FastMap, 40, 90
Fat-factor, *60*, 88, 114, 118
   absolute, 61
   relative, 62
Fixed Quantiles Fixed Queries Array, 72
Fixed Queries Array (FQA), 70

Fixed Queries Tree (FQT), 69, 71, 81
Fixed Slices Fixed Queries Array, 72
Fixed-Height Fixed Queries Tree (FHFQT), *69*, 71
Furthest neighbor search, 26

Generalized Hyperplane Tree (GHT), *77*, 80, 83, 85, 169
    distributed (GHT*), 167, 179
Geometric Near-neighbor Access Tree (GNAT), *82*, 85, 106
Good fraction approximation, 98, *148*, 157, 159

Hausdorff distance, 14, 15
Hotspot, *163*, 167, 168

Image adjustment, 168, *175*
Improvement in efficiency, *46*, 155, 156, 159
Incremental similarity search, 19, 25
Index structure, 67
    centralized, *105*, 144, 167
    distributed, 161, *163*, 167
    parallel, 161, *162*, 164
Induced footrule distance, 50
Insertion algorithm, 107, 112, 113, 119, 130, 132, 171
Interquery parallelism, 189
Intraquery parallelism, 189

Jaccard's coefficient, *13*, 14, 66, 137

Karhunen-Loeve transform, *39*, 40, 90
Key dimension, 122

Levenshtein distance, *see* Edit distance
Lipschitz embedding, 39
Logarithmic replication, *177*, 180, 183
Lower-bounding function, 36, *36*
L_p distance, *see* Minkowski distance

M^+-tree, 121
M^2-tree, 124
Manhattan distance, *see* Minkowski distance
Metric, *8*, 9
    pseudo, 8
    quasi, 9
    super, *see* Metric, ultra
    ultra, 9
Metric space, *6*, *8*
    distance function, *see* Metric
    domain, 6, 8
    embedding, 36, 39, 40
    postulates, *8*, 26, 57, 76, 127
    transformation, 35, 42
Metric tree (M-tree), 87, *105*, 113, 118, 121, 124, 138, 179
    parallel, 164, 167

MetricMap, *40*, 90
Minimum Spanning Tree (MST), 113
Minkowski distance, *10*, 14, 37, 39, 40, 89, 121, 122, 137
Monotonous Bisector Tree (MBT), *76*, 78
Multi Vantage Point Tree (MVPT), 81
Multi-set metric, 37
Multi-way insertion, 112
Multi-way Vantage Point Tree (mv-VPT), 74

Natural join, 17
Nearest neighbor search, 22, 59
    algorithm, *23*, 25, 85, 91, 173
    approximate, 47, 48, 90, 96, 146, 148, 150, 153
    incremental, *see* Incremental similarity search

Optimistic Vantage Point Tree, 74
Outlier, *64*, 66

Partitioning
    ball, *20*, 27, 63, 67, 72
    excluded middle, *21*, 75, 89, 126
    extensions, 21, 83
    generalized hyperplane, 21, 33, 76
Peer-to-Peer (P2P) data network, *164*, 167, 168
    joining, 178
    leaving, 178
Performance evaluation, 136, 154, 179
Performance prediction, 58
Pivot, 20, 63, 72, 106, 169
    filtering, *see* Bounding constraints, pivot filtering
    selection, 63, 108, 171
Pivoting M-tree (PM-tree), 118
Point query, *see* Exact match
Precision, *46*, 50, 97
Principal Component Analysis, 39
Priority queue, 23–25, 91, 121, 123, 158, 165, 173
Probably Approximately Correct (PAC), 99, *153*, 157
Proximity-based approximation, 99, *152*, 155, 159
Pruning condition, *see* Bounding constraints
    approximate, 43, 45, 93, 148, 150, 153, 154

Quad-tree, 91
Quadratic form distance, 137
Quadratic form distance, *11*, 15, 37

Range search, 22, 58
    algorithm, *23*, 27, 39, 68, 72, 77, 80, 84, 86, 108, 120, 124, *130*, 172
Recall, *47*, 50, 97, 155
Reference object, *see* Pivot

Region, 22, 43
 ball, *23*, 55, 58–60, 106
 proximity, 24, 45, *55*, 56, 60, 61, 153, 166
 ring, 118
Relative error approximation, 98, *145*, 154, 155, 157, 159
Relative error on distances, *48*, 145, 153
Relaxed branching, 43, 44, 146, 153, 158
ρ-split function, 89, *126*, 131
 n-order, 127
 binary, 127
Routing mechanism, 163, *169*
Routing object, *see* Pivot

Scalability, 136, *141*, 143, 161, *163*, 164, 166, 170, *189*
Scalable and Distributed Data Structure (SDDS), *163*, 164, 167
Scaled distance function, 36
Scaleup, *162*, 166
Scaling factor, *36*, 37
Separable bucket, 126, *128*
Separable property, *127*
Separable set, 88, *127*, 131
Sequential scan, 22, 28, 71, 85, 95, 125, 138, 161, 183
Similarity, 6
Similarity algebra, 19
Similarity Hashing (SH), 88
Similarity join, *17*, 131
 algorithm, 131, *133*
 self join, *17*, 18, 131
Similarity query, 6, *15*
 combined, 18
 complex, *18*, 25, 124
 execution, *22*, 58, 59, 165

 nearest neighbors, *16*, 18
 range, *15*, 18
 reverse nearest neighbors, 17
Sliding window, 133
Slim-down algorithm, 114
 generalized, 116
Slim-tree, 88, *113*
Small chance improvement approximation, 98, *150*, 157, 159
Spaghettis, 80
SparseMap, 39
Spatial Approximation Tree (SAT), 85
Speedup, 143, *162*, 166, 167
Sperman footrule distance, 49
Splitting, 108, 110, 113, 120, 122, 170, 175, 177
 deferred, 113, 115
SS-tree, 92
Stop condition, 42, 44, 92, 97, 148, 150, 151, 154
Suffix tree, 71

Tanimoto similarity, 14
Tree edit distance, 13, 15
Triangle inequality, *see* Metric space, postulates
Twin node, 121

User-defined function, 36, *38*

Vantage Point Tree (VPT), *72*, 74, 78, 81, 84
Vector Approximation file (VA-file), 90
Vector Quantization index (VQ-index), 95
Viewpoint, 54
 discrepancy, 54
 homogeneity, 55, 58, 149
Voronoi Tree (VT), 77

Abbreviations

AESA	Approximating and Eliminating Search Algorithm
Ak-LAESA	Approximating k-LAESA
AST	Address Search Tree
bps	Ball-Partitioning Split
BBD	Balanced Box Decomposition
BID	Bucket Identifier
BKT	Burkhard-Keller Tree
BPATH	Bit Path
BST	Bisector Tree
B-tree	Balanced Tree
BT	Big system elapsed Time
BTBP	Big system elapsed Time on Big Problem
Clindex	Clustering for Index
CPU	Central Processing Unit
D-index	Distance Index
DNA	Deoxyribonucleic Acid
eD-index	Extended Distance Index
ED	Error on Distances
EP	Error on Position
FHFQT	Fixed-Height Fixed Queries Tree
FQA	Fixed Queries Array
FQT	Fixed Queries Tree
GHT	Generalized Hyperplane Tree
GHT*	Distributed Generalized Hyperplane Tree
GNAT	Geometric Near-neighbor Access Tree
kNN	k-Nearest Neighbors
$kRNN$	k-Reverse Nearest Neighbors
IAM	Image Adjustment Message
IE	Improvement in Efficiency
IFD	Induced Footrule Distance
I/O	Input/Output
KLT	Karhunen-Loeve Transform
LAESA	Linear Approximating and Eliminating Search Algorithm
mM_RAD_2	Minimum Maximum Radius
MBT	Monotonous Bisector Tree
MST	Minimal Spanning Tree
M-tree	Metric Tree
MVPT	Multi Vantage Point Tree
mw-VPT	Multi-Way Vantage Point Tree

NL	Nested Loop
NNID	Network Node Identifier
OJ	Overloading Join
P2P	Peer-to-Peer
PAC	Probably Approximately Correct
PM-tree	Pivoting M-tree
PR	Pending Request (Priority) queue
RAM	Random Access Memory
RJ	Range Join
ROAESA	Reduced Overhead Approximating and Eliminating Search Algorithm
R-tree	Rectangular Tree
SAT	Spatial Approximation Tree
SDDS	Scalable and Distributed Data Structure
SH	Similarity Hashing
SFD	Sperman Footrule Distance
ST	Small system elapsed Time
STSP	Small system elapsed Time on Small Problem
STR	String (Sentence) dataset
SVD	Singular Value Decomposition
TLAESA	Tree LAESA
URL	Uniform Resource Locator dataset
VEC	Vector dataset
VPF	Excluded Middle Vantage Point Forest
VPT	Vantage Point Tree
VQ-index	Vector Quantization Index
VT	Voronoi Tree